CHARLIE PIECHART

and the case of the
Missing Pizza Slice

Katherine Tegen Books is an imprint of HarperCollins Publishers.

Charlie Piechart and the Case of the Missing Pizza Slice

ISBN 978-0-06-237054-9
Library of Congress Control Number: 2014946657

The artist used pencil, paper, Adobe Illustrator, and Adobe Photoshop to create the digital illustrations for this book.
Typography by Eric Comstock and Dana Fritts
15 16 17 18 19   SCP   10 9 8 7 6 5 4 3 2 1
❖
First Edition

CHARLIE·PIECHART
and the case of the
Missing Pizza Slice

written by
ERIC COMSTOCK & MARILYN SADLER

illustrated by **ERIC COMSTOCK**

KT KATHERINE TEGEN BOOKS
An Imprint of HarperCollins Publishers

a
CHARLIE
PIECHART
mystery

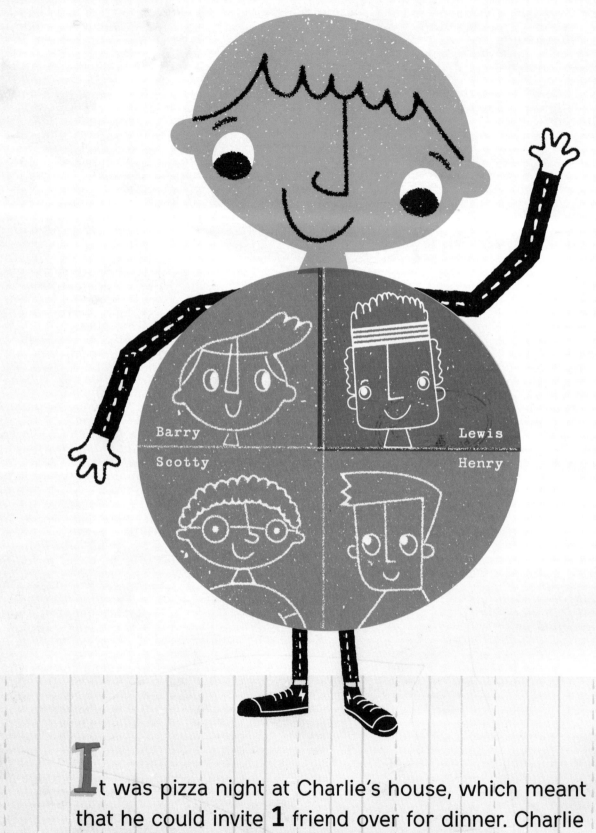

It was pizza night at Charlie's house, which meant that he could invite **1** friend over for dinner. Charlie had **4** friends: Lewis, Henry, Scotty, and Barry.

Lewis was **1/4** of Charlie's friends, but he was his best friend. So Charlie invited Lewis over for pizza night.

There were **6** pizza eaters: Charlie; Lewis; Charlie's sisters, Kate and Alice; and Charlie's mom and dad.

Small
8 Slices

Medium
10 Slices

Large
12 Slices

FIDO'S PIZZA

Toppings:

Cheese

Veggies

Anchovies

Bacon

Mushrooms

Pepperoni

Hawaiian

We Deliver!

Everyone agreed on the size: LARGE!
That meant everyone would get 2 slices.

But No One Could Agree on the Same Topping.

yelled **4/6** of the pizza eaters.
And no one wanted anchovies.

AUTHOR'S NOTE: Anchovies are tiny little fish, and why anyone would want them on their pizza is a mystery that may never be solved.

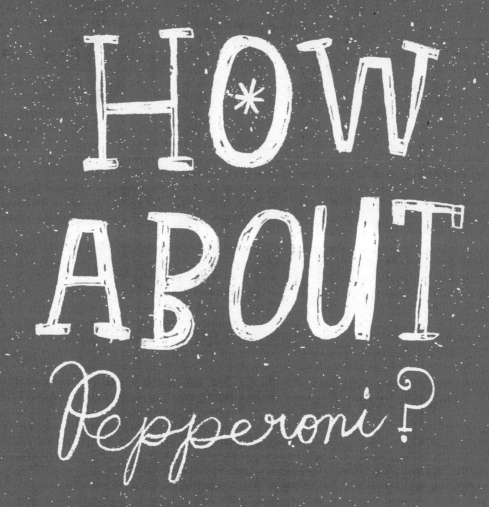

All of the pizza eaters liked that decision best,
including Charlie's dog, Watson.

WARNING! Whatever you do,
DON'T give any pepperoni
to Watson.

Dad paid the pizza boy, and Kate and Alice took the pizza into the kitchen.

Mom set the table while Dad
poured a grape soda for Lewis.

The next thing everyone knew, Kate and Alice were screaming!

Charlie wondered what happened to the missing piece.

He looked for clues but couldn't find any.

It was time to talk to his suspects.

Charlie had **5**:

Mom

Dad

Alice

Kate

Lewis

Dad was **1/5** of his suspects.
But Dad was in the kitchen with Mom.

Mom didn't take the pizza slice, either, so it could have been Lewis. There were **3** suspects left. Lewis was **1/3** of the remaining suspects.

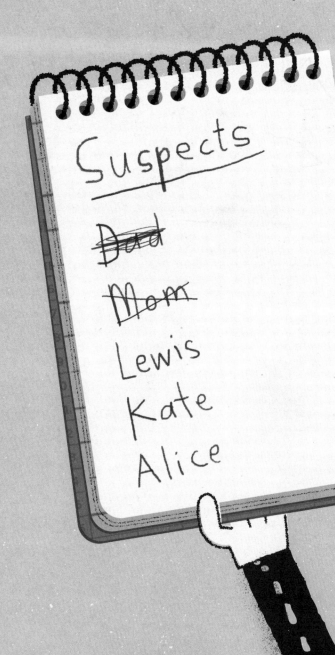

But I was drinking a **Grape Soda** in the kitchen.

Charlie saw a purple spot on Lewis's shirt. It smelled like grapes, not pepperoni, and it was still wet.

fig. A: SPILLED GRAPE SODA

Alice and Kate were **2** out of **2** suspects left.
Charlie was sure they were in it together.
Little sisters were always guilty. To be sure,
Charlie had them do the burp test.

Then he heard their stomachs growl.

Grooooooowl
Grooooooowl
EMPTY!

Suspects
~~Dad~~
~~Mom~~
~~Lewis~~
Kate
Alice

There were no suspects left.

Charlie hadn't solved the mystery, but his dad
had a solution.

"I'll eat only one slice," he said.

Everyone liked that idea, so they finally sat down to eat before the pizza got cold.

DAD of the YEAR!

Mom shared **1/2** of **1** of her **2** slices of pizza with Dad. Mom and Dad each got **1 1/2** pieces.

Everyone was finishing their pizza when
Watson walked into the kitchen.

Charlie knew that Watson had
taken the missing slice of pizza.

thp. thhhhhp, thhhhhhhp.

¹⁄₄ Ball

¹⁄₂ Shoe

Ohhhs

¹⁄₄ Cereal Box

¹⁄₃ Pizza Slice

And Charlie was **100%** certain that it would happen again.

↖ 7/8 Peanut Butter

FUN with FRACTIONS

$\frac{1}{8}$ of the **Pie is gone.**

$\frac{1}{4}$ of the Pencils are **YELLOW.**

$\frac{1}{2}$ of my **Bike tires are Flat!**

$\frac{2}{3}$ OF THE **Donuts** HAVE **SPRINKLES.**

Watson ate $\frac{1}{12}$ of the **PIZZA!**

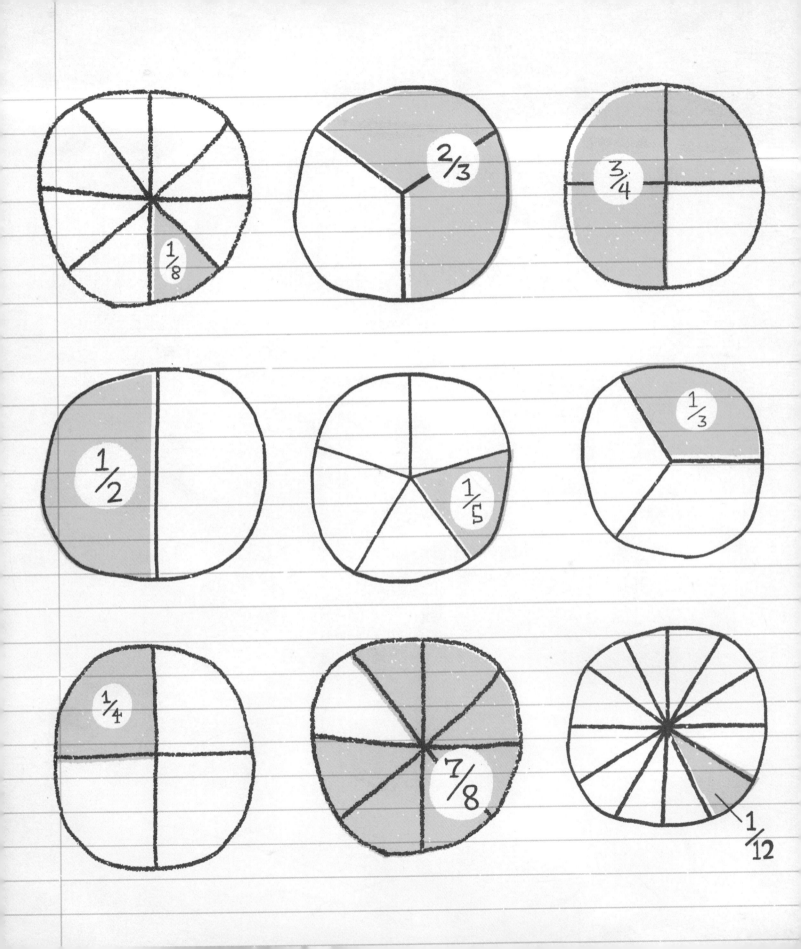

For my dear parents: Stan, an engineer who
loved math, and Anne, an amazing cook
whose favorite food was pizza!

—M.S.

For Julie and my kids, Ethan, Kate, Abby, and Jack.
And while I'm at it, for our dog, Suki, who never ate a pizza,
but if she had we'd know it right away.

—E.C.

DISCOVER CANADA

British Columbia

By Isabel Nanton with Nancy Flight,
Barbara Tomlin, Yvonne Van Ruskenveld and
Lois Richardson, Editors

Consultants

Desmond Morton, FRSC, Professor of History,
University of Toronto

Jean Barman, Ed. D., Department of Social and Educational Studies,
University of British Columbia

Alan McMillan, Department of Social Sciences,
Douglas College, and Department of Archaeology,
Simon Fraser University

 Grolier Limited
TORONTO

Downtown Vancouver seen from the south side of False Creek
Overleaf: Long Beach, Pacific Rim National Park, Vancouver Island

Canadian Cataloguing in Publication Data

Nanton, Isabel, 1951-
  British Columbia

(Discover Canada)
Includes index.
ISBN 0-7172-3148-8

1. British Columbia — Juvenile literature.
I. Flight, Nancy. II. Title. III. Series: Discover
Canada (Toronto, Ont.)

FC3811.2.N35 1996   j971.1   C96-931903-7
F1087.4.N35 1996

Printed and bound in Canada.
Published simultaneously in the United States.
  2 3 4 5 6 7 8 9 10 DWF 99 98 97 96

Front cover: North head of Ellerslie Lake, near
Bella Bella
Back cover: Totem pole at 'Ksan, a recreated
Gitksan village near Hazelton

The sunken Butchart Gardens, outside Victoria, have been planned to bloom year-round.

Table of Contents

CHAPTER 1

Land of Promise

Leonard George, chief of the Burrard Native Band, has said, "If there is still an Eden in the world, it would be British Columbia." Other people have referred to British Columbia as paradise or the Promised Land. Perhaps you have heard another well-known nickname for the province — Lotusland. All of these names reflect the special quality that has attracted many people to British Columbia.

The spectacular natural beauty of the province is one feature that makes British Columbia seem like Eden or paradise. Snow-capped mountains, deep blue fjords and inlets, lush rain forests, picturesque lakes and orchards, rolling grasslands and rushing rivers are all part of British Columbia's breathtaking landscape.

The richness of the land and its natural resources has generally provided a good life for the people of British Columbia. The Native peoples harvested salmon from the sea, built houses and totem poles out of cedar, made clothing from cedar bark and caught sea otters and other fur-bearing animals to trade for European goods. Later, people mined gold and other minerals from the earth. Today the B.C. economy still depends heavily on resource-based industries such as forestry, fishing and mining.

British Columbia is also a place where new ideas are welcome, where people can express their individuality and where there is plenty of economic opportunity. As a result, people from other parts of Canada and from nearly every country in the world have moved to British Columbia. Today a rich mosaic of people from many cultural backgrounds live in this land of promise by the Pacific.

The giant Douglas firs of Cathedral Grove in Vancouver Island's MacMillan Provincial Park

CHAPTER 2

The Land

British Columbia is Canada's third-largest province and covers an area of 948 600 square kilometres (366 280 square miles), or 9.5 percent of Canada's land area. It is nearly four times larger than Great Britain, two and a half times larger than Japan and larger than any American state except Alaska. From the beaches of the Pacific Ocean to the rocky peaks of its many mountain ranges, British Columbia is famous around the world for natural beauty.

Taking Shape

The huge mountains and deep valleys of British Columbia's landscape look solid and ancient, but the forces that created them are still at work beneath the earth's surface.

The rocks of British Columbia are not part of the original ancient continent of North America. They are separate huge chunks of rock originating far to the west and south that were pushed up against the continent millions of years ago by the forces of plate tectonics. According to the theory of plate tectonics, the earth's crust is broken up into huge plates that slowly move across the planet. Sometimes plates collide. As one plate pushes against another, the force of the collision can crumple solid rock, pushing it upwards to form mountains. British Columbia lies where plates meet. Some of its mountains are still being pushed up — the St. Elias Mountains in the northwest corner of the province are moving upwards at a rate of about four centimetres (1.6 inches) per year.

When two plates collide, they do not stop moving. One plate

Overleaf: **Alpine meadow in the Selkirk Mountains of southeastern British Columbia**

Above left: Fjord near Desolation Sound, one of many inlets that cut deep into the B.C. coastline. *Above right:* The Spectrum Range is part of a belt of volcanoes and lava plateaus that stretches from northwestern B.C. into the Yukon. *Left:* Monarch Ice Fields in the Coast Mountains, near Tweedsmuir Provincial Park

is forced under the other, sometimes causing earthquakes. British Columbia has the highest risk of earthquakes in Canada.

As a plate is pushed deeper into the earth, it gradually melts, and some of the magma finds it way to the surface, creating volcanoes. British Columbia has many volcanoes. None has erupted recently, but Native legends describe an eruption 200 years ago in the northwestern part of the province.

British Columbia's landscape has also been shaped by the grinding force of huge glaciers. During many ice ages, glaciers advanced and retreated, gouging out large valleys and carving out the coastal fjords that cut in from the Pacific Ocean.

Today you can still see remnants of the ice ages as small glaciers glisten in the sun on the tops of some of the province's tallest mountains.

Topography

British Columbia can be divided into four main topographical areas: the coastal area, the interior, the Rocky Mountains and the northern lowland.

The coastal area contains some of the province's most rugged landscape, in its mountains, and some of its gentlest, in the Fraser Valley. The Coast Mountains, the highest in North America, stretch northwest from Vancouver in a 1440-kilometre (895-mile) arc about 160 kilometres (100 miles) wide. The highest peak completely in the province is in the Coast Mountains: Mount Waddington at 4016 metres (13 175 feet).

The only flat part of the coastal area is in the south, where most of the population of British Columbia lives. The lower mainland, as it is known, contains the province's largest city, Vancouver, as well as the delta of the Fraser River, a rich farming area.

The coastal area also includes many islands. The largest are Vancouver Island and the Queen Charlotte Islands. They too are part of a mountain range, which continues into the far north of the province. On the mainland, this mountain range is the St. Elias Mountains. One of its peaks, Fairweather Mountain, right on the Alaska border, is the highest point in the province at 4663 metres (15 300 feet).

The islands and island groups off British Columbia's coast form a shield against the wind and waves of the open Pacific Ocean. They create the sheltered "Inside Passage" used by tugs with log booms, ferries, fishing boats, pleasure craft and other boat traffic.

The B.C. interior is a region of plateaus, valleys and mountain ranges. This varied area includes the snow-capped peaks of the Cassiar, Omineca, Monashee, Purcell and Selkirk mountain ranges

as well as the rolling grasslands of the Cariboo-Chilcotin. The southern interior valley of the Okanagan contains a semi-desert complete with cacti and rattlesnakes.

The dividing line between the interior and the Rocky Mountains is the Rocky Mountain Trench. This huge valley, 3 to 20 kilometres (2 to 12 miles) wide, extends from Montana in the United States to the Yukon border. It was formed by faulting and erosion over millions of years.

The Rocky Mountains are the best-known mountains in Canada. They extend 1200 kilometres (745 miles) from the border with the United States almost to the Yukon. Along part of that distance, they form the border between British Columbia and Alberta. They also form part of a natural boundary known as the continental divide. This is the dividing line between North America's watersheds, where some rivers flow west to the Pacific Ocean, others flow north to the Arctic and still others flow east to empty eventually into the

Below left: **Mount Robson, the highest peak in the Canadian Rockies**
Below right: **The semi-desert lands of the southern Okanagan**

Atlantic Ocean. The highest peak in the Rockies is Mount Robson at 3977 metres (13 048 feet).

The northeastern corner of British Columbia, which lies east of the Rockies, is an extension of the high plains of western Alberta. Although it is part of the plains, this lowland is not completely flat. There are low, flat-topped hills and wide valleys. The Peace River flows through the southern part of the area, and the whole region is often called the Peace River Lowland.

Water

Thousands of lakes, rivers and streams shape British Columbia's landscape by erosion and deposition, but the landscape also strongly affects the shape and direction of the waterways.

A map of the province shows that most of the large lakes, such as Okanagan Lake in the south and Babine Lake farther north, are long and narrow. They lie in valleys formed by the many mountain ranges and plateaus. Most of the major rivers flow in a generally

Right: The clear waters of the Thompson River (right) disappear into the muddy, silt-laden Fraser near Lytton. *Far right:* Glacier-fed Takakkaw Falls plunges 254 metres (833 feet) into the Yoho River in Yoho National Park.

north-south direction for much of their route — following the valleys between the mountain ranges. Only three major rivers have found a way through the Coast Mountains to the Pacific Ocean: the Fraser, Skeena and Stikine. All three are important salmon rivers.

The Fraser River is the major river in British Columbia as it drains about one-quarter of the total area of the province. It rises as a tiny, clear trickle in the southeast corner of Mount Robson Park in the Rockies. Gathering silt and debris, it empties as a massive waterway 1280 kilometres (795 miles) later in the Pacific Ocean at Vancouver. Over millions of years, the Fraser has cut deep into the interior plateau and created a spectacular canyon. At Hell's Gate, the river rushes through canyon walls 1000 metres (3300 feet) high.

In the southeast corner of the province, the Columbia River flows north from its headwaters through the Rocky Mountain Trench. It turns sharply south at the north end of the Selkirk Mountain range and flows down into the United States. Many dams have been built along the Columbia both to control flooding and to produce hydroelectric power.

The biggest lakes in the province are the Williston and Nechako reservoirs that were created by damming rivers for hydroelectricity. Williston Lake covers 1660 square kilometres (640 square miles). British Columbia also has many natural lakes. Babine Lake is the largest one, covering 497 square kilometres (192 square miles).

Climate

British Columbia's climate is as varied as its landscape. Often areas separated by just a mountain range or a lake experience completely different climates. For example, the west coast of Vancouver Island is very wet. Over 250 centimetres (98 inches) of rain fall here annually, so a lush rain forest thrives. Yet the Gulf Islands in the Strait of Georgia on the opposite side of Vancouver Island lie in a rainshadow. On average, the yearly rainfall is only 80 centimetres (31 inches). Cacti grow there in the warm climate.

People living in the southern coastal zones and the southern Fraser River Valley enjoy Canada's longest frost-free period — over 200 days a year. This means that the last spring frosts occur in early April and the first fall frosts occur after Halloween.

The interior of the province is drier and hotter than the coast in summer and colder in the winter. The Okanagan Valley records an average of 2000 hours of sunshine each year. The long hours of sunshine and high summer temperatures have made the Okanagan one of Canada's major fruit-growing regions. Farther north, winters can be very harsh. The settlement of Smith River has recorded temperatures as low as -58.9 °C (-74 °F), and early morning frosts are common by the second week in August.

The northeast lowland has long, cold winters like the rest of the western plains. However, summers here are hot, and the frost-free period is long enough to grow grain, forage and other crops.

Below left: **Irrigated farmlands in the Okanagan Valley, near Vernon.** *Below right:* **Autumn colours along the Peace River.** *Right:* **Winter near Fairmont Hotsprings in the Columbia Valley**

Wildlife

From ocean to mountaintop and rain forest to desert, British Columbia's many habitats are home to hundreds of species of animals. Because the Coast Mountains have acted as a barrier, some of these animals have developed differently from their relatives east of the mountains. The coastal blacktail deer, for instance, is a smaller version of the mule deer common elsewhere, and coastal black bears are larger than those found inland.

The largest animals in British Columbia are the whales. Passengers on the ferries between Vancouver and Victoria sometimes see orcas swimming by in large family groups called "pods," and grey whales migrate every year on a route along the west coast of Vancouver Island. Other mammals that inhabit these waters include sea otters, harbour seals and sea lions.

The five species of salmon found in B.C. waters are important food for both animals and humans. Pink, chum, coho, chinook and

Left: Orcas in Queen Charlotte Strait. *Bottom left:* Sea lions in Kyuquot Sound on the west coast of Vancouver Island. *Below:* Spawning sockeye salmon in the Adams River

sockeye salmon all live as adults in the open ocean but migrate inland along streams and rivers to lay their eggs in fresh water. Halibut and herring are also fished commercially.

The best place to see the small animals that live in the ocean's intertidal zone (between low and high tides) is in tidal pools on the rocky Pacific shore. There you might find sea anemones, starfish, sea urchins, snails, mussels and tiny crabs. On a sandy beach, you might find sand dollars.

On land, the British Columbia wilderness is home to large carnivores such as the grizzly bear, the cougar and the wolf. Members of the deer family, including the large wapiti (elk), are plentiful. Caribou live mainly in the northern part of the province, and mountain goats and bighorn sheep are common in mountainous areas. Moose browse along interior lakes and black bears roam the forests. Besides the cougar, two other wild cats are native to British Columbia: the lynx and the bobcat.

Smaller mammals include squirrels, chipmunks, badgers, rabbits, porcupines, raccoons, fishers, marmots and pikas. Amphibians and reptiles, such as Pacific tree frogs, rattlesnakes and alligator lizards, add to the large number of animal species that live in the province.

In the lakes, rivers and streams swim several kinds of trout, such as rainbow, brown, cutthroat, steelhead, and their relatives the Dolly Varden and lake trout. Squawfish and carp are very common, but less well known than the trout and char. While sea-going salmon return to fresh waters to spawn, one type of salmon, the kokanee, is landlocked — it never leaves its lake environment.

British Columbia's many species of birds add sound and colour to wilderness, farmland, towns and cities. Albatrosses, puffins, cormorants, oystercatchers and gulls are just some of the seabirds that live along the coast. Ducks are abundant throughout the province. The great blue heron picks its way cautiously through shallow waters, both salt and fresh. Birds of prey range in size from golden and bald eagles with wingspans of almost two metres (6.6 feet) to the tiny pygmy owl, which may weigh as little as 50 grams

Far left: The white Kermode bear, found only on Princess Royal Island and a small stretch of coastal B.C. south of Prince Rupert, is really a very rare colour variation of black bear. The two bears seen here are brother and sister. *Top left:* A family of mountain goats, barely visible as they make their sure-footed way along a rocky slope. *Bottom left:* Tufted puffins

(two ounces). The smallest birds in the province are the tiny hummingbirds that arrive early each spring from their winter homes in Mexico.

The mouth of the Fraser River is especially important to migrating waterfowl and shorebirds. Millions of them stop here during their spring and fall migrations, including thousands of snowgeese from Siberia.

Forests

Forests cover almost two-thirds of British Columbia. On the wet west coast are the huge trees of the temperate rain forest. The gentle climate, long growing season, fertile soil and large amount of rain allow some trees here to grow more than 90 metres (295 feet) tall. Some of these huge trees are over 1000 years old.

The main rain forest trees are western red cedar, western hemlock, amabilis and Douglas firs and Sitka spruce. They grow in a very limited area: no more than about 80 kilometres (50 miles) inland and no higher than about 300 metres (985 feet) above sea level.

Also on the coast are the dry coastal woodlands of southeastern Vancouver Island, the Gulf Islands and the extreme south of the Fraser Valley. Forests in this area contain a mix of coniferous and deciduous trees. While Douglas fir and lodgepole pine are plentiful, so are Garry oak and alder. Canada's only broad-leaved evergreen, the arbutus, grows here.

East of the Coast Mountains, the forests of the interior reflect a variety of climates from the dry, hot grasslands to the wetter, western-facing mountain slopes. The semi-desert grasslands are not heavily forested, but treed areas are common. The trees here include ponderosa pine, Douglas fir, juniper, birch, trembling aspen and chokecherry. Similar trees are found in the dry montane forests of the plateaus and on lower slopes of mountains. Higher still are the subalpine forests that include spruce, mountain hemlock, alpine fir, lodgepole pine, alpine larch, whitebark pine and trembling aspen. Westward-facing mountain slopes receive more rain than the rest of the interior because they catch the moisture-laden clouds moving east from the Pacific Ocean. On these slopes, western red cedar, western hemlock, Douglas fir, western larch, spruce, yew and bitter cherry grow.

The boreal forest that covers most of the rest of Canada with a mix of conifers, birches and poplars is only found in the northern parts of British Columbia.

Wildflowers

In the densest, darkest part of the rain forest, few wildflowers grow, but elsewhere in British Columbia, flowers and other plants thrive. The mild climate of southwestern British Columbia brings flowers out early: even in January several species of wildflowers may

bloom on Vancouver Island and the Gulf Islands. In these dry coastal woodlands, flowers such as blue camas, chocolate lily, shooting star and sea blush colour the landscape.

Some of the most spectacular displays of wildflowers are seen on high alpine meadows. Here the growing season may be as short as 25 days, and summer blizzards can occur. Plants must grow quickly. Lupines, paintbrushes, daisies, western anemones and columbines are just some of the flowers that brighten these meadows during the short summer.

Deep in the forest of Carmanah Pacific Park. *Inset left:* Glacier lilies in the Cascade Mountains. *Inset right:* Along with the trees that are native to the province are apple and other fruit trees that now thrive in irrigated areas of the Okanagan Valley.

CHAPTER 3

The People

People have come from all over the world to live in British Columbia. Over the past 200 years or so, they have come from 140 countries and from other parts of Canada.

For thousands of years before that, the area's first inhabitants, the Native people, lived on the abundant natural resources of the coast and the interior. Experts estimate that there were more than 80 000 Native people in the land that became British Columbia when the first Europeans arrived.

First Nations

In the beginning, an ocean covered all of the earth. Then Raven created an island. Plants, animals and the first people appeared on the island. People and animals could talk to each other and change what they looked like. Over time, Raven transformed the people, animals and landscape into what they are today.

This is the story of creation that is told by some of the Native people living on the coast of British Columbia. They believe they have always lived there. Modern archaeologists agree that Native people have occupied what is now British Columbia for a very long time — 10 000 to 12 000 years.

The people lived in groups that were very different from each other. Thirty-four different languages were spoken. Some groups traded with each other; others fought wars with each other. Today, these groups are called First Nations because they were here first — before Europeans came.

British Columbians at work and play

Coastal Nations

From north to south, the Native nations living on the coast were the Tlingit, Tsimshian, Haida, Bella Coola, Kwakiutl, Nootka, and Coast Salish. Within some of these groups were smaller groups that spoke different, though closely related, languages.

Each nation had its own culture and traditions, but each also held some things in common. Many had a class system that included nobles, commoners and slaves captured in wars. Marriages were usually arranged to unite families. On the north coast, women held more important positions than on the south coast. Among the Haida on Haida Gwaii (the Queen Charlotte Islands), families traced their ancestry through the mother, and women sometimes became chiefs.

The Native people believed that everyone had a soul, which still lived after the person died. They believed that certain men or women, called shamans, had the power to heal those who were sick or had lost their soul. If too many of a shaman's patients died, the shaman might be killed by the villagers.

The coastal economy was based on the sea and the forests. Seals, salmon, halibut, mussels, clams, herring roe and seaweed provided food and trade items. So many shellfish were eaten that all along the coast today you can see large mounds of discarded

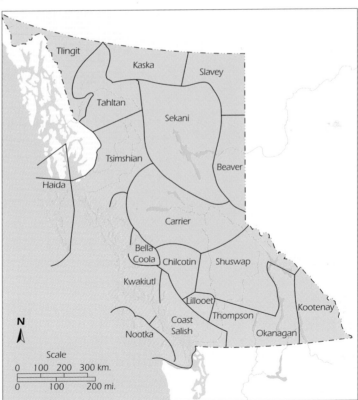

This map shows the areas occupied by the main Native groups when the first Europeans arrived.

shells that piled up over the centuries. The Nootka, on the west coast of Vancouver Island, also hunted whales in their eight-person canoes. And every spring, the Tsimshian set up camp at the mouth of the Nass River to catch the small, oily eulachon or candlefish that came there in huge numbers to spawn. Eulachon oil, extracted by cooking the fish in wooden vats, was used as a buttery sauce and a berry preservative. Tsimshian traders carried it in wooden boxes along "grease trails," well-used paths to the interior. The trails included bridges and canoe routes.

All Native people had great respect for the land and the animals. The coastal nations believed that salmon were people who had eternal life and lived in a large house deep in the ocean. Every spring these people took on the form of salmon and gave themselves to humans for food. After the Native people ate salmon, they put the bones in the water to wash out to sea and change again into salmon people.

During the summer, men fished and women gathered berries and plants for food. Most of the winter was spent indoors in large

Left: The interior of a Coast Salish house, by Paul Kane. Coast Salish women were skilled weavers who made beautiful blankets from spun mountain goat wool and dog hair. *Below:* Traditional houses and totem poles at 'Ksan, a reconstructed Gitksan village near Hazelton. The Gitksan are one of the three Tsimshian peoples (the Nishga and the Coast Tsimshian are the others).

"longhouses" that might hold ten families, each with its own living area. The houses were made of planks that were split from cedar logs and fitted into a frame of cedar posts. The posts and walls were often decorated with carvings and paintings. Sleeping benches were built along the outer walls. Cedar mats and wooden storage boxes were used as walls to divide the living areas. Fish were hung to dry on racks hanging from the ceiling.

During the cold, rainy winter, the adults and children gathered around a large central fire to tell stories or play games. The men built canoes and tools and carved masks, and the women wove baskets and clothing from strips of bark and roots.

Carved totem poles representing family histories or Native legends were often placed at the front of a house. Ravens, eagles, whales, bears, beavers, mythical beings and human figures were carved on the poles. Some poles were raised as a memorial when an important person died or when someone became a chief.

When a new totem pole was raised, a potlatch was usually planned. The potlatch was like a big party held to celebrate important events such as a marriage or a newly built house or a new chief taking power. Sometimes the potlatch just celebrated a family's high status.

Guests came to the potlatch from many villages. They sometimes stayed for days, feasting, dancing, singing and telling stories about their history. The host gave many valuable gifts to all the guests. The gifts included beautifully carved canoes, masks and bowls, skins, fishing rights and even slaves. To show their wealth, everyone tried to give more and better gifts than others had given.

Interior Nations

Native nations living in the interior were the Interior Salish, which includes the Okanagan, Lillooet, Thompson and Shuswap peoples; the Athapaskan, which includes the Chilcotin, Carrier, Sekani, Tahltan, Kaska, Slavey and Beaver peoples; and the Kootenay.

Life in the interior was harder than on the coast. The weather was

Far left: **In winter, the Interior Salish lived in pit-houses called *kikulis*.**
Left: **The distinctive shape of Kootenay bark canoes — with pointy ends that extended underwater — was well suited to the rushing rivers of the B.C. interior.**

harsher, and it took more effort to find food. People moved around more — they were nomadic. Because of this, they did not have as many possessions as coastal Natives did, and there was more equality among people.

Some interior groups lived beside rivers where they could catch salmon, which came far upstream to spawn. Other groups often spent the summer near lakes and streams where they could fish, but they depended primarily on hunting for food.

All interior groups hunted, even during the snowy winters, using spears or bows and arrows to kill large animals, such as deer and elk, and snares made of rope to catch groundhogs, rabbits and other small animals. They also gathered berries and edible roots.

As on the coast, Native people living in the interior respected the spirits of the fish and animals they killed. For example, when the Athapaskan killed a bear for its meat and fur, they apologized to it and honoured it by placing its skull in the fork of a tree.

Some people, such as the Kootenay, lived in lodges made from buffalo hides that could be taken down easily and moved. In winter,

the Interior Salish lived in *kikulis*. The bottom half of these dwellings were pits dug into the earth, which provided good insulation from the cold. The dome-shaped roof was made of logs and poles that were covered by soil. Several families might live together in a kikuli.

The Native peoples of the interior traded such things as mountain goat skins, lichen dyes, obsidian and soapberries for dried seaweed, shells and eulachon oil from the coast.

Contact with Europeans

Europeans began exploring the coast of British Columbia in the late 1700s. First to come were Spaniards from Mexico, then came the British, who soon established a profitable trade in sea otter furs with China. In the early 1800s, the British also began coming into British Columbia by land from the east to set up fur-trading posts.

After the arrival of Europeans, the trading activities of the Native people changed. The newcomers wanted furs, and so Native people hunted otter and trapped beaver to trade for blankets, buttons, iron and other items they could barter from the Europeans. They were sharp traders and were said to check the quality of European trade goods carefully and reject inferior items.

The fur trade did not do much to change the culture of the Native people other than to increase the wealth of some groups. The European traders, especially those who came overland from the east or south, depended on help from Native people, who shared food and housing with them and guided them over the mountains. Some Native women married Europeans.

New Settlers

Fur traders came and went, but few people settled in British Columbia. By 1855, only about 500 non-Natives lived around Fort Victoria on Vancouver Island, and another 150 around Nanaimo. There were even fewer settlers on the mainland.

Some Black immigrants became policemen in Victoria and later formed a militia unit, the Victoria Pioneer Rifle Company. For a time, this was the only organized defence force in the colony.

All this changed with the gold rush, which began in 1858. More than 30 000 Americans, Chinese and Europeans streamed into British Columbia over the next few years. Most came looking for gold in the Fraser River near Hope and later in the Cariboo, but others came to supply goods and services to the gold-seekers. Among the Americans who came were a large number of Black men and women who had left California because of racial discrimination. A few of them headed for the gold fields, but most settled around Fort Victoria and on Saltspring Island, where they farmed, started businesses and worked in a variety of jobs. Many, but by no means all, returned to the United States after the American Civil War.

Most of the gold and the gold-seekers were gone by 1866, but many of the new people stayed on. They began farming on Vancouver Island and in the Lower Fraser Valley. They raised cattle in the Cariboo and hunted whales and seals off the coast of Vancouver Island. They mined coal on Vancouver Island, and they logged the giant trees in the coastal forests.

The next great influx of settlers came after British Columbia joined Confederation, when construction finally began on the promised railway that would link it to the rest of Canada.

Building the railway through British Columbia was an enormous job. Chinese labourers were brought from China and San Francisco

Vancouver's Chinatown at the turn of the century and today

to help with the work. In the early 1880s, about 4000 Chinese lived in British Columbia. By the early 1890s, after the railway was built, the Chinese population had doubled.

During the same period, the European population more than tripled. Most of these new arrivals came from other parts of Canada, especially Ontario and the Maritimes. They came because farm land and jobs were available. Japanese people also began coming to British Columbia in the 1880s, mainly to fish, and Sikhs came from India to work in logging camps and sawmills.

Among the new settlers, most of the adults were men. In some areas in the interior, men outnumbered women by ten to one. Among the Native people, the number of men and women was more equal, but the entire Native population was declining.

Conflict of Cultures

After gold was discovered and settlers began to move into the area, conflict developed between the Native people and the newcomers. The Europeans wanted to own land to farm and to build houses on. Native people did not believe anyone could own the sacred land — they just travelled over it.

The Europeans began to take the land, without treaties and

without adequate compensation, and made laws that forced the Native people to live only in certain areas called reserves. Some Native peoples, such as the Nishga living in the Nass Valley, protested. In 1888, when the government wanted to give them a piece of land to live on, a Nishga spokesperson said, "How can they give it when it is our own.... They have never bought it from us or our forefathers. They have never fought or conquered our people.... It has been ours for thousands of years...."

There were other problems, too. The Native people had no immunity to European diseases, and many thousands died of smallpox, measles and tuberculosis spread by Europeans.

The Canadian government wanted the Native people to live like Europeans. The potlatch was outlawed. Laws were passed to control the way Natives fished. Native children were forced to live in schools run by Europeans, where they were not allowed to speak their own languages, but had to speak English. Missionaries taught them Christianity.

The Twentieth Century

By 1901, for the first time, the majority of the people living in British Columbia were of British heritage. Almost 11 percent of the population were people of Asian heritage, the same as today.

More and more British moved to British Columbia, attracted by the mild climate, the jobs in resource industries, such as forestry and mining, and the hunting and fishing. The province was so British, in fact, that people drove on the left side. One visitor wrote that a person from Ontario would not feel at home in Vancouver.

Meanwhile, people from other countries continued to immigrate. Scandinavians, Greeks, Italians and Basques built their own communities. Doukhobors, a Christian group originally from Russia, moved to British Columbia from Saskatchewan. They bought land as a group in the Kootenays and remain there today.

The Doukhobors and the Mennonites, another religious group

In the 1920s, Japanese British Columbians put together their own baseball team, the Vancouver Asahis. It was one of the best baseball teams of the twenties and thirties.

from Europe, tried to stay apart from other British Columbians. They wanted to live according to their religion and not according to Canadian ways. Other newcomers wanted to be part of Canadian life, but sometimes were not allowed to be. Asians, in particular, suffered many forms of discrimination during the first half of the century.

After the Second World War, many Europeans came to British Columbia looking for a better life. They came from Italy, Germany, Portugal, Czechoslovakia, Ukraine and Holland. Later political upheavals around the world brought many more immigrants to the province — from Hungary in the mid-1950s (all the teachers and students from one Hungarian forestry school came as a group to UBC); from India, Pakistan and Tibet in the 1960s and 1970s; from Vietnam and Cambodia in the 1970s and 1980s; from Hong Kong after 1984, the year the British agreed to return Hong Kong to Chinese rule in 1997.

In the 1960s and 1970s, another group of newcomers made an impact on British Columbia. Thousands of young people from other parts of Canada and from the United States moved here. Many stayed in Vancouver, but others settled in the Gulf Islands, the Kootenays, and the Shuswap lakes to live simply in the country.

In the past few decades, the province has also welcomed immigrants from Korea, Thailand, Uganda, Latin America, South Africa and the Caribbean. Very recently, people from Romania and from the former East Germany and Yugoslavia have made their way to British Columbia.

British Columbia has welcomed many new groups of immigrants in recent decades.

Native Rebirth

During the early and middle 1900s, many Native people in British Columbia suffered from the destruction of their way of life. They were not allowed to follow their own customs and faced discrimination when they tried to live away from the reserves. On reserves, many bands lived with constant unemployment, poverty, alcoholism and family problems. Their numbers continued to decline — in 1929, the total Native population was only 22 605.

Then the long downward trend reversed itself. By 1950, there were almost 30 000 Native people living in the province. At the end of 1992, there were over 90 000.

Left: Master carver Charles Edenshaw (c. 1839-1920) was one of the first Haida artists to gain widespread recognition. *Above:* Argillite carving is a specialty of Haida artists as the beautiful soft stone is found only in the mountains of southern Graham Island.

In recent years, the First Nations have been asserting their rights. In 1982, "existing aboriginal rights" were recognized by the Canadian Constitution. Native people began talking about returning to Native self-government. They have filed "land claims" to reclaim ownership rights to their land. They have led protests against the government. They have found new pride in their history, traditions and art. Native artists are now famous throughout the world for their prints, masks, sculpture and modern totem poles.

Today's People

Today, about three and a half million people live in British Columbia. Fewer than half the non-Natives were born in the province. Some 30 percent moved here from other provinces, 20 percent from other countries. Although their numbers continue to grow, Native people are now only 2.69 percent of British Columbia's population, down from 100 percent barely two centuries ago. About half live on reserves all over the province.

People from other parts of Canada come to British Columbia for jobs, for the milder climate and for the mountains and the sea. Many come when they retire. People from other countries come to British Columbia to join their families, to flee persecution, to seek freedom or to enjoy a better life.

More than half of the province's people live in the Lower Mainland. It is still growing rapidly, especially in the suburban areas south of the city. The next largest population areas are around Victoria, Prince George, Kamloops, Kelowna and Nanaimo.

The cultural mix of people in British Columbia means that a number of different religions are practised here. Many aboriginal people are rediscovering their Native spiritual roots. Almost 75 percent of British Columbians today say they are Protestant. Nearly 15 percent are Roman Catholic. Among the others are Hindus, Muslims, Jews and Buddhists.

Just as Christians celebrate their special holidays of Christmas and Easter, British Columbia's other cultural and religious groups

A couple of today's citizens, and of tomorrow's

celebrate special days. Hindus and Sikhs celebrate Diwali, the festival of lights, with fireworks in the fall. The Chinese have colourful parades and dragon dances to celebrate their New Year in January or February. Jews celebrate their New Year, Rosh Hashanah, in early fall.

The Future

In the early 1990s, British Columbia was Canada's fastest-growing province. It will probably continue to attract people from other places.

From the time the first Europeans arrived, the First Nations have seen new groups moving in. The newcomers often wear different clothes, eat different food and speak different languages. This great variety among the people in British Columbia makes it an exciting and challenging place to live.

CHAPTER 4

Early Exploration and Settlement

During the 1700s, ships from many nations sailed the seas looking for new trade routes and new worlds to explore. A growing European population wanted more spices, silks, tea, gold, furs and fish. Fleets from Russia, Britain, Spain, France, Portugal and Holland competed with each other in an effort to claim new lands and obtain access to these and other resources.

First European Explorers

Russian interest in the Pacific Northwest began in the early 1700s and increased after Vitus Bering's 1740 expedition returned with several hundred sea otter pelts. The Spanish, who had claimed the entire Pacific coast in the sixteenth century, became concerned about this Russian presence in the north and dispatched ships from Mexico to establish Spain's sovereignty.

The first of three Spanish expeditions left from Mexico under Commander Juan Pérez Hernández and reached the Pacific Northwest in 1774. Hernández's ship, the *Santiago,* dropped anchor first off the Queen Charlotte Islands and then in Nootka Sound, halfway down the west coast of Vancouver Island. At both places, local Natives visited the Santiago and exchanged sea otter pelts for clothing, beads and knives. The next year, a Spanish ship commanded by Juan Francisco de la Bodega y Quadra travelled as far north as the Alaska Panhandle and erected a large wooden cross to claim the coast for Spain. After a third voyage in 1779, the Spanish felt confident that their claim to the area was well established.

Captain James Cook at Nootka Sound, April 1778

Captain James Cook

In 1776, Captain James Cook left Britain in search of the Northwest Passage — a sea route from Europe to the Orient that many people believed would be found through North American waters. British ships had been searching for this route for more than 200 years when Cook was sent to look for the passage from the Pacific side.

After voyaging through the South Sea islands, Cook reached Nootka Sound in 1778. Thirty canoes filled with Nootka people greeted his ships. The Nootka chief, Maquinna, waved a bird-shaped rattle in formal welcome and scattered eagle down on the water. Cook and his crew stayed for four weeks, repairing their ships and brewing up enough spruce beer to prevent scurvy on their onward journey. After sailing farther north without finding a passage, the expedition travelled south to the Sandwich Islands (now known as Hawaii) to pass the winter. Cook died in the islands in 1779, but his crew continued on to China as planned. There the sea otter pelts obtained for next to nothing from the Native people were sold for large sums of money. While the expedition did not succeed in finding the Northwest Passage, it did succeed in starting a fur trade that lasted for the next 50 years and in establishing Britain's presence in the area.

Captain George Vancouver

The maritime trade in sea otter pelts that grew up after Cook's expedition led to the arrival of many explorers and mapmakers. In 1792, Captain George Vancouver travelled from England and began the job of surveying and charting the coastline. At Nootka Sound he met the Spanish commander Bodega y Quadra. Although their countries were involved in a dispute over control of the area, the two became friends. In fact, Vancouver named the land where he had met the Spanish commander "Quadra's and Vancouver's Island." (Mapmakers later shortened it to "Vancouver Island.")

Vancouver explored the area over the course of three summers, mapping much of the coastline and naming many places.

Captain George Vancouver and his survey team off the B.C. coast. Vancouver first visited the area as a young midshipman with Cook's expedition. He is now considered to have been one of the world's great navigators and mapmakers.

Alexander Mackenzie

While Vancouver and Quadra were surveying the Pacific coast, other explorers were charting routes down rivers and through the mountains. One of them was Alexander Mackenzie, the first of the Pacific Northwest's great fur-trader explorers.

Mackenzie began working in the fur trade when he was 15 years old. He was 25 and a partner in the North West Company when he began looking for a canoe route from Lake Athabasca to the Pacific Ocean. In his first attempt he travelled down the river that now bears his name and reached the Arctic Ocean. In his second attempt, he travelled down the Peace and Fraser rivers.

Mackenzie's second great exploration, like his first, depended on the strength of voyageur paddlers and the skills and knowledge of Native guides and interpreters. On the journey to the Pacific, his party paddled through narrow canyons and dragged heavy canoes up hill sides. Struggling over many obstacles, the group crossed the Rocky Mountains and the interior plateau, then followed the

centuries-old Grease Trail, used by Native people to transport eulachon oil into the interior.

In 1793, Mackenzie finally reached salt water at Bella Coola, the first European to travel overland to the Pacific. On his arrival, he used a mixture of vermilion and melted grease to record his achievement on a rock just above the tide line.

Simon Fraser

Simon Fraser, another of the Pacific Northwest's fur-trader explorers, joined the North West Company at age 16 and was 29 when he was put in charge of fur-trading operations in the area now

Right: Simon Fraser and his party at Hell's Gate. Fraser later wrote of the experience in his diary: "I have been for a long period among the Rocky Montains, but have never seen anything to equal this country, for I cannot find words to describe our situation at times. We had to pass where no human being should venture." *Below:* Mackenzie's inscription. Rain eventually washed the words away, but in 1926 the Historic Sites and Monuments Board had them carved in the rock and filled with red cement.

known as central British Columbia. After building four trading posts in the area, Fraser tried to find a safe canoe route to the Pacific Ocean. Accompanied by 19 voyageurs, and ignoring the advice of Native people, Fraser set out in 1808 to travel down the river that now bears his name. Shooting through rapids and whirlpools, the members of Fraser's group navigated treacherous waters until they were forced to abandon their canoes at the narrow gorge known as Hell's Gate. There they had to drag their baggage over a faint trail that ran along a sheer rock wall high above rushing waters. Supplies ran out after this and everyone had to eat berries and moss. Yet the expedition members survived, and after they obtained some canoes from Native people, they continued on to the coast.

Even though the river travelled by Fraser never became a useful fur-trade route, it did become an important travel "corridor." Almost 200 years after Simon Fraser's journey, people are still travelling by road and by rail along the banks of the Fraser River.

David Thompson

While Simon Fraser was looking for a canoe route to the Pacific, British-born David Thompson was exploring the Rocky Mountains in search of another possible canoe route. Like both Fraser and Mackenzie, Thompson entered the fur trade as a young man. He began working for the Hudson's Bay Company (HBC) when he was 14. After learning the skills of a surveyor, Thompson left the HBC to work for the rival North West Company. He soon became its leading mapmaker.

In 1807, Thompson followed the Columbia River to Lake Windermere and constructed a trading fort. Using the fort as a base, he continued to explore and map the area that is now southeastern British Columbia. Often his Métis wife and their three small children travelled with him.

Thompson finally reached the mouth of the Columbia River in 1811, but he was too late to claim the territory for Britain — Americans had already arrived and built a fort. Today Thompson is

remembered for his accurate maps and the colourful journals he wrote about his explorations.

The Fur Trade

As the newly charted riverways opened up the West, the land-based fur trade expanded, and competition intensified between the North West and Hudson's Bay companies.

The Montreal-based North West Company controlled trade in the area now known as British Columbia through a network of forts that included Fort St. James, Fort Fraser, Fort George, Fort Kamloops and Kootenay House. The Hudson's Bay Company was a powerful firm based in England and, until 1820, had no forts west of the Rocky Mountains. In 1821, the two companies finally realized that competition was ruining them both and agreed to merge under the name of the Hudson's Bay Company.

The 20 years after the merger were relatively stable ones. The HBC's governor in North America, George Simpson, worked to make the company more powerful and more efficient. In 1841, Simpson decided to move the company's west coast headquarters from Fort Vancouver on the Columbia River to Vancouver Island. He sent HBC Chief Factor James Douglas to choose a suitable location, and in 1843 the construction of Fort Victoria began in a cove on the southern tip of Vancouver Island.

But even before Fort Victoria was finished, the fur trade in the Pacific Northwest had started to change. Some fur-bearing animals were declining in numbers, and ownership of the area west of the Rocky Mountains was in dispute. Britain had granted the HBC trading rights over territories that extended as far south as present-day Oregon, but some American political leaders insisted that all the lands between California and Alaska belonged to the United States. There was even talk of war before the two parties reached an agreement in 1846 and signed a treaty that gave Britain all of Vancouver Island and established the border with the United States

James Douglas supervises early construction work on Fort Victoria in 1843.

at the 49th parallel. The fur trade did not revive, however. European demand for furs lessened, and the trade that had once been a source of great wealth continued to decline.

The Native people who had been essential to the trade continued to feel the effects of the changes it brought them for many, many years. Traditional ways had been undermined, alcohol had disrupted community life, and diseases like smallpox and influenza had ravaged whole villages. Unfortunately, the decline of the fur trade did not mean the end of these problems.

As the heyday of the fur trade came to a close, the days of the settler began. The farming and fishing activity that had been carried on around forts in order to feed the traders increased as more settlers arrived. Then came an event that added impetus to the drive to settle the land west of the Rockies — the discovery of gold.

The Rush for Gold

In 1858, news of gold found on Fraser River sandbars reached San Francisco, and boats filled with miners streamed north to Victoria.

Within days, Victoria's population grew from a few hundred to thousands. A huge tent city sprang up to shelter an international community of gold-seekers: native-born Americans, Chinese, Germans, Italians, Spaniards and many others who had already tried their luck in the California gold fields.

The miners bought supplies and licences, then boarded a variety of vessels to cross Georgia Strait to the mainland. Some of the boats were no bigger and no safer than bathtubs, and many people drowned. The miners who reached the mainland then had to tramp through dense forest and over rugged mountains. Some of them were rewarded for their efforts — before the end of 1858 about $1.6 million worth of gold was taken from the stretch of river between Hope and Lillooet.

The arrival of more than 25 000 people during 1858 changed the sparsely populated mainland. Shanty towns grew up with the influx of miners and the arrival of innkeepers, builders and merchants who saw the possibility of profit in the Fraser River Gold Rush.

Since many of the miners in the new shanty towns came from the United States, there was renewed fear of American domination. James Douglas, who had been made governor of the Vancouver Island colony in 1849, was quick to let leaders in Britain know about this fear. When Britain decided to assert its authority by creating another colony on the mainland, Douglas was asked to take on a second governorship. In 1858, he became governor of the new colony of British Columbia.

The mainland government soon had a second gold rush to deal with. In 1862, an Englishman named Billy Barker struck "paydirt" after digging a 13-metre (42-foot) shaft at Williams Creek near present-day Quesnel. Within two weeks a new town, Barkerville, had sprung up, with hotels, bakeries, blacksmith shops, stores, banks and even a theatre. Men made fortunes and then lost them as they drank, gambled and danced with the hurdy-gurdy girls. Billy Barker himself lost his fortune and died a pauper.

Above: For a time, Barkerville was the gold rush capital of the world. Much of it burned down in 1868, but by then the Cariboo Gold Rush was virtually over. *Left:* Camels were introduced as pack animals into the Cariboo in 1862. It no doubt seemed like a good idea, since camels could carry a lot more than a mule or a horse, but it turned out that their feet were unsuited to the rocky, muddy terrain.

The Fraser River and Cariboo gold rushes dramatically increased the populations of Vancouver Island and British Columbia. Prospectors of every nationality flocked to the two colonies. More people often meant more trouble. The man who helped Governor Douglas control lawlessness during and after the gold rush was the legendary Judge Matthew Baillie Begbie.

Judge Begbie almost singlehandedly upheld law and order from

Catherine Schubert was the only woman among a group of gold-seekers known as the Overlanders of '62, who travelled overland to the Cariboo from present-day Winnipeg. The trek through the mountains was harrowing for everyone, but especially for Mrs. Schubert, who gave birth to a daughter only a few hours after arriving in Kamloops. The baby, Rose, was the first non-Native child born in the B.C. interior.

New Westminster on the coast to the Cariboo gold fields. He was often seen riding on horseback as he travelled to every corner of the colony to hear trials in halls, tents and open fields. Between 1859 and 1872 he presided over 52 murder trials. Twenty-seven of the people found guilty by the juries were hanged.

As well as contributing to the establishment of a justice system, the gold rushes led to the development of new and better routes for transporting people and goods. In 1859, the Royal Engineers arrived and began the work of choosing sites for cities and ports, planning the layout of communities and building bridges and roads. The largest road-building project was a wagon route stretching north from Yale to the Cariboo. Under the command of Colonel Richard Moody, the Royal Engineers laid out a 650-kilometre (400-mile) route and did most of the dangerous rock-blasting work in the Fraser Canyon. The Cariboo Wagon Road was completed in 1865 and immediately made travel by ox-drawn wagon and stagecoach much easier. Settlers began using the road to reach homesteads and communities in the interior. Several of the "Mile Houses" that catered to travellers along the way can still be seen from the Trans-Canada Highway, which follows some of the route.

Becoming a Province

During the gold rush period, ranchers began raising cattle on the natural grasslands of the southern Cariboo, Catholic priests planted the first fruit orchards and grape vines in the Okanagan Valley, and

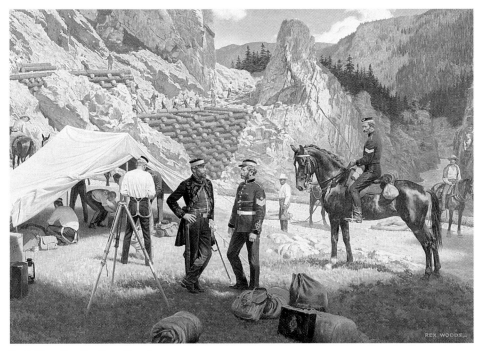

Building the Cariboo Road

Chinese settlers on Vancouver Island grew vegetables for local use. Soon land rather than gold began to attract people who saw the economic potential of farming, fishing and logging in the two colonies.

In the mid-1860s, British authorities decided that the development of Vancouver Island and British Columbia would be strengthened if they were united. Accordingly, in November 1866 the two colonies became the United Colony of British Columbia. The new colony had a 23-member legislative council with nine elected members, four from the island and five from the mainland. New Westminster became the first capital, but lost its position two years later when government officials voted to move the seat of government to Victoria.

One of the chief forces behind the move from New Westminster to Victoria was a man who stands first in a long line of colourful British Columbia politicians — Amor De Cosmos. Born in Nova

Scotia, William Alexander Smith was a journalist who travelled to the California gold fields and changed his name to Amor De Cosmos — "Lover of the Universe." After arriving in Victoria, the outspoken De Cosmos started the *British Colonist* newspaper and was soon deeply involved in politics.

De Cosmos was one of the most active promoters of union with the new Dominion of Canada. In 1867, the colonies of New Brunswick, Nova Scotia, and the United Province of Canada

Coaling station at Nanaimo, 1859. Even before the gold rush, the discovery of coal in the Nanaimo area was attracting miners to Vancouver Island. By the mid-1880s, coal would overtake gold as the province's most valuable mineral.

(Quebec and Ontario) had joined in a Canadian Confederation. Some British Columbians agreed with De Cosmos and wanted to become part of the Dominion; others thought the colony should join the United States. When the Dominion promised a transcontinental rail link, opponents to the plan were won over. In 1871, British Columbia entered Confederation with the assurance that a railway joining the province with the rest of the Dominion would be built by 1881.

Even with the promise of a rail link, the new province was far from strong. The decline of the fur trade and the end of the gold rush had left the economy in an uncertain state. The population of 40 000 consisted of almost 30 000 Native people and a mixture of Europeans, Chinese and Americans. In some areas there were hardly any non-Native women to share in the work of building and maintaining settlements. These settlements consisted of Native villages, some fur trade depots, fading gold-mining towns and a few well-established communities — all scattered across a large and rugged territory. The province builders had their work cut out for them.

Fort Street, Victoria, about the time of Confederation

CHAPTER 5

The Province Grows

When British Columbia entered Confederation on July 20, 1871, life was difficult for the fur traders, miners, merchants and settlers in the new province, but it was particularly difficult for the Native peoples of the region. Over one-third of the Native population had died during the smallpox epidemics of the early gold rush years. Those who survived soon faced an entirely different social, economic and political order. With the decline of the fur trade and the end of the gold rush came a push to clear and use the land in a way that was foreign to Native culture. Europeans lived by cultivating and building and settling on land, practices that were incompatible with the hunting and gathering traditions of Native peoples. Tension between the two groups increased. Although no treaties were signed, Native lands were reduced to small reserves. Discouraged by government (the potlatch would even be banned), Native traditions gave way to European ones, despite the fact that there were more Native people than Europeans living in British Columbia until well into the 1880s.

The Canadian Pacific Railway

After Confederation, fishers, miners, loggers and farmers had spread out across the province and settled close to the major transportation routes in an effort to use the province's resources and earn a living. Canneries were built all along the coast to process salmon caught in the major runs on the Fraser, Skeena and Nass rivers. Sawmills were built to turn trees into lumber, and crops were planted. The railway

Logging camp, Vancouver Island, in the early 1900s

Above: **The Honourable Donald Smith, one of the founders of the Canadian Pacific Railway Company, drives in the ceremonial last spike symbolizing the completion of the railway from Halifax on the east coast to Port Moody on the west.** *Right:* **Chinese railway workers had their own separate camps, which were usually little more than a group of flimsy tents.**

that colonists had been promised before Confederation was needed more than ever. The wagon roads, trails and riverways could not transport all the supplies required or the goods produced.

After many delays, the construction of the British Columbia portion of the Canadian Pacific Railway (CPR) finally began in 1880. The railway builders soon discovered that the province's rugged terrain made building a route to the coast a massive undertaking. Surveyors working in the Rocky Mountains studied several routes before choosing the Kicking Horse and Rogers passes. While looking for the pass that would later bear his name, CPR engineer Major A.B. Rogers

and his surveyors ran into terrible weather and were forced to pitch their tents in the snow. Almost frozen, the men then had to beat each other with their pack straps to keep warm.

While the survey crews endured hardships, the construction crews suffered even more. Tunnelling through solid rock, balancing on half-built bridges over fast-moving water and living in cold and uncomfortable camps, many workers died from accidents and disease. Among the workers were over 15 000 Chinese labourers who were brought from China and San Francisco to blast railbeds and place ties. The hard work and the poor conditions in their segregated camps led to the death of at least 600 Chinese workers.

Despite delays and difficulties and the death of many workers, the railway was completed at last. On November 7, 1885, a crowd of CPR officials and railway workers gathered at Craigellachie in the Selkirk Mountains. There they watched as the "last spike" was driven in, and a railway joining British Columbia to Canada was finished.

Vancouver's Rise

The completion of the Canadian Pacific Railway had a direct effect on Coal Harbour, the small logging settlement that had grown up on the south shore of Burrard Inlet to process the massive trees covering what is now North Vancouver. Many people in the community worked at Hastings Mill and then gathered in "Gassy Jack" Deighton's hotel to drink and tell tall tales. When the decision was made to make Coal Harbour the western terminal of the Canadian Pacific Railway, the rough-and-ready settlement was transformed.

In 1885, the newly named townsite of Vancouver was laid out, and in 1886 Vancouver was incorporated. Two months later, a fire burned most of the city to the ground. Almost 800 buildings were destroyed and 13 people were killed. Rebuilding began immediately, and when the first transcontinental train rolled into Vancouver's Burrard Inlet terminal in 1887, the city boasted 5000 inhabitants.

With the advantages of a railway and a good natural harbour,

Vancouver continued to grow. Cargo ships brought tea and silk from Asia, pleasure liners carried visitors, and the railway transported settlers and entrepreneurs from other parts of Canada. Streets were paved, schools were built and factories were started. By 1900, Vancouver had outgrown the capital city of Victoria and was on its way to becoming the busiest city in the province.

At the same time as Vancouver was developing into a major commercial and manufacturing centre, communities in other parts

The tiny community of Coal Harbour was renamed Vancouver and grew by leaps and bounds once it was chosen as the CPR's western terminal. Seen here: the arrival in 1887 of the first trans-continental train into the city *(right)*; the Old Hastings Mill Store, now a museum, is Vancouver's oldest building, one of the few that escaped the 1886 fire *(above left)*; a stroll in Stanley Park, which opened in 1888, quickly became a favourite way to spend a Sunday afternoon *(above right)*.

of British Columbia were expanding. Since mineral production was so important to the province's economy, many of these communities were mining towns. On Vancouver Island, Nanaimo grew to serve workers who mined coal in damp, dark and often dangerous conditions. On the mainland, rich deposits of copper, silver and lead were discovered in the Kootenay region and hastened the establishment of Nelson as a supply centre. While neither Nanaimo nor Nelson rivalled Vancouver in size, they represented the kind of growth that was opening up more parts of the province.

Railway Expansion

From the 1880s to the early 1900s, the Canadian Pacific Railway played as large a role in British Columbia's development as the Hudson's Bay Company had played 50 years earlier. After completing its cross-Canada route in 1885, the CPR purchased hotels and ships, moved into mining and expanded its rail lines.

New routes built by the CPR and rival railway companies began to criss-cross British Columbia. The Canadian Northern Railway built a line that used the Yellowhead Pass through the Rockies and proceeded along the North Thompson River to Kamloops before running parallel with the CPR line through the Fraser Canyon to the coast. The Grand Trunk Pacific Railway began work in 1906 on a line that crossed from the Yellowhead Pass to Prince George and then continued on to the coast at Prince Rupert. Communities grew up all along these railway routes, and speculators bought land in the hope of selling it later at a profit. As rail lines spread, more and more settlers arrived from across Canada and around the world.

Immigration

In the 30 years that followed the completion of the CPR, British Columbia's Native population decreased dramatically, and the non-Native population increased even more so. Most of this

increase resulted from immigration. Chinese immigrants arrived to join relatives who had come earlier to mine for gold and build the railway. Doukhobors came to escape religious persecution in their homeland. English, Irish, Scottish, Scandinavian, Italian and German immigrants came looking for opportunities not available in their crowded home countries, as did immigrants from India and Japan.

The vast majority of new arrivals in the 1880s, however, came from other parts of Canada. Looking for good farmland and better wages, young men and women left Ontario and the Maritimes to work as loggers, schoolteachers, cooks and shopkeepers in British Columbia. Canadian immigrants continued to arrive throughout the 1890s, outnumbering all other groups of new arrivals until the early 1900s, when British immigrants became the largest group of new British Columbians.

Throughout this period of steady immigration, people from Britain, northern Europe, the United States and other parts of

Below: **Japanese shop damaged during the 1907 anti-Asian riots.** *Right:* **Would-be Sikh immigrants aboard the *Komagata Maru*. After two months in harbour, the ship was finally persuaded to leave by the arrival of a Canadian navy cruiser.**

Canada were considered more desirable than immigrants from southern Europe and Asia. As the province grew, so did racist attitudes and policies. Chinese and Japanese people were termed an "Oriental menace" while East Indians were all called "Hindoos," even though most were Sikhs. Asian workers were excluded from many occupations, and Chinese immigrants had to pay a large "head tax" before entering the country. In Vancouver in 1907, a protest meeting of working men opposed to Asian immigration was followed by rioting in Chinatown and the Japanese area nearby. Later, the federal government passed laws to limit the numbers of people from Asia allowed into Canada.

One of the laws used to restrict Asian immigration required immigrants to travel directly from their country of origin to Canada. This law was challenged in the summer of 1914 by a wealthy Sikh who tried to bring in 376 Sikh and Muslim Punjabi immigrants on the *Komagata Maru*, which had made stops at Shanghai and Japan on its way to Canada from Hong Kong. Officials upholding the "continuous passage" law refused to let the ship land. The immigrants were kept on board the crowded steamer for two months while the Sikh organizer of the trip argued with immigration officials. Finally the officials had their way and the *Komagata Maru* and her passengers left for Hong Kong.

Unrest and Reform

Tensions caused by racial differences were not the only ones felt by British Columbians in the years before the First World War. Conflicts between workers and their employers were common in both the mining and fishing industries. In the early 1900s, British Columbia had more strikes than any other province, as workers fought against long hours, poor pay and unsafe working conditions.

In 1909, a gas explosion at a Vancouver Island coal mine killed 32 men. An investigation suggested that the company was more interested in making money than in protecting workers. Miners

responded by joining a mine worker's union. A few years later, the company's refusal to act on a workers' gas safety report led to a two-year strike. From 1912 to 1914, almost 7000 miners refused to work, and the company kept its mines in partial operation using nonunion labour. In the summer of 1913, the striking workers learned that the company planned to bring in even more nonunion labour and riots broke out. Over 250 miners were arrested, and some were sentenced to as long as two years in prison. The provincial and the federal governments were clearly on the side of the employers, and the next year strikers were forced to accept a settlement that did not include recognition of the union.

The unrest among miners was matched by the unrest among fishers and cannery workers. The cannery owners controlled both the price paid for fish and the wages offered to workers. Labour leaders tried to improve wages and working conditions, but little was achieved because Native, Japanese and white workers in the fishing industry were unable to unite against their employers.

Later in the twentieth century, workers in both the fishing and the mining industries achieved better pay, hours and working conditions, but they did not have great success in their early campaigns for labour reform. Similarly, the campaign for women's suffrage — the right to vote — did not make much progress in the first years of the twentieth century. But this changed after 1910, when more suffrage associations were founded, and reformers like Helen Gregory MacGill and Helena Gutteridge became active in the campaign to improve the position of women in British Columbia. MacGill worked to change the legal status of women and children, who had little control over their own lives, and later became the first woman judge appointed in the province. Gutteridge campaigned for the rights of working women, who were paid much less than men, and later was elected to Vancouver City Council.

Campaigns for workers' and women's rights in the early 1900s were part of a larger reform movement that sought economic and

Helen Gregory MacGill in 1938, just after she received an honorary Doctor of Laws degree from the University of British Columbia. This was the first honorary degree conferred on a woman by the provincial university.

social change. In British Columbia, as elsewhere, the pace of change quickened after the outbreak of the First World War.

The First World War

On August 4, 1914, Britain declared war on Germany, and Canada, as part of the British Empire, was automatically drawn into the conflict. For four years, Canadians stood beside soldiers from Britain, France, Russia and other countries against soldiers from Germany, Austria-Hungary and Turkey. Millions of Canadian men fought in the war's muddy trenches, and over 3000 women served as nurses — called "bluebirds" because of their blue uniforms.

The war changed many aspects of life in British Columbia: communities became smaller as men and women left for Europe, certain industries expanded to serve the war effort, and the building of roads, bridges and other public works stopped. British Columbia contributed a larger share of its population to the war than any other Canadian province. Men and women of all backgrounds volunteered to serve as soldiers, cooks, ambulance drivers and nurses. Japanese, Sikh and Native British Columbians were among

the 43 000 men who went overseas. By the end of the war, 6225 were dead and over 13 000 were wounded. Cities and towns across the province lost many of their young men. In Walhachin, a fruit-growing centre near Kamloops Lake in the central interior, all 43 young men in the 150-member community volunteered.

While the war disrupted family and community life, it also forced employers to negotiate with workers, who were needed to keep important industries running, and hastened women's suffrage (women were given the right to vote in provincial elections in 1917). As well, the wartime need for wood, certain metals and fish maintained the British Columbia economy.

After the War

Immediately after the war, the demand for British Columbia's natural resources decreased and the number of unemployed increased. Soldiers came home from Europe to find a province in economic difficulty. Everywhere in the province, the logging industry suffered when wood was no longer needed to manufacture British airplanes. In the interior mines and smelters were closing, and on the coast the fishery was in trouble. Problems in the fishery had started before the war with the building of the Canadian Northern Railway. In 1913, landslides caused by construction had partially blocked the Fraser River at Hell's Gate. Native fishers had made a heroic effort to net individual salmon and carry them upriver past the slide debris, but too few salmon had survived to spawn. The "lost generation" of fish and the blocked river meant that the Fraser River sockeye run was reduced to a fraction of its original size in the postwar years.

To stimulate the economy and help returning soldiers, Liberal premier John Oliver encouraged settlement in undeveloped areas like the Bulkley Valley and the Kootenays. Oliver's predecessor, Richard McBride, had focused on railway building and the expanding resource industries during his largely prosperous

1903-1915 term as premier. Oliver, a Delta farmer, concentrated instead on road building and farming during his less prosperous 1918-1927 term. One of the farming schemes involved draining Sumas Lake in the Fraser Valley south of Chilliwack and starting dairy farms. Another scheme involved irrigating the southern end of the Okanagan Valley and establishing fruit-growing communities. Oliver also negotiated the return to the province of a rich square of farmland known as the Peace River Block, which had been transferred to the federal government in 1884 as part of the terms for the completion of the Canadian Pacific Railway.

From 1920 onwards, the province experienced increased economic growth. In Vancouver, shipping was becoming the city's biggest industry, and many new homes and larger buildings were constructed. Victoria was expanding as well, becoming a popular tourist destination and a desirable retirement community. Throughout the province labour unrest lessened as more British Columbians found employment and benefited from new workers' compensation and pension programs. To British Columbians driving along the province's new dirt roads in Model-T Ford cars and trucks, the "good life" seemed within reach.

Left: Irrigation in the southern Okanagan Valley was first undertaken in the 1920s. The result over the next few decades was to transform the area into the major fruit-producing region it is today. *Below:* Vancouver Harbour in the 1920s

CHAPTER 6

New Challenges

The mid- to late 1920s were good years for most British Columbians. Prairie grain was shipped out of Vancouver in ever-increasing amounts, and the province's wood, minerals and fish were in demand around the world. Jobs were easy to find, and wages had increased since the war.

Greater prosperity meant that more people were buying things that they had once made at home — clothing, furniture and numerous food products. Local merchants did well, as did manufacturers in central Canada, who produced almost all of the province's manufactured goods. The government continued to promote farming schemes — even though most parts of the province did not have the right kinds of soil or climate for agriculture — while mining, logging and fishing expanded.

The Great Depression

On Black Thursday, October 29, 1929, prosperity ended when the New York stock market collapsed and a worldwide depression began. Unlike previous "slumps," or recessions, this was a deep and far-reaching economic disaster. British Columbians who had become used to prosperity suddenly found themselves out of work in a world that could no longer afford the province's natural resources or products. Prairie grain shipments fell, first because of reduced demand and then because of a drought that turned rich farmlands into dusty wastelands. Across Canada, the United States and

Vancouver's stunning Canada Place was built as the Canadian pavilion for Expo 86. It now houses a trade centre, a convention centre, a 500-room luxury hotel and a cruise ship terminal.

Europe, factories closed and unemployed men and women lined up to receive some form of government relief.

All British Columbians suffered during the years now known as the Great Depression. People lost their homes when they could not pay their taxes, and families were separated when breadwinners travelled away to find work. Some British Columbians suffered more than others. Women were not considered to be part of the workforce in the same way that men were. When single unemployed women in Vancouver tried to get relief money, they were told to find jobs as domestic servants. When unemployed Chinese British Columbians were given relief money, they were given less than non-Chinese British Columbians.

The hardships of the Depression forced everyone to manage with very little. People borrowed, bartered and improvised. Some wore clothes made out of old flour sacks and lived on home-grown produce, game and bannock. Some made soap from bear oil and moose fat, and coffee from roasted grain. Many chopped firewood and built their own homes, returning to the pioneering traditions of earlier years.

People in rural British Columbia had some advantages over city-

Police armed with clubs and tear gas drive unemployed demonstrators out of Vancouver's main post office, July 20, 1938.

dwellers. In the country, people were used to providing for themselves and helping each other. In cities, hunting and fishing were not practical ways of putting food on the table.

Cities were also places where large numbers of unemployed men gathered. In Vancouver in 1938, there were 6000 jobless men, many from the drought-stricken Prairies. When the provincial government refused to give relief payments to non-British Columbians, 1000 unemployed men took over the main post office, the art gallery and the Georgia Hotel. Those occupying the art gallery and the hotel agreed to leave on their own, but the group occupying the post office had to be driven out by police using tear gas and clubs. Many people were wounded in the confrontation.

The Second World War

On September 3, 1939, Britain declared war on Germany after the German army invaded Poland. A week later, Canada declared war on Germany and became part of a conflict that eventually would involve many more countries and would rage for six years in Europe, Africa, Asia and the South Pacific. During the conflict, 42 042 Canadians lost their lives.

In British Columbia, the declaration of war led to an immediate drop in the number of unemployed when many men enlisted in the army, navy or air force. Later, women became directly involved in the war effort as well. By the end of the Second World War, over 4000 nurses had served in more than 100 hospital units, and many more women had served in the Royal Canadian Air Force, Canadian Women's Army Corps and Royal Canadian Naval Women's Service.

Men and women served on the home front as well as the battle front throughout the war. Shipbuilding became an important industry, employing over 30 000 workers in Victoria and Greater Vancouver. The logging industry also employed large numbers of people. Sitka spruce from the Queen Charlotte Islands was needed

to build the light frames of Mosquito bombers, and fir was needed for war-time housing. The mining industry benefited from war-time demands for metals and fuels, but also from the opening up of British Columbia's north.

The Alaska Highway — stretching 2445 kilometres (1519 miles) from Dawson Creek in the Peace River country to Fairbanks, Alaska — was completed as an American defence project in 1943. As well as providing the U.S. army with access to territory that was vulnerable to Japanese attack, the highway provided access for mineral exploration. Old fur-trade posts like Fort St. John and Fort Nelson developed into modern communities to serve prospectors and mine employees as well as people travelling the Alaska Highway.

Although many British Columbians prospered from war-time growth and change, some did not. After Japan bombed Pearl Harbour in 1941, British Columbians of Japanese descent were treated as potential allies of a country many had never seen, much less supported. At first, only a few Japanese men, along with German and Italian "enemy aliens," were evacuated from coastal areas. Then, as fear of a Japanese invasion increased, full-scale evacuation and internment began. Thousands of Japanese men, women and children — most of them Canadian citizens — were rounded up and sent to inland communities and work camps. Many were given little time to gather their possessions, and many had to watch as government officials took away their property. The loss of homes, fishing boats and businesses made it very difficult for evacuees to re-establish themselves after the war. There was some improvement in 1949 when people of Japanese ancestry were allowed to live on the West Coast again and were given the right to vote in federal and provincial elections. However, it was not until 1988 that the Canadian government officially apologized to Japanese British Columbians and attempted to compensate them for losses during the war.

Left: **A famous photograph of a Vancouver family's leave-taking early in the Second World War.** *Above:* **In British Columbia, as in the rest of Canada, the war years saw many women take on jobs traditionally done by men.**

"The Golden Age"

After the Second World War, British Columbia entered a new era of growth and prosperity. Demand for the province's natural resources did not end with the close of the war, and once again forestry, mining, agriculture and fishing were able to provide jobs and products for many people. Tourism and manufacturing also began to play larger roles in the provincial economy.

From 1947 onwards, a wave of Dutch, German, Italian, Greek and Portuguese immigrants joined the flow of British immigrants arriving in the province. Many "war brides" from England and Europe arrived to join their Canadian soldier husbands. In 1951, the population of British Columbia was 1 165 210.

In 1952, dissatisfaction with the previous Conservative, Liberal and coalition governments led to the election of the province's first Social Credit government. Socred Premier W.A.C. ("Wacky")

Bennett, a Kelowna hardware merchant, was a charismatic man of the people who kept the party in power for the next 20 years. Early on, the Social Credit government undertook a range of major projects designed to "open up" British Columbia. From 1955 to 1968, the energetic minister of highways, P.A. "Flying Phil" Gagliardi, pushed roads into every corner of the province, making areas in the northeast and northwest accessible for industry and tourism. In 1958 alone, 62 bridges and six ferry landings were built. In 1962, the final B.C. portion of the Trans-Canada Highway was completed.

As roads were built to link remote parts of the province and air travel became more common, water transport changed. The Union Steamship Company had been running boats between tiny coastal communities for 70 years when it stopped operating in 1959. A year later the provincial government began operating ferries to Vancouver Island. Soon a fleet of blue-and-white vessels was transporting commuters and visitors.

Big hydroelectric projects were also popular during the years Bennett was in power. In the 1950s, Alcan built an aluminum smelter at the head of Kitimat Arm on the north coast and dammed the Nechako River south of Fraser Lake to provide power. The entirely new community of Kitimat was built for the many families that moved into the area. In 1968, the Peace River development in the northeast began providing low-cost electricity to major companies investing in the province.

The Aluminum Company of Canada built a giant smelter in the northern B.C. wilderness in the early 1950s, then built the town of Kitimat around it. The facility remains the only aluminum smelter in Canada outside Quebec.

Prosperity and a greater sense of confidence during the postwar years led to a greater interest in the arts and education. The Queen Elizabeth Theatre and the Vancouver Playhouse were built, and an opera company was formed. Museums, galleries, schools and colleges opened. In Hazelton, Native and non-Native people worked together to build a carving school, workshop and museum in a recreated 1880s Gitksan village called 'Ksan. Victoria College in the capital became the University of Victoria in 1963, and in Burnaby, Simon Fraser University welcomed its first students in 1965. British Columbians in most parts of the province benefited from a buoyant North American economy.

Towards the Twenty-First Century

As W.A.C. Bennett's 20 years in power came to an end, unemployment and labour unrest once again began to affect British Columbians. Hopes for continued prosperity were disappointed as inflation increased and businesses failed. In 1972, the New Democratic Party (NDP) came into power in the province for the first time. Under Premier Dave Barrett, a former social worker from working-class East Vancouver, the NDP government tried to make changes it considered long overdue. During its first year in power, the new government rushed 400 bills through the legislature. Among other things, the bills reorganized social services and created new labour laws. But with the world economy entering a severe recession, the Barrett government's push for change and continued spending made many voters unhappy.

In 1975, the Social Credit Party was returned to power under W.A.C. Bennett's son, Bill Bennett. Subsequently, another "Bill," Wilhelmus Vander Zalm, became leader of the Social Credit Party and premier of British Columbia. A colourful and controversial premier, Vander Zalm was eventually rejected by many Social Credit supporters. His successor, Rita Johnston, became the province's first woman premier, but her time in office was brief.

Since being taken over by the government in 1960, B.C.'s ferry system has grown and modernized. Today, it is one of the largest and most sophisticated in the world.

The 1991 election, held shortly after Johnston became party leader and premier resulted in an NDP government headed by Mike Harcourt. In the 1996 election, the NDP was elected for a second term as government for the first time in the province's history. The newly elected premier, Glen Clark, soon faced many challenges — some that would have been familiar to his predecessors; some that were new.

Issues Old and New

Today, British Columbia is still the vast and rugged province it was at the time of Confederation. But instead of an 1871 population of 36 000, it now has a population of 3.8 million. Rather than living on homesteads and in small mining or logging communities, most British Columbians now live in the expanding cities of the province's southwest.

Economic uncertainty continues to plague British Columbia. The fishing industry is suffering because of shrinking fish populations. Mining is suffering from fluctuations in demand for particular minerals. And the forest industry is suffering because of dwindling supplies of trees — years of overcutting now mean that tough decisions must be made about how many trees can be cut in the future.

The forest industry is also being forced to decide where trees can be cut. Individuals and environmental groups are opposed to logging in certain areas of the province. As well, some British

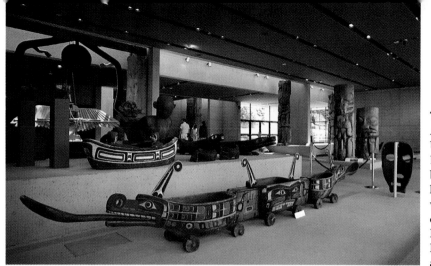

The Museum of Anthropology at the University of British Columbia, built in the 1970s, houses one of the world's finest collections of Northwest Coast Native art and artifacts.

Columbians are opposed to clearcut logging, and a number of Native groups want any kind of logging stopped on lands they claim as their own.

Today, a variety of Native organizations in the province are working to reclaim traditional territories and move towards self-government. One on the Sunshine Coast in southern British Columbia negotiated a self-government agreement with federal and provincial officials. Since 1988, the Sechelt Nation has been in control of its reserve lands and has operated like a municipality. Its success has made many British Columbians and Canadians recognize the need to agree to self-government and settle Native land claims. In 1996, the Nishga Tribal Council from the Nass Valley in northwestern British Columbia signed an agreement-in-principle with the province and Canada after over 100 years of negotiations. They expect to sign a final treaty in 1997.

Even with the positive changes in attitude towards Native peoples, racism is still very much an issue in British Columbia. As immigrants and refugees continue to arrive from all parts of the world — Asia, Eastern Europe, Central America, Africa — the face of British Columbia is changing. Along with economic and environmental challenges, British Columbia's leaders face various social challenges. Over the next decade, they will be working to make citizens of both sexes, all income levels and every colour, culture and background feel included in provincial decision making.

CHAPTER 7
Government

Like all the provinces, British Columbia has a government based on the British parliamentary model. At the head is the lieutenant-governor, the Queen's representative, who is appointed for a five-year term by the governor general of Canada on the advice of the prime minister. The province is divided into 75 legislative constituencies. The people of each constituency or riding elect a representative to be their MLA (Member of the Legislative Assembly). Elections cannot be more than five years apart.

Following an election, the lieutenant-governor calls on the leader of the political party with the largest number of elected members to serve as premier. The premier then chooses a cabinet from the elected members of the party. Members of the cabinet head government ministries such as forestry, finance and tourism. The premier and cabinet form the executive council, which runs the government, while the legislature enacts laws. These laws concern all aspects of life in British Columbia: economic development, social services, road building and, of course, taxes.

The provincial government administers a wide range of programs for British Columbia. Taxes are used to provide social services and to encourage development of the provincial economy. Provincial social services include major programs for health, education, child protection, income assistance and housing. Other provincial programs safeguard human rights, provide law enforcement and protect the environment. The province shares the cost of some programs, such as the public school system, with

The British Columbia Legislative Building, Victoria. Rising above the central dome is a statue of Captain George Vancouver.

municipalities. As well, the federal government shares the costs for some services.

Through the first half of the 1900s, Liberals and Conservatives dominated British Columbia politics. In 1952, the Social Credit Party was established by former Conservatives led by W.A.C. Bennett. Until 1991, the Social Credit Party and the New Democratic Party (NDP) controlled the province's political life. However, in the 1991 election, the Social Credit Party was reduced from a majority to a small minority in the legislature. The Liberal Party, which had not been a force in B.C. politics for many years, formed the official opposition. And a new party, the British Columbia Reform Party, entered the political scene with a few members in the legislature. During that session of the legislature, another new party, the Progressive Democratic Alliance, was established by two former members of the Liberal party. In the 1996 election, the NDP returned for a second consecutive term.

Other Levels of Government

British Columbia is represented by 32 members of Parliament in the House of Commons. Canada's first female prime minister, Kim Campbell, came from British Columbia. There are also six appointed representatives in the Senate.

The province has 43 cities, 50 district municipalities, 14 towns, 43 villages and 29 regional districts. These cover 80 percent of the population but only one percent of British Columbia's total area! The other 99 percent of the province is classified as "Unorganized Territory" with no specific local government.

The Court System

The judicial system has come a long way in British Columbia since Judge Matthew Baillie Begbie rode his horse to makeshift courts set up in the bush around the province. Today, three levels of courts maintain the law in the province.

Contrasting courthouses: Kamloops (*left*) and the Vancouver Law Courts, designed by Arthur Erickson

The Provincial Court is the first level in British Columbia's court system, and it is here that most cases are heard. There is no jury in this court. The provincial government appoints the judges. These 125 judges deal with minor criminal offences, such as shoplifting, family and youth problems, traffic violations and money claims under $10 000.

The next level in the court system is the Supreme Court. Here most cases are heard by judge and jury, or sometimes by judge alone. The federal government appoints judges to this court, which hears many civil cases, including divorce, libel and financial disputes greater than $10 000. It also hears serious criminal cases that include murder and manslaughter, aggravated assault, bank robbery and major drug crimes. As well, the Supreme Court hears some appeals from Provincial Court.

The Court of Appeal is the highest court in the province. It is not a trial court. Three to five judges sit together on a panel and hear appeals from the two other courts concerning criminal and civil cases. The chief justice of British Columbia heads the Court of Appeal. An appeal case involves only the judges and lawyers. Court of Appeal judges are appointed by the federal government.

Education

British Columbia has 75 local school districts in its public education system. Under the School Act, each district is governed by an elected board of trustees. In 1995, approximately 595 000 students attended 1697 public schools, which included 1188 elementary schools and 485 secondary and combination schools.

Public education is non-denominational and paid for through provincial taxes. The province also has 343 independent schools with 52 000 students. Families must pay a fee or tuition for their children to attend these schools.

While the majority of students attend public or independent

Above : Simon Fraser University was built in the 1960s on top of Burnaby Mountain just outside Vancouver. *Right:* Students and teacher gather around a computer at a Sikh school in suburban Vancouver. *Far right:* The First Nations House of Learning at the University of British Columbia opened in 1993.

schools, some students study at home. Pioneers in British Columbia were often so isolated that no schools were available to them. As a solution, provincial correspondence education was introduced, first in 1919 at the elementary level, and ten years later at the secondary level. It is still used by British Columbians living in remote areas.

A wide range of academic, technical, vocational and career education programs is offered at 16 community colleges throughout the province, and at the British Columbia Institute of Technology and the Emily Carr College of Art and Design.

British Columbia has five publicly funded universities, which offer a host of courses in undergraduate, graduate and professional programs. The University of British Columbia is in Vancouver; Simon Fraser University is in Burnaby; the University of Victoria is in Victoria; and the main campus of the University of Northern British Columbia is in Prince George. The new Royal Roads University is just outside Victoria. Some community colleges also offer university programs in partnership with the universities.

Because of its many remote communities, the province has placed a high priority on distance education. The Open University offers degree programs in the arts, while the Open College offers programs in such fields as health, business and tourism. The Knowledge Network provides general public education for adults and children on television.

Health

The Hospital Insurance Act ensures that all permanent residents of British Columbia have access to medical care. One group that receives special attention is the elderly. The province's pleasant, mild climate is very attractive to senior citizens, and as a result, a larger proportion of retired people live in British Columbia than in other provinces. One-quarter of the population of Victoria is over 65. Government-sponsored long-term care programs ensure good quality care for the elderly.

The Economy

Over the centuries, different products have been important to the economy of British Columbia. Five hundred years ago, the Native peoples of the region made and traded a variety of goods: dried berries, jewellery, cedar boxes, blankets made of mountain goat wool, and many other items. Later, European settlers arrived in large numbers and began to make and exchange goods: furs, gold, salmon and lumber for shipbuilding. Today British Columbians offer numerous services and make and sell many products, from gourmet foods to award-winning films.

Natural resources form the backbone of British Columbia's economy. Wood, metals, hydroelectricity and fish have all played their part in the past and continue to do so. Four important sectors of today's provincial economy are forestry, mining, energy and fishing. These industries earn approximately 80 percent of the money made from exporting goods.

Most of the goods exported go to the United States, Japan and South Korea. Although the United States is British Columbia's chief trading partner, countries in the Asia-Pacific region buy 40 percent of its exports. Trade experts think that these countries will play an even larger role in the province's economy in the future.

Forestry

Forests and the forest industry are very important to British Columbians. Thousands of people work at jobs in the forest industry, and more than half of the province's exports are forest

The Hugh Keenleyside dam on the Columbia River was built in the late 1960s as part of a huge hydroelectric development project.

products. Most of the trees harvested are softwoods — spruce, lodgepole pine, true fir (or balsam), hemlock, cedar and Douglas fir — and are used to make lumber, pulp and paper products, shingles and shakes. Some of the people involved are loggers, biologists, truck drivers, paper mill workers and tree planters.

Whether they are employed making forest products or not, all British Columbians have a stake in the forest industry. Eighty-five percent of the province's area is designated as Provincial Forests and is owned by the people of the province. This land is managed by the government through the B.C. Forest Service (BCFS), which grants Forest Licences and Tree Farm Licences to forest companies. These licences give the companies cutting rights and responsibilities. The companies' responsibilities include road building and tree planting (or reforestation) in the logged areas.

Before the Second World War, the methods and equipment used to harvest and process wood required many workers. Logging operations and small mills were found in and near the forests all over the province. After the war, logging changed. Forest products began to be processed in large, centrally located plants. Fewer people were needed to harvest and process the wood.

Right: "Fallers" in a stand of Douglas fir on Vancouver Island. *Far right:* Vancouver sawmill. B.C. produces about two-thirds of Canada's sawn lumber.

Today, as more efficient logging equipment has become available, trees are cut at a faster rate and supplies of easy-to-reach trees have grown smaller. Even with reforestation programs, not enough trees have grown to replace the ones logged.

The dwindling supply of trees is not the only problem the forest industry faces. Today there is a great deal of conflict between forest companies and other groups in the province. Some British Columbians are unhappy about certain land-use decisions. There have been disputes over whether logging should be allowed in some places, including the Queen Charlotte Islands, the Cariboo Mountains area, the Walbran Valley and Clayoquot Sound. There have also been disputes about logging methods. Many people oppose clearcutting — the removal of large areas of forest at one time — which they say damages the environment.

Everyone in British Columbia wants something when it comes to forests and forestry. First Nations governments want their land claims settled. Forest workers want to protect their jobs and communities. Resort operators want to prohibit unsightly clearcuts

Clearcut area in Vancouver Island's Carmanah Valley. In recent years logging practices — particularly the logging of old-growth forests and clearcutting — have stirred up a great deal of opposition from environmentalists and other groups.

in places tourists visit. Pulp and paper mill owners want a reliable supply of wood for the future. Environmental groups want to preserve the old-growth forests and watersheds that support animal life and contain trees that are hundreds of years old.

In an attempt to take the values of different groups into account and improve overall forest management, the government introduced the Forest Practices Code in 1995. The new code was developed through consultation with the public, industry, environmental groups, First Nations and government officials. It sets standards for logging, limits the size of clearcuts and contains regulations to protect streams and wildlife. It also includes penalties that can be enforced when these standards are not met.

The government also has established a fund called Forest Renewal BC to create more employment and economic benefits from the province's forests. The money for the fund comes from the stumpage fees and royalties paid by forest companies to the government for the right to harvest trees. A board of directors that includes representatives from industry, labour, communities, First Nations, environmental groups and government officials distributes money from the fund. Projects financed by the fund include studies to improve the way forests are tended in British Columbia, repairs to environmental damage, development of new products, and providing training and new skills for forest workers. An important part of the fund is community involvement in developing and managing projects.

Mining

Most of British Columbia lies within the Western Cordillera, a geological formation that contains a wide variety of valuable minerals. Minerals found in the province include gold, coal, asbestos, sulphur, copper, silver, zinc, lead and molybdenum.

The miners, prospectors, engineers, heavy equipment operators, clerical workers and others employed in the mining industry might live in one of many areas. On the north coast, the smelter at Kitimat

Left: **Open pit coal mine in the Elk River Valley.** *Below:* **Lead-zinc mine and the Cominco smelter at Trail where its ore is processed**

processes aluminum. Sulphur is produced in Peace River country; coal is mined in the southeast corner of the province. And in the southern Okanagan, silver, lead and zinc are extracted.

Mining suffers more than most industries from changes in the market for its products. The need for particular minerals can swing dramatically, carrying a town from "boom" to "bust" in a very short time. This has happened often in the province, particularly in communities where the mine is the main employer.

Besides having to deal with unpredictable markets, the mining industry also has to deal with some public opposition. British Columbians have become concerned about the damage mineral extraction can do to an area's plant life, soil and water. In 1993, the government responded to public concerns and declared that there would be no mining in the Tatshenshini River Valley in the far northwest, even though vast copper deposits are present there. In

the future, other cases where mining may be in conflict with the preservation of an environmentally sensitive area will be considered through land use planning.

Energy

British Columbia is rich in energy resources. Oil and natural gas are found in the northeast, and coal is found in the north, southwest and southeast. Waterways that can be used to generate electricity are found almost everywhere in the province. Only petroleum, which comes mainly from Alberta, must be imported.

From various parts of British Columbia, transmission lines carry electricity made by harnessing the power of the province's great rivers: the Peace, the Fraser, the Skeena and the Columbia. Eighteen percent of British Columbia's requirement is provided by hydroelectric dams. One of the largest of these is the W.A.C. Bennett Dam on the Peace River.

Although British Columbia has abundant energy resources, the production, transportation and use of these resources is not problem-free. The public today is concerned about environmental damage caused by coal mining, dam building and pipeline construction. The

Right: **On the Sechelt Peninsula, workers get ready to join sections of pipe on the Vancouver Island gas pipeline.** *Far right:* **"Nodding donkey" at sunrise in the northeastern corner of the province, where B.C.'s only oil fields are found**

air pollution caused by burning fossil fuels worries many people as well. Cleaner fuels, alternative energy sources and more efficient resource use will all need to be part of the energy industry in the future.

Fishing

Fishing has supported people in British Columbia for thousands of years. Many Native groups obtained food and materials for tools and artwork from the sea and the rivers of the area. European settlers have relied on ocean resources as well.

Today the fishing and aquaculture industry in British Columbia harvests more than 40 species of fish and marine animals. Fishing here is big business.

Some of the people employed in the industry are fishboat operators, marine biologists, processing-plant workers and fish farmers. Prince Rupert in the north and Steveston in the south are important fishing centres where many of these people work.

The several species of salmon found in B.C. waters are the focus of a lot of industry attention. Most fish farms raise salmon, and many

Left: Worker at the Kootenay Trout Hatchery, Bull River. *Below:* Wharf with nets and fishing boats at Port Edward, at the mouth of the Skeena River

commercial fishers make their livelihood catching pinks, sockeye, coho, chum and chinook. B.C. salmon — whether fresh, frozen or canned — is prized around the world and makes up more than half of the province's ocean exports. Herring, different kinds of groundfish and shellfish make up the rest.

Japan is the main customer for exports of B.C.'s fish and seafood products, followed by the United States and the European Community. In Japan, the mass of eggs or roe found in herring is a traditional delicacy. Each spring the B.C. herring fishery gears up to satisfy this export market. Tonnes of herring are caught, the roe is taken out of the mature female fish, and the carcasses are processed for animal feed and fertilizer. Millions of dollars are made from the herring roe fishery.

Fishing, like forestry and mining, is not without opponents and difficulties. Shrinking salmon populations have become a major concern in British Columbia. Several groups have been accused of overfishing: commercial fishers, sport fishers and Native fishers. Fisheries biologists are working to assess the situation. Whoever and whatever is to blame for the decline in fish stocks, changes are being made in fishing practices and regulations over the next few years.

The federal government has put in place a controversial "revitalization" program to reduce the number of commercial fishers. The goal is to reduce the capacity of the commercial fleet by 50 percent by buying back fishing licences, increasing licence fees and changing the way licences are assigned by area and type of fishing equipment. Government officials hope this program will help to protect the salmon stocks but many commercial fishers think the program is unfair. "Catch-and-release" programs for the sport fishery in some areas are also designed to protect salmon stocks.

Manufacturing

British Columbia's manufacturing industry is based mainly on natural resources. The processing of logs, the refining of petroleum or

minerals and the production of food employ many British Columbians. Manufactured items include wood and paper products, as well as a range of food products: fruit drinks and wine, processed fish, poultry and various products made from milk, eggs, beef or pork.

Some of the secondary manufacturing industries involve metal and chemical products, printing and publishing, electronics and clothing.

Manufacturing activity is centred in the Vancouver area and on the east coast of Vancouver Island. Efforts are being made to develop other manufacturing centres and to expand the manufacturing sector by "adding more value" to natural resources. Furniture and plastics are examples of value-added products that British Columbians hope to see more of in the future.

Tourism

Tourism is a major dollar earner in British Columbia. In 1995, revenue from overnight visitors reached over $6 billion, and the industry employs large numbers of British Columbians all over the province.

On the southern coast, the mild climates of Vancouver and Victoria attract visitors year-round. In the past, Expo 86 and the Commonwealth Games in 1994 brought many visitors and focused world

Magnificent scenery and a wide range of recreational activities are just two of the attractions that draw millions of tourists to British Columbia.

attention on the province. Other events, like the World Cup Ski Races at Whistler and the annual Indy 500 Car Races, draw sports fans on a regular basis.

On the east and west coasts of Vancouver Island and on the northern coast of the mainland, visitors from around the world catch salmon, trout and steelhead. River rafting, canoeing, kayaking and surfing are other activities that draw visitors to these areas. Away from the coast, resorts attract downhill and cross-country skiers in the winter, and golfers, tennis players, hikers and cyclists in the summer. Other visitors are interested in the province's history, and probably more are interested in the wide variety of wildlife to be seen.

Whatever their interests, most of the province's visitors come from other parts of Canada and the United States. Overseas visitors come principally from Japan, then from the United Kingdom and Germany. To improve service for these visitors, the provincial government has designed a training program called SuperHost, which teaches front-line workers in the industry how to give pleasant and efficient assistance to tourists. The program has been so successful that other provinces, American states and many countries have developed programs based on SuperHost.

Agriculture

Only 4 percent of the land in British Columbia is considered farmland, yet agriculture is the province's third-largest industry, ranking behind forestry and tourism. A third of the farmland is used to raise crops; the rest is used for pasture or grazing.

Throughout the province, British Columbians are busy operating dairy farms, market gardens, herb farms, cattle ranches, and pig and poultry farms. Farmers are at work in the vast wheat fields of the Peace River country and the small, intensively planted ginseng plots of the dry Nicola Valley. (Ginseng roots are highly prized in Asian medicine.) In the south and central interior, ranchers tend cattle on rolling rangeland. In the Okanagan Valley, fruit farmers

Far left: Farm in the Chilliwack area. *Left:* Irrigated vineyards along the Similkameen River contrast sharply with the arid terrain beyond.

grow apples, cherries, peaches, apricots and plums as well as grapes for the thriving wine industry. And in the mild climate of the Fraser Valley outside Vancouver, farmers grow vegetables, berries, mushrooms, bulbs and ornamental flowers.

Film Industry

One of British Columbia's fastest growing and most glamorous industries is the movie business. In 1995, 95 film and television shows were shot here, and the film industry spent just over $432 million in the province.

While everyone agrees that the province's scenery is the real star of the industry, producers from all over the world like the variety of locations and appreciate the highly skilled workforce. British Columbia can provide actors, camera operators, makeup artists, special effects co-ordinators, location scouts and the many other specialists needed to work on film or TV productions.

TV series shot here over the years include the *Beachcombers, The Commish* and *The X-Files*. Notable among movies made in the province are *Little Women, Jumanji* and *Legends of the Fall*.

Transportation

People and goods are transported in British Columbia by water, by rail, by road and by air. Vancouver is the province's main port and

Above: **Coast guard and float plane dock, Prince Rupert. Planes like these provide important service to the province's remote communities.** *Right:* **The** *Royal Hudson***, North America's only steam locomotive in scheduled mainline service**

the second largest port in North America. Ships from Korea, Poland, South Africa, Japan and the Philippines can be seen in the deep waters of Burrard Inlet on any day of the year. Other year-round deep-sea ports are located at Prince Rupert, New Westminster, Victoria, Esquimault, Nanaimo, Port Alberni, Campbell River and Powell River. B.C. ports accommodate a range of cargo ships, freighters, research vessels, fishing boats and naval ships. Many also accommodate vessels belonging to the British Columbia Ferry Corporation. BC Ferries operates one of the largest ferry systems in the world. It has 24 routes between the Lower Mainland, Vancouver Island and various coastal ports. The corporation's superferries, launched in 1993, are some of the most sophisticated in the world.

British Columbia's railway system is less sophisticated but no less important. Over the years, 6800 kilometres (4225 miles) of railway track have been laid across the province. CN Rail and CP Rail operate freight lines, and VIA Rail operates a passenger line between Victoria and Courtenay. BC Rail operates both freight and passenger lines. A

commuter rail line runs between Mission and downtown Vancouver.

Every day in the summer, BC Rail's *Royal Hudson* chuffs from North Vancouver to Squamish, sending up great plumes of steam as it skirts the sparking blue waters of Howe Sound. In summer and winter, BC Rail passenger cars shuttle between North Vancouver and Prince George, a trip that is rated one of the "top ten" scenic excursions in the world.

Although less scenic, air travel is also important in British Columbia. Vancouver International Airport is the province's largest airport, handling ten million passengers, on average, a year.

British Columbia's road network includes 23 000 km (14 260 mi.) of paved roads, 19 300 km (11 966 mi.) of unpaved roads and 2700 bridges. The mountainous terrain, the extremes in climate and the size of the province are all challenges to road builders.

Communications

British Columbia's communications network links remote areas and numerous communities with each other and with locations around the world.

Over 98 percent of B.C. homes and businesses have telephone service. Even remote areas of the province have service, although this often takes the form of radio phones.

There are 83 radio stations. Over 89 percent of British Columbians subscribe to cable television services, and many people in remote areas pull in television signals with the help of a satellite dish. There are 11 television stations that broadcast original programs, 259 rebroadcasting stations and 137 cable systems. Both television channels and radio stations offer multicultural programs.

Two newspapers, *The Vancouver Sun* and the *Province,* are produced daily in Vancouver and shipped all around the province. Presses in other communities turn out 15 daily newspapers and over 160 weekly or community papers. Magazine and book publishers also keep British Columbians informed.

CHAPTER 9

Arts and Recreation

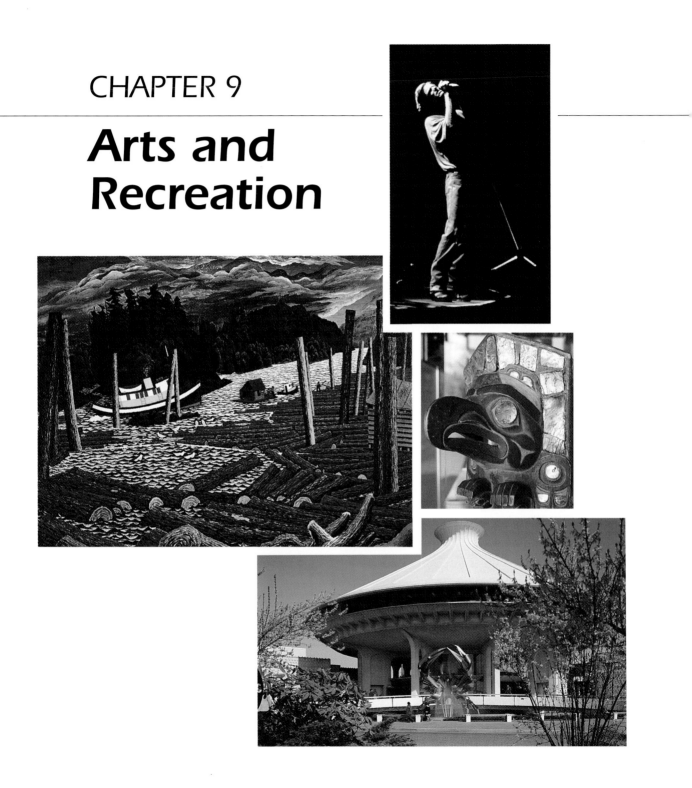

For centuries, the people of British Columbia have enjoyed a wealth of cultural traditions. Long ago, the Native peoples along the coast told legends that were passed on from one generation to the next. Dancers wearing elaborately carved masks often acted out these legends. Nootka and Kwakiutl shamans used the glimmering firelight in the longhouses and magic quartz crystals to create dramatic effects in their theatrical performances. Coastal peoples also carved totem poles and made bentwood boxes from a single piece of wood and decorated them with carvings and paintings. In the interior, Native peoples also told legends and sang songs, which were sometimes accompanied by drums, rattles and flutes.

Early immigrants from Europe brought their culture with them. During the gold rush, stock theatre companies performed English comedies and dramas. Sometimes they even staged scenes from Shakespeare's plays. The works of early painters and writers were European in style and technique. Gradually, however, artists began to paint and write about what they saw in British Columbia and to experiment with new styles.

Today the arts and recreation in British Columbia reflect the diversity of its population. You can admire Native totem poles and masks, enjoy Shakespeare on the beach, listen to music by Doukhobor choirs and watch Sikh wrestling.

Clockwise from top: **Bryan Adams in concert; Native mask, inlaid with mother-of-pearl, on display at the Museum of Anthropology, University of British Columbia; The H.R. MacMillan Planetarium, Vancouver;** *Logs: Ladysmith Harbour,* **by Vancouver Island landscape painter Edward John Hughes**

The Performing Arts

People in British Columbia who enjoy theatre, music, opera and dance have much to choose from. The province has more than 50 professional performing arts groups, ranging from traditional orchestras and theatre companies to experimental dance troupes and a horse-drawn stage company.

Theatre

Professional theatres began to emerge in British Columbia in the 1960s. The Vancouver Playhouse opened in 1963 and four years later created a sensation when it presented George Ryga's *The Ecstasy of Rita Joe*, the story of a young Native woman who suffers at the hands of white society. Today you can see both classic and modern plays, including Canadian premieres and Broadway plays, at the Playhouse.

Vancouver is also the home of the Arts Club Theatre, the largest regional theatre in Western Canada. Located on bustling Granville Island, it offers drama, comedy and musicals, with an emphasis on twentieth-century productions. For those who prefer more experimental works, Tamahnous Theatre specializes in avant-garde theatre and has presented many plays based on dreams or fantasies. (The name "Tamahnous" comes from the Chilcotin word for "magic.") Touchstone Theatre and the Headlines Theatre Company often present plays that deal with social issues. Many other groups put on experimental plays at the Vancouver East Cultural Centre, a beautifully restored old church.

In 1995, a new facility was added to Vancouver's lively theatre scene when the Ford Centre for the Performing Arts opened just a couple of blocks away from the new Vancouver Public Library. The new theatre opened with a long-running lavish production of the musical *Showboat* and will continue to offer productions on a grand scale.

In summer, the Bard on the Beach Theatre Society presents Shakespearean favourites in an open-ended candy-striped tent in Vanier Park, affording a magnificent view of the city, the sea and the

Far left: **With Vancouver as a backdrop, Torquil Campbell plays Romeo in the Bard on the Beach production of** *Romeo and Juliet.* **Left: British Columbia's reputation as a film and television production centre continues to grow. Seen here are Jillian Anderson and David Duchovny from the popular series,** *The X-Files.*

mountains. Summer is also the season for Broadway-style musicals staged at Stanley Park's Malkin Bowl Theatre under the Stars.

In the fall, both Vancouver and Victoria buzz with the lively Fringe Theatre festivals. Performers from all over the world present small-scale productions that might not be presented by a conventional theatre company, perhaps because of subject or style. Fringe productions can range from one-person readings to several-person musicals on just about any subject imaginable.

The first professional theatre in Victoria was the Bastion Theatre, founded in 1971. Today, the McPherson and the Royal theatres present dramas, comedies, musicals and opera.

Throughout the province, hundreds of theatre groups entertain British Columbians. Every summer the Gold Rush Theatre in Barkerville puts on old-fashioned shows like those from the gold rush days. Also in the summer, the Caravan Stage Company travels by horse-drawn wagons to perform in small communities in the interior. In the little town of Horsefly, the whole community participates in the annual Follies. And on the Sunshine Coast, theatre buffs can hop into a four-wheel-drive "taxi" and go up a mountain to see a play staged in a Scout hall.

Besides George Ryga, well-known B.C. playwrights include John Gray and Carol Bolt. John Gray has written several musicals, and Carol Bolt writes plays about the problems of urban living. She also helped create the children's TV show *Fraggle Rock*. British Columbians who have gained fame on stage, screen and/or TV include Chief Dan George, Bruno Gerussi, Michael J. Fox and Pamela Lee.

Music

Music holds a prominent place in the cultural life of Vancouver. The Vancouver Symphony Orchestra and the Vancouver Bach Choir perform at the legendary Orpheum Theatre, where 100 glittering chandeliers light the halls. For something a little different, there is the ten-day International Jazz Festival in June, and every July, the Folk Music Festival held at Jericho Beach attracts thousands of folk music enthusiasts. Rock music fans can hear their favourite groups at B.C. Place Stadium or General Motors Place.

At the Royal Theatre in Victoria, the Victoria Symphony performs pops, classics concerts and the Masterworks Series, which features

Right: **In keeping with its image as the "Bavarian City of the Canadian Rockies," Kimberley hosts the International Accordion Championships every summer.** *Below right:* **Every year on the long weekend at the beginning of August, the Victoria Symphony holds its Symphony Splash, a free, open-air concert performed on a harbour barge to enthusiastic audiences that number in the tens of thousands.**

music and artists from all over the world. Members of the symphony also put on special performances for schools. The Greater Victoria Youth Orchestra, composed of 60 musicians between the ages of 11 and 25, performs three or four programs of symphonic music a year.

In summer, music sounds throughout the province. Old-time piano music at the Theatre Royale in Barkerville echoes the sounds of the gold rush days. In early June, Doukhobor choirs come to Castlegar from all over Canada to celebrate their music and traditions. The International Accordion Championship is held in Kimberley in July, and that same month Burns Lake hosts the Bluegrass Music Festival.

And, every summer, a grand piano is swung by helicopter to the top of Whistler Mountain, where Vancouver Symphony musicians provide an afternoon of classical music in the alpine meadows.

Notable among B.C. musicians who have achieved national and international recognition are classical composer Jean Coulthard, mezzo-soprano Judith Forst, tenors Ben Heppner, and Richard Margison, children's entertainer Charlotte Diamond, country singer Patricia Conroy and rock superstar Bryan Adams, who grew up in

Far left: **A scene from** *Hansel and Gretel,* **performed by the Vancouver Opera as part of its Opera in the Schools program.** *Left:* **Kokoro Dance's** *Rage* **is an extraordinary theatrical experience that combines dance, live music and film images to present a searing commentary on Canada's treatment of its citizens of Japanese ancestry during the Second World War.**

North Vancouver. Tom Cochrane is another rock musician who lives in Vancouver.

Opera

Opera has always been strong in Victoria. The Pacific Opera Victoria puts on three operas a year at the McPherson and Royal theatres, including timeless masterpieces like *Madame Butterfly* and *The Marriage of Figaro,* as well as twentieth-century works such as *The Merry Widow.* The company also presents special programs for students from elementary school through university.

For more than three decades, the Vancouver Opera has presented four operas a year at the elegant Queen Elizabeth Theatre. The company performs classic works but in the 1993-94 season it staged a new Canadian opera entitled *The Architect.* The singers also perform mini-operas in elementary schools. A special high school program invites students to dress rehearsals and gives them a tour backstage.

Dance

Dance is alive and thriving in British Columbia. From September to June, Ballet B.C. stages bold, innovative works, which have included a dance set to popular love songs. The company has earned glowing reviews throughout Canada and the United States.

Choreographers such as Lola MacLaughlin, Karen Jamieson and Judith Marcuse present exciting, imaginative modern dance programs each year. Kokoro and Jumpstart dance companies also entertain dance enthusiasts with highly original and sometimes startling performances.

Canada's largest alternative dance festival, Dancing on the Edge, features new dancing from around the world. Over a two-week period, 60 to 70 shows are performed in every kind of setting, from traditional stages to the beautiful beaches of Vancouver.

Visual Arts

Many Native artists live and work in British Columbia. Bill Reid, a Haida artist living in Vancouver, makes carvings and sculptures out

Left: Bill Reid's *Raven and the First Men. Far left:* The grizzly bear design in this button blanket by Florence Davidson was adapted from a nineteenth-century Haida tunic. Davidson is also the link in a long artistic tradition that began with her father, master carver Charles Edenshaw, and continues with her grandson Robert Davidson.

of wood, argillite, ivory and bronze. His luminous cedar sculpture entitled *Raven and the First Men,* showing the first people emerging from a clamshell, is on display in the Great Hall in Vancouver's Museum of Anthropology. Reid also creates beautiful silver and gold jewellery, including tiny gold chests and masks that are worn as necklaces and pins.

On the Queen Charlotte Islands, Haida carver Rufus Moody works in argillite. This blue rock acquires a soft black shine when it is polished. Other well-known Native artists are Robert Davidson, who has carved totem poles for various places in Canada, and Tony Hunt, a Kwakiutl carver who learned his art from his father, Henry Hunt, and his grandfather, Mungo Martin. Native masks, totem poles, baskets, carvings and jewellery are displayed in shops, galleries and museums throughout British Columbia.

Many non-Native artists have been strongly influenced by Native art. Emily Carr, who was born in 1871, is probably British Columbia's most famous artist. She was deeply influenced by Native culture and by the mysterious beauty of the rain forests. The permanent collection of her work at the Vancouver Art Gallery is in great demand for exhibits overseas in places like China, where her art is highly prized and admired.

One of Canada's pre-eminent painters today is Jack Shadbolt, who lives in Burnaby. His abstract paintings combining primitive

Right: Sign **by Jack Shadbolt. *Far right: Indian Church*, a 1929 painting by Emily Carr**

and modern styles have inspired a generation of students. Like Carr, Shadbolt has been influenced by Native art.

Another famous B.C. artist is Toni Onley, who is known for his coastal scenes. Younger British Columbia artists who enjoy an international reputation are Jeff Wall and Kati Campbell. Using advertising techniques and forms, Jeff Wall creates gigantic photographic displays showing scenes that have a social message. Kati Campbell uses photographs to explore ideas about women's work and how we raise children.

Pottery and architecture are two other visual arts that are well represented on the coast. John Reeve, Wayne Ngan and Walter Dexter are highly admired potters. Arthur Erickson, Geoffrey Massey and the late Ron Thom have designed superlative buildings across the province and around the world.

Literature

Books are important to British Columbians, who buy more of them per capita than any other Canadians. There are about 230 publishing companies, including self-publishers, who are a growing force in the

province. All told, B.C. publishers have approximately 2600 titles in print.

In 1995, the impressive new main branch of the Vancouver Public Library was completed. Designed by the Canadian architect Moshe Safdie, the dramatic structure contains 1.2 million items, including books, periodicals, microfilms and audiovisual materials.

Poetry

Pauline Johnson, the daughter of a Mohawk chief and an Englishwoman, wrote poetry in the 1890s and early 1900s. Dressed in fringed buckskins, she toured Canada, the United States and Britain giving dramatic readings of her work. In 1901, she moved from Ontario to Vancouver, where she wrote stories based on Native folk tales.

Two well-known twentieth-century B.C. poets are Earle Birney and Dorothy Livesay. Both have won Governor General's awards for their work. Today Susan Musgrave, George Bowering and bill bissett are popular poets.

Prose

One of British Columbia's most admired fiction writers was Ethel Wilson, who wrote her first book in 1947 at age 59. Her most highly praised novel, *Swamp Angel*, tells the story of a woman who leaves her unhappy marriage in Vancouver for a fishing camp in the interior. A provincial park is named after Wilson.

Malcolm Lowry, author of the internationally acclaimed *Under the Volcano*, lived in British Columbia from 1940 to 1954. For a time his home was a shack on the beach near North Vancouver. It had no heat, electricity or plumbing. While living there, Lowry wrote a collection of short stories that won a Governor General's Award.

Important fiction writers today include Audrey Thomas, Jane Rule, crime writer L. R. (Bunny) Wright and science fiction writer William Gibson. Poet and novelist Joy Kogawa, who as a child during the Second World War was interned at a camp in the B.C. interior along with thousands of other Japanese Canadians, wrote about this experience in her 1981 novel *Obasan*.

In recent years, several B.C. writers have enjoyed worldwide recognition. Douglas Coupland's books, starting with *Generation X*, explore the lives of young adults living in the 1990s. Nick Bantock's beautiful *Griffin and Sabine* and its sequels, which he wrote and illustrated, follow a correspondence between two friends.

British Columbians have also produced some of Canada's finest nonfiction. Artist Emily Carr won a Governor General's Award in 1941 for *Klee Wyck*, a collection of literary sketches. George Woodcock, one of Canada's leading men of letters, published dozens of books, mostly works of literary criticism and political writings. A dedicated conservationist, Roderick Haig-Brown wrote numerous books containing his reflections on nature and on fishing, as well as several children's books and adult novels. Journalist Bruce Hutchison, who also wrote eloquently about nature and life in the country, was best known for his volumes of biography and history. Shuswap activist George Manuel wrote forcefully about the plight of his own peoples and indigenous people around the world.

Several of Canada's most popular children's authors live in British Columbia. Eric Wilson, who sets his series of mystery books in Canadian locations, lives in Victoria. Vancouver-based Kit Pearson won the Governor General's Award for *The Sky Is Falling*, and author-illustrator Ann Blades produced one of Canada's best-known picture books, *Mary of Mile 18*.

Recreation

British Columbia is a mecca for outdoor sports enthusiasts. With more than 5800 square kilometres (2240 square miles) of wilderness, several national parks and hundreds of provincial parks, there is something for everyone. People hike, camp, go horseback riding, bicycle and fish in rivers, lakes and the ocean. Hang-gliders soar with the eagles. Spelunkers explore underground caves the size of football fields, bristling with stalactites and stalagmites. In winter, many people enjoy downhill or cross-country skiing, and in the interior people ice fish. During the summer, water sports like swimming, kayaking, rafting, sailing, canoeing and scuba diving are very popular.

Organized sports are also popular in British Columbia. Games like soccer, rugby, cricket, ice hockey, football and baseball thrive throughout the province, as do lesser-known sports such as harness racing, kabaddi (Sikh wrestling) and rhythmic gymnastics.

Spectator Sports

Spectator sports are a major pastime in British Columbia. In cities and towns, amateur baseball, soccer, rugby, football and hockey teams compete in front of keen home-town crowds.

Vancouver's Empire Stadium was built in 1954 to host the British Empire Games and later became the home of the B.C. Lions football club. The Lions, who won the Grey Cup championship in 1964, moved their home games to B.C. Place Stadium in the 1980s.

In 1970, the Vancouver Canucks joined the National Hockey League. The Canucks' Pavel Bure, also known as the Russian Rocket, is a favourite among junior league hockey players. In 1995, the Canucks moved from the Pacific Coliseum to the new General Motors Place near B.C. Place Stadium.

The new General Motors Place is also home to the Vancouver

Given the province's geography, it is not surprising that water sports and skiing are among British Columbians' favourite outdoor activities.

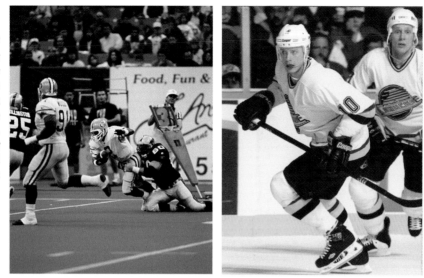

Right: B.C. Lions' quarterback Danny Barret, protected by All-star guard Rob Smith, completes a pass against the Edmonton Eskimos. *Far right:* Vancouver Canucks star Pavel Bure in action

Grizzlies basketball team. In the 1995-1996 season, the Grizzlies, along with the Toronto Raptors, became one of the first non-U.S. teams to join the National Basketball Association since 1946.

Other Vancouver sports teams include the Vancouver Canadians AAA baseball team and the Vancouver 86ers, who play soccer at Swanguard Stadium in Burnaby.

Champions

British Columbia has had its share of sports champions. In 1928, sprinter Percy Williams won two Olympic gold medals, an achievement that remains unique in Canadian track and field history. Another famous B.C. sprinter, Harry Jerome, tied the world record for the 100-metre dash in 1960 and for the 100-yard dash in 1962. He also won a bronze medal in the 1954 Olympics.

Nancy Greene Raine is well known as the champion skier who won the World Cup in 1967 and 1968, after winning Olympic gold in the giant slalom and silver in the slalom.

Canada's best female swimmer ever was Elaine Tanner. She set world records in the 220-yard individual medley and the 200-yard butterfly in 1966, and that same year, at age 15, became the youngest person to receive the Lou Marsh Trophy as outstanding athlete of the year. In 1969, she received the Order of Canada.

Far left: **Terry Fox, running in eastern Ontario during his Marathon of Hope.** *Left and above:* **Two B.C. champions: sprinter Harry Jerome and swimmer Elaine Tanner**

Rower Silken Laumann became a national hero at the 1992 Olympics in Barcelona when she won a bronze medal after suffering a serious leg injury in training just eight weeks before the games. At the Atlanta games in 1996, she won silver. Also at the Atlanta games, double-scull rowers Marnie McBean and Kathleen Heddle won a gold medal, to add to their two gold medals from Barcelona. They became the first Canadians ever to win three gold medals at Olympic summer games. Alison Sydor won a silver medal in mountain biking at the Atlanta games — the first time a mountain biking competition was held as an Olympic event.

There have been other B.C. champions — figure skater Karen Magnussen, rhythmic gymnast Lori Fung, wrestler Jeffrey Thue, to mention just a few — but no athlete ever aroused as much admiration as a young runner from Port Coquitlam who set no records and won no competitions. In 1980, after losing most of his right leg to bone cancer, Terry Fox set out to run across Canada to raise money for cancer research. He had completed two-thirds of his journey when the disease spread to his lungs and ended his personal Marathon of Hope. Over the next few months, his example inspired Canadians to donate almost $25 million to cancer research, and thousands still participate in the annual fund-raising runs that are held in his name.

A Tour of British Columbia

The province advertises itself as "Super, Natural British Columbia," offering both cosmopolitan cities and rugged wilderness. Even in the cities, the wilderness is never far from anyone's doorstep.

The easiest way to appreciate this huge and varied province is by looking at its two most important cities and then at the nine main regions identified by the Department of Tourism.

Vancouver

Rimmed by mountains and ocean beaches, Vancouver boasts one of the most spectacular settings of any city in the world.

Stanley Park, home of the Vancouver Aquarium, is a 406-hectare (1000-acre) peninsula of tall cedars and landscaped gardens. The 10-kilometre (6.5-mile) sea wall surrounding the park is a popular pathway from which Vancouverites can watch the bustle of Vancouver Harbour — one of Canada's busiest and most important ports. Freighters from all over the world, gleaming white cruise ships travelling to and from Alaska, and oil tankers are all guided and pushed around by sturdy tug boats. Sea planes land and take off amid the shipping traffic. The tiny ferry known as the SeaBus scoots across Burrard Inlet, linking Vancouver and North Vancouver.

Stanley Park is not the only natural oasis in busy Vancouver. Pacific Spirit Park, once part of the University Endowment Lands

Clockwise from top: **The Vancouver Aquarium in Stanley Park; a spring stroll among Okanagan peach blossoms; rainforest trail in Pacific Rim National Park; summer tourists on Horstman Glacier, atop Blackcomb Mountain; night view of the Legislative Building, Victoria**

Top: The Lion's Gate Bridge connecting Vancouver to North Vancouver. *Bottom left:* Dr. Sun Yat-Sen Classical Chinese Garden. *Bottom right:* Gastown is Vancouver's oldest district. Vancouverites and visitors alike enjoy the nineteenth-century atmosphere provided by the cobblestone streets, old-fashioned lampposts and dozens of restored buildings that now house boutiques, antique shops, restaurants and art galleries.

of the University of British Columbia, is a 400-hectare (990-acre) woodland. Nearby on the university grounds, the Nitobe Memorial Gardens recreate a traditional Japanese garden.

Another of Vancouver's garden treasures is the Dr. Sun Yat-Sen Classical Chinese Garden in Chinatown. The only classical Chinese garden outside China, it was built using traditional Chinese methods and materials. Outside its walls, Vancouver's Chinatown, the second largest Chinatown in North America (after San Francisco), hums with activity. Just north and west of Chinatown is historic Gastown where Vancouver began. This area of old restored brick buildings and cobbled streets is named after John "Gassy Jack" Deighton, who built the first saloon here.

To learn more about Vancouver's history, visitors go to Vanier Park on the city's west side. The park is actually a museum complex that includes the Vancouver Museum, the H.R. MacMillan

Planetarium, the Gordon Southam Observatory, the Maritime Museum and the City of Vancouver Archives.

One of the most fascinating museums in Vancouver is the Museum of Anthropology at the University of British Columbia. This striking building was inspired by the traditional cedar houses of Northwest Coast Natives and contains one of the world's finest collections of their art. Natives are one of many cultural groups that give Vancouver its dynamic, cosmopolitan atmosphere. As a Pacific Rim city, it has strong traditional links with Asia through its thriving Chinese, Indian and Japanese communities. Its natural beauty, mild climate and diverse economy have attracted people from across Canada. This cultural mix has nurtured a vibrant artistic community.

Victoria

Located at the southern tip of Vancouver Island, the provincial capital, Victoria, is known as Canada's City of Flowers. The climate is so mild that flowers bloom year-round. Victorians take great pride in their annual Flower Count in February when they tell the rest of Canada how many millions of blossoms fill the city. Butchart Gardens, near Victoria, is one of Canada's most famous gardens.

Overlooking the city's inner harbour are the imposing Parliament Buildings and the magnificently restored Empress Hotel, for decades the heart of Victoria's social life. Many beautiful old brick buildings make the city's downtown attractive to both tourists and local citizens.

One of the best museums in Canada is located in Victoria. The Royal British Columbia Museum focuses on the province's natural and human history. Next to the museum, Thunderbird Park is filled with totem poles and a Native longhouse. Victoria's long naval history is celebrated at the Maritime Museum.

Greater Victoria includes the municipalities of Esquimalt, still an important naval base, Saanich and Oak Bay. North of Greater Victoria stretches the Saanich Peninsula, known for its fruit and

Above: **A Victoria residential district.**
Right: **The elegant Empress Hotel.**

vegetable farms, its dozens of beaches and Western Canada's oldest agricultural fair, held every September since 1871 at Saanichton.

Victoria and its neighbouring communities are isolated from the rest of the island by the high rocky ridge known as the Malahat. This ridge offers wonderful views of mainland mountains and of the Gulf Islands and the Saanich Peninsula.

Vancouver Island and the Gulf Islands

Once over the Malahat, travellers have easy access to the entire east coast of Vancouver Island. The west coast is not so easily accessible, however, because of the island's mountainous interior. Only two highways cross the island from east to west.

Just north of the Malahat is the Cowichan Valley and the city of Duncan. This is dairy farming and logging country. Known as "The City of Totems," Duncan celebrates its large Native population with over 60 totem poles and a Native Heritage Centre.

Farther north is the town of Chemainus, "The Little Town That Did." In the early 1980s, the citizens decided to keep their town alive through tourism after the local sawmill closed. They commissioned huge murals for the walls of the downtown

110

Top left: The port of Nanaimo. *Bottom left:* Getting ready for the city's annual International Bathtub Race, which sees hundreds of variously powered bathtubs and other outlandish craft head out across the Strait of Georgia to Vancouver. *Above:* One of the famed Chemainus murals. Tourists can take walking tours to the 32 murals, following footprints on the sidewalks.

buildings. The murals, showing scenes from the area's history, have made Chemainus an important tourist attraction.

The second-largest city on the island is Nanaimo, a rapidly growing retirement centre. Among the city's attractions are a picturesque waterfront, many well-preserved historic buildings, and some two dozen parks, which include bird sanctuaries and ancient Native stone carvings. At Parksville, also a growing retirement area, one of the cross-island highways begins. Along this road is the famous Cathedral Grove, a carefully preserved stand of old-growth forest. Some of the hundreds of Douglas firs here are over 800 years old.

The largest community in the island's interior is the logging town of Port Alberni. Although it is located in the middle, it is a port because it is situated at the head of long, narrow Alberni Inlet. From here, the small freighter M.V. *Lady Rose* travels to Bamfield and Ucluelet on the west coast, carrying supplies, mail and people.

The road west from Port Alberni becomes narrower and more

winding as it approaches the island's rugged west coast. The two communities here, Tofino and Ucluelet, rely on logging, fishing, and tourism. Tourists come here because of the wild beauty of Pacific Rim National Park, which includes Long Beach, the Broken Group Islands and the West Coast Trail.

North from Parksville on the east coast, Courtenay is located in the farming area of the Comox Valley. It provides access to the skiing areas of Forbidden Plateau and Mount Washington and to Strathcona Park. The highest peak on the island, the 2200-metre (7200-foot) Golden Hinde, is in the centre of the park, and Della Falls, the waterfall with the highest vertical drop in Canada (440 metres/1440 feet), is in the southern part of the park. The most northerly large community on Vancouver Island is Campbell River, a popular fishing resort as well as a logging and mining centre.

Between southern Vancouver Island and the mainland lie almost 200 islands of various shapes and sizes known as the Gulf Islands. Sheltered and dry, the islands are warm enough to grow cactus.

The largest Gulf Island is Saltspring. With its mix of mountains, gentle farmland, lakes, and ocean beaches, it attracts many visitors from the mainland and Vancouver Island. Because of its popularity, Saltspring is experiencing high land prices and rapid development.

The other popular islands are North and South Pender, Galiano and Mayne islands. The larger Gulf Islands are accessible from Vancouver Island and the mainland by regular ferry services.

Southwestern British Columbia

Southwestern British Columbia is a wedge stretching from the American border northwest up the Sunshine Coast and east into the interior of the province.

The most heavily populated part of the province is the Lower Mainland in the southwest corner. Here Vancouver and other cities and towns surround and cover the delta of the Fraser River. Due east of Vancouver is Burnaby, home to Simon Fraser University.

Due south, the city of Richmond is built on islands in the Fraser River delta. Southeast of Burnaby is "The Royal City" of New Westminster, British Columbia's first capital city. Nearby is Fort Langley National Historic Park where the Crown Colony of British Columbia was inaugurated in 1858. Surrey, located south of New Westminster, is the largest district municipality in the province and one of the fastest growing in Canada. There are some 60 parks in the Surrey area, as well as a marsh — the Serpentine Fen — that is home to more than 100 species of birds. North of Vancouver, on the north shore of Burrard Inlet, are the two large cities of North Vancouver and West Vancouver. Built on the lower slopes of the Coast Mountains, these cities get more rain than Vancouver because the mountains trap the clouds moving inland from the Pacific.

The highway leading west from West Vancouver passes through Horseshoe Bay where travellers can take a ferry to the aptly named Sunshine Coast. As well as an average 2000 hours of sunshine a year, this stretch of coast offers some of the world's best scuba diving. The largest community on the Sunshine Coast is Powell River with one of the world's biggest pulp and paper plants.

Swaying above North Vancouver's Capilano River is the Capilano Suspension Bridge, the longest and highest footbridge in the world. *Inset top:* Recreating life at a Hudson's Bay Company Post, Fort Langley National Historic Park. *Inset bottom:* Peace Arch Park is maintained jointly by British Columbia and the state of Washington. The arch itself straddles the Canada–U.S. border.

Instead of taking a ferry at Horseshoe Bay, travellers can continue north along the shore of Howe Sound through the town of Squamish. Above Squamish looms Stawamus Chief, a 762-metre (2500-foot) mountain that is a popular climbing and hiking spot. Beyond Squamish, the road climbs past the world-famous ski resorts of Whistler and Blackcomb to Mount Currie, a Native village surrounded by snow-capped mountains. In the 1860s, gold seekers trudged through this wilderness on their way to the Cariboo gold fields.

In the southern part of southwestern British Columbia lies the more tranquil countryside of the Fraser Valley. Dairy farms, market gardens and flower nurseries thrive in this lush green valley on the province's most fertile farmland. The largest communities in the valley are Abbotsford, Mission, Chilliwack and Hope.

Okanagan-Similkameen

The dry sunny climate of this region has made it a favourite of fruit farmers and tourists alike. The northern part of the Okanagan Valley is a dairy and vegetable-growing area. Vernon, at the head of Okanagan Lake, began as a commercial centre for the huge ranches in the area. The O'Keefe Historic Ranch offers a glimpse of these cattle empires of the past. Today Vernon is the business and tourist centre for the north Okanagan.

Kelowna is the largest city in the Okanagan. Its name means "grizzly bear" but no grizzly bears prowl the Okanagan today. The city is a commercial centre for the local orchards, canning plants, vineyards and wineries in and around it. With its sunny climate and pretty setting, it is a growing retirement centre.

The name of Penticton, at the foot of Okanagan Lake, means "place to stay forever." With its warm climate, beaches on two lakes and ski hills, the name suits the city. The southernmost city of the Okanagan-Similkameen is Osoyoos, close to the border with the United States and surrounded by desert. With heavy irrigation,

Far left: Campground on Osoyoos Lake, the warmest freshwater lake in Canada. *Left:* Historic O'Keefe Ranch, built about 1867. *Bottom left:* Statue of Ogopogo, the monster of Okanagan Lake. Tales of a fearsome lake monster have persisted since long before European settlers came to the area.

farmers have made the desert a rich orchard area that produces some of the earliest fruits in Canada.

The Similkameen River Valley in the southwest is a traditional mining area that had its own gold rush in the 1890s. The area is rich in copper, gold and other metals. Mining continues, but agriculture, tourism and logging are also important to the economy.

Kootenay Country

Born of many mining booms, Kootenay Country, east of the Okanagan, is a mix of snow-capped mountains and green valleys.

Castlegar is known locally as the "Crossroads of the Kootenays." Doukhobors settled here in the early 1900s, and their culture is showcased in the local Doukhobor Historical Museum. Trail is a major mining centre with a large smelter, and Rossland is an old gold town. At the turn of the century, Rossland was the province's fourth-largest city, producing half of its gold. Today "prospectors" can visit the LeRoi Gold Mine at the Rossland Museum, the only hardrock gold mine in Canada open to the public.

The city of Nelson is nestled on the West Arm of Kootenay Lake in the heart of the Selkirk Mountains. Nelson is called the "Heritage

Above: **Kootenay Country is mining country. Most of the ore extracted in the area is processed at Trail, seen here on a winter evening.** *Right:* **The S.S.** *Moyie,* **now permanently anchored at Kaslo, was one of a whole fleet of sternwheelers that once plied Kootenay Lake.**

Capital of the Kootenays" because of the 350 turn-of-the-century buildings that date from its mining heyday.

Kootenay Country is hot springs country. At Nakusp in the northern part of the region and at Ainsworth Hot Springs, on Kootenay Lake, visitors can soak in hot, mineralized waters year-round. At Kaslo on Kootenay Lake, the S.S. *Moyie,* last of the sternwheelers that brought supplies and people to pioneer settlements before the railway and good roads were built, is now a museum. It was retired in 1957 after 60 years of service.

Rocky Mountains

The Rocky Mountains region of British Columbia lies in its southeast corner along the border with Alberta. Over half the province's elk population lives in this area, which is also a major migration route for birds travelling the Columbia River flyway.

The Rocky Mountains region is home to three of the six national parks located in British Columbia. Glacier National Park contains over 400 glaciers. With one of the heaviest snowfalls in the world, Rogers Pass in the park is the site of the world's largest avalanche control program. Yoho National Park gets its name from the Cree word meaning "how magnificent." Kootenay National Park,

Left: A clear mountain lake provides a perfect reflection of the granite spires of the Bugaboo Range. *Above:* A few of the restored buildings at Fort Steele, named for Major Sam Steele, who established B.C.'s first North-West Mounted Police post nearby in 1887.

bordering on the southeast portion of Yoho, is actually the floor of an ancient ocean. It was established to protect the area's many canyons, mineral hot springs and waterfalls.

From here the road leads south to Kimberley, Cranbrook and Fort Steele. Kimberley is known as the "Bavarian City of the Canadian Rockies" and looks like a village in southern Germany. There is a fine Railway Museum in Cranbook. Nearby, at Fort Steele, 60 restored buildings and costumed townspeople recreate the community's gold-mining past.

High Country

British Columbia's High Country, with its lakes, turbulent rivers and rolling rangeland, juts southwest from the mountains of the Alberta border through the houseboating waters of Shuswap Lake to the ranch country of Douglas Lake.

The region includes Mount Robson Provincial Park, Wells Gray Provincial Park and Mount Revelstoke National Park. Mount Robson (3977 metres/13 048 feet) is the highest peak in the Canadian Rockies. Wells Gray Provincial Park contains a dozen large waterfalls and an extinct volcano.

In Monck Provincial Park, on the north shore of Nicola Lake, are the remains of a *kikuli* (pit house), the winter dwelling used by the Interior Salish and Athapaskan peoples.

Shuswap Lake is a popular summer resort area because of its sandy beaches and protected anchorages. The Adams River, which flows into Shuswap Lake, is famous for its fish. Every four years (1994, 1998, 2002, and so forth), a "dominant" sockeye salmon run fills the river, turning the waters blood red as crimson salmon head for their spawning grounds. The largest community in the High Country is the city of Kamloops, which lies where the North and South Thompson rivers meet. It began as a fur-trading post in the early 1800s and is now a forestry, mining, ranching and tourism centre. Its name means "meeting place."

Cariboo-Chilcotin

Rolling from east to west almost clear across the province, the wild, untamed Cariboo-Chilcotin is British Columbia's "true west." Here, under wide blue skies, some of Canada's largest ranches spread across the high plateau. The snow-covered peaks of the Coast and Cariboo mountain ranges dominate the region.

Clockwise from top left: **Float plane at the Monarch Ice Fields near Tweedsmuir Provincial Park, one of the most varied wilderness areas in Canada; small town rodeo; whitewater rafting in Wells Gray Provincial Park; marina near Salmon Arm at the southern end of Shuswap Lake**

The Cariboo to the east and the Chilcotin to the west each has its own unique character. The communities of the Cariboo were shaped by the historic gold rush that began in 1858. Quesnel, the area's largest town, developed as a supply centre for the gold miners. At Barkerville Historic Park, restored and reconstructed buildings give visitors a taste of a real gold rush town.

From Williams Lake west to the Coast Mountains is the cowboy country of the Chilcotin. Cattle from these rangelands are sent to markets across Canada. On the western edge of the plateau, Tweedsmuir Provincial Park offers a widely varied wilderness that includes glaciers, alpine meadows and grassy valleys.

Far to the west is the coastal community of Bella Coola, separated from the rest of the province by the Coast Mountains. The road into the community was built only in the 1950s when the residents completed it themselves rather than wait for the government to do it. The communities of Ocean Falls and Bella Bella are even more remote and can be reached only by water or air.

Northwest

Home to the legendary Klondike Gold Rush Trail, the Tatshenshini River and totem poles, the Northwest region of British Columbia is a vast L-shaped wilderness. It stretches from the Rockies in the east to the Queen Charlotte Islands and Alaska in the west, and from Cariboo Country to the Yukon border.

The mist-cloaked Queen Charlotte Islands are the homeland of the Haida people, whose name for them is Haida Gwaii. The remains of ancient Haida villages are scattered throughout the dense rain forest along the islands' coasts. Today, the Haida are not the only residents of the islands. Natives and non-Natives work in the fishing, logging, mining and tourism industries.

Prince Rupert, built on an island near the mouth of the Skeena River, is the second most-important port in the province, and it is the commercial and transportation centre for the northwest.

Southeast of Prince Rupert is the "aluminum city" of Kitimat. A huge aluminum smelter built here in the 1950s has been joined by a large methanol plant. This modern industrial city is surrounded by wilderness. A single road leads north to Terrace, named for the terraced bank from which it overlooks the Skeena.

Human history is an important attraction in this region. Kitwanga Fort National Historic Site was part of a Native trading network and the location of several famous Native battles. At the village of Kitwancool is the oldest standing totem pole in the world, known as "Hole-through-the Ice." Nearby at Hazelton, the 'Ksan Indian Village recreates a Gitksan community that stood at the junction of the Bulkley and Skeena rivers until the 1870s. Six longhouses are decorated with carved poles and painted fronts.

In the eastern part of the region, visitors can explore a Hudson's Bay fort of the late 1800s at Fort St. James National Historic Site. The village of Fort St. James is the oldest non-Native community in the province. To the south, Vanderhoof is the geographical centre of British Columbia. The largest city in northern British Columbia is Prince George, located where the Nechako and Fraser rivers meet. Today it is a major commercial and transportation centre and home of the new University of Northern British Columbia.

Below: **Farm near McBride.** *Right:* **Totem poles at Kispiox, in the Hazelton area**

Atlin, the main centre of the extreme northwest, sits beside a turquoise lake, backed by snow-clad mountains. Due west of Atlin lies the legendary Klondike Gold Rush Trail. Miners' gear litters the trail and is protected from vandalism by law.

Peace River

Explorer Alexander Mackenzie called the Peace River region a "magnificent theatre of nature" because of its mountains, powerful rivers and rolling grasslands. Today this region has fields of grain, huge hydroelectric dams, mines and oil wells.

From Mile 0 at Dawson Creek on the southeast edge of the region, the Alaska Highway winds northwest to the Yukon border and beyond. A popular tourist route in summer, the highway is also an important supply route for northern communities.

Northwest of Dawson Creek, Fort St. John is the largest community north of Prince George. The first oil well in British Columbia was drilled near here. Fort Nelson, farther north, is also an important centre for petroleum and natural gas development.

The largest "lake" in the province is in the southwest corner of the region — Williston Lake, formed when the W.A.C. Bennett Dam was built.

Far left: **Harvesting barley in the Peace River Valley.**
Left: **Dawson Creek signpost marking the beginning of the Alaska Highway**

Facts
at a Glance

General Information

Provincehood: July 20, 1871

Origin of Name: Queen Victoria suggested the name of British Columbia for the colony that had existed since 1858.

Provincial Capital: Victoria

Provincial Nickname: The Pacific Province

Provincial Flag: The upper part of the flag is a Union Jack with a golden crown in the centre. This symbolizes the province's origins as a British colony. The lower part shows a golden half sun superimposed over three wavy blue bars that represent the Pacific Ocean. The sun setting over the ocean is symbolic of British Columbia's position as Canada's most westerly province.

Motto: *Splendor Sine Occasu:* The Latin words are translated "Splendour without diminishment."

Provincial Flower: Pacific dogwood

Provincial Bird: Steller's jay

Provincial Tree: Western red cedar

Provincial Mineral: Jade

Population

(1991 census)

Population: 3 282 061

Population Density: 3.7 people per km² (9.58 per sq. mi.)

Population Distribution: 55.8% of British Columbians live on 4.2% of the land area in the southwestern corner of the province.

Greater Vancouver	1 542 744
Greater Victoria	299 550
Kelowna	75 950
Prince George	69 653
Kamloops	67 057
Nanaimo	60 129

Population Growth: British Columbia is Canada's fastest-growing province.

1871	36 247
1881	49 459
1891	98 173
1901	178 657
1911	392 480
1931	694 263
1941	817 861
1951	1 165 210
1961	1 629 082
1971	2 184 600
1981	2 713 615
1991	3 282 061

Geography

Borders: British Columbia lies between the 49th and 60th northern parallels of latitude and between the 120th and 144th meridians of longitude. It is bordered by the

American states of Washington, Idaho and Montana on the south, and Alaska on the northwest, by Alberta on the east and by the Yukon and Northwest Territories on the north.

Highest Point: Fairweather Mountain (on the border with Alaska), 4663 m (15 300 ft.). Mount Waddington, 4106 m (13 175 ft.), is the highest point entirely within the province.

Lowest Point: Sea level along the coast

Area: 948 596 km² (366 281 sq. mi.) of which about 2% is fresh water

Rank in Area Among Provinces: Third

Time Zone: Most of B.C. is on Pacific Time; the Peace River region and the Kootenays are on Mountain Time.

National and Provincial Parks: British Columbia's spectacular natural beauty is protected in six national parks (Gwaii Haanas, Pacific Rim, Mount Revelstoke, Kootenay, Yoho and Glacier) and over 400 provincial parks and recreation areas.

Rivers: Rivers draining into the Pacific Ocean include the Fraser, Skeena, Stikine, Nass and (via Oregon) the Columbia. The Liard and the Peace rivers drain eventually into the Arctic Ocean.

Lakes: British Columbia has thousands of lakes. The largest are Williston, Nechacko and Upper and Lower Arrow lakes formed behind dams. Atlin, Babine, Kootenay, Stuart and Okanagan are the largest natural lakes.

Topography: British Columbia is a sea of mountains, interspersed with plateaus, plains and lowlands. The major mountain ranges are: the Coast, Skeena, Cascade, Cassiar, Omineca, Cariboo, Monashee, Selkirk, Purcell and Rocky Mountains. The northeastern corner of the province is an extension of the high plains of western Alberta. The southwestern corner is a flat lowland formed by the delta of the Fraser River. The biggest offshore islands are Vancouver Island and Graham and Moresby islands in the Queen Charlottes.

Climate: Moisture-laden clouds from the Pacific Ocean rise when they meet the mountains, and the moisture in them condenses to form rain. As a result, rainfall on the west side of the mountains tends to be greater than on the east. Vancouver Island's climate is mild because of the Pacific Ocean. In Victoria, the average January and July temperatures are 4.1°C (39.3°F) and 15.4°C (60°F), respectively. Winters on the mainland coast are generally mild and wet. In the interior they are colder, and summers are hotter. In Princeton, the average January temperature is -8°C (17°F), and the average July temperature is 18°C (65°F). Although very little snow falls at the lower elevations along the coast, snow is an expected part of B.C. winters at higher coastal elevations and in the interior.

Nature

Trees: About 60% of the province is covered with forests. Important trees

include Douglas fir, western red cedar, hemlock, Sitka spruce, western red pine, lodgepole pine, balsam fir, poplar, Garry oak, and birch.

Young grizzly bear

Wild Plants: B.C. is home to hundreds of varieties of wild plants. These include various kinds of grasses, mosses, ferns and lichens, mushrooms, sedges, wildflowers and wild berries.

Animals: The 112 species of mammals in the province include grizzly bear, cougar, mountain goat, bighorn sheep, moose, black-tailed deer, elk, hoary marmot, Townsend vole, pika, orca, grey and humpback whales, seals, sea otters, and sea lions. Fifteen species of reptiles and 19 species of amphibians are found here.

Birds: Among the hundreds of bird species are 266 species of water birds, including ducks, pelicans, herons, swans and geese; and 34 species of raptors, such as ospreys and hawks. Other species include rufous hummingbirds, whiskey jacks and rhinoceros auklets. Twenty-eight of the bird species found in B.C. are endangered, threatened or of special concern.

Fish: Five species of salmon, lingcod, halibut, rainbow, brown and cutthroat trout, steelhead and Dolly Varden are the main fish species.

Government and the Courts

Governments: British Columbia has 32 seats in the federal House of Commons and five seats in the Senate. Provincial laws are passed by an elected single-chamber Legislative Assembly of 75 members. Municipalities of various kinds are responsible for local government services. The province has 43 cities, 14 towns, 43 villages, 50 district municipalities, 29 regional districts and 300 improvement districts.

The Courts: British Columbia has a three-tiered court system. At the first, or lowest, level is the Provincial Court, which hears most of the criminal cases. At the second level is the Supreme Court of British Columbia, which hears civil cases as well as very serious criminal cases. At the highest level is the Appeal Court of British Columbia. This court hears matters appealed from the decisions of lower courts.

Education

Seventy-five local school districts administer public school education.

Education is offered from kindergarten through to grade 12. In 1995, the province's 1697 public schools enrolled 595 000 pupils, while 343 independent schools enrolled 52 000 pupils. The language of instruction in most schools is English. Various French programs are available in many areas, and other languages such as Japanese, Chinese, Spanish and German are also taught.

A number of post-secondary programs are offered at 16 community colleges and 3 institutes located throughout the province. During 1995-1996, 35 500 full-time and 61 000 part-time students took courses.

Four university colleges, located in Kamloops, Chilliwak, Nanaimo and Kelowna, offer courses leading to bachelor degrees. Five publicly funded universities offer a wide range of undergraduate, graduate and professional programs: the University of British Columbia in Vancouver, Simon Fraser University in Burnaby, the University of Victoria in Victoria, Royal Roads University near Victoria and the University of Northern British Columbia in Prince George. There is also one privately funded university. In 1995-1996, approximately 46 000 full-time and 22 000 part-time students were enrolled in university programs.

Economy and Industry

British Columbia's economy is based on natural resource extraction, manufacturing and service industries.

Primary Products

Wood: B.C. lumber, newsprint, pulp and paper, shingles and shakes are in demand throughout the world.

Minerals: Mines produce copper, gold, silver, lead, zinc, molybdenum, asbestos, sulphur and coal.

Energy: The energy industry produces coal, hydroelectricity, oil and natural gas. Some hydro-electricity, some natural gas and almost all of the coal produced are exported.

Agriculture: B.C. ranks sixth among the provinces in farm earnings. One-third of farmland is used to raise crops; the rest is for pasture or grazing. Crops include grains, fruit, vegetables and herbs.

Fish: More than 40 species of fish and marine animals are harvested and marketed by the province's fishing and aquaculture industries. There are 240 fish-processing plants on the coast and a fishing fleet of 6200 vessels. The federal government has a program to reduce the number of vessels in order to help conserve salmon stocks.

Secondary Products and Services

Manufacturing: Items manufactured include petroleum products, food products, metal and chemical goods, computer technology, communications equipment and clothing.

Tourism: In 1991, British Columbia residents and visitors made over 23 million overnight trips in the province. Countless excursionists also took one-day trips. These travellers helped create tens of thousands of jobs and generated over $6 billion.

Transportation: All B.C. ports are ice-free year-round. The Port of Vancouver is the second largest port in North America. The BC Ferry Corporation has 24 routes between the Lower Mainland, Vancouver Island and coastal ports. The province has 6800 km (4225 mi.) of railway track. Vancouver International is the province's largest airport. It handles 10 million passengers a year and is served by major Canadian and international airlines. B.C.'s highway network is made up of 23 000 km (14 260 mi.) of paved roads and 19 300 km (11 966 mi.) of unpaved roads.

Communications: British Columbia has 83 originating radio stations and 11 originating television stations. There are 15 daily newspapers and 160 weekly or community newspapers, some of which publish in languages other than English. There are over 230 book publishers.

Social and Cultural Life

Museums and Art Galleries: British Columbia has about 190 museums. Some, like the Royal British Columbia Museum in Victoria, are internationally renowned. Others, like the tiny museum in the former jail at Miner's Bay on Mayne Island, are much smaller and are not well known outside the area.

In Vancouver, important museums include the Museum of Anthropology, the H.R. MacMillan Planetarium and the Vancouver Museum. The maritime museums in both Vancouver and Victoria are well worth visiting. Other museums of interest are the mining exhibits at Britannia and Rossland, the Burnaby Village Museum, the British Columbia Forest Museum near Duncan and the Museum of Northern British Columbia in Prince George.

A CPR freight train winds its way through the mountains along the Yoho River.

The work of prominent artists is displayed in galleries such as the Emily Carr Gallery in Victoria, the Kamloops Public Art Gallery and the Vancouver Art Gallery.

Notable among museums devoted to Native art are 'Ksan at Hazelton, the Kwakiutl Museum in Cape Mudge Village on Quadra Island and the U'Mista Cultural Centre at Alert Bay.

Festivals: Countless festivals take place around the province.

On Vancouver Island, summer music festivals include the Victoria Folkfest and Jazz Festival, the Choirfest in Port Alberni and the Bluegrass Festival in Coombs.

In Vancouver, the festival season begins with the Children's Festival and continues with the International Dragon Boat Festival, the Diwali Festival of Lights, the Vancouver Sea Festival, and the International Writers and Readers Festival.

Festivals held elsewhere in southwestern British Columbia include the Salmon Festival in Steveston, the Seabird Island Indian Festival in Harrison Hot Springs and the Agassiz Fall Fair and Corn Festival.

In the Okanagan, the Penticton Peach Festival and the Osoyoos Cherry Fiesta Parade take place in July, and the Okanagan Wine Festival is celebrated throughout the region in the fall. Festivals in the Kootenays, the Rockies and the Cariboo include the Sunfest in Castlegar, Sam Steele Days in Cranbrook and the Williams Lake Stampede. Up north, Prince Rupert

celebrates Seafest, and Prince George hosts Simon Fraser Days.

Performing Arts: There are several large theatres in Vancouver and Victoria and smaller ones across the province. British Columbians enjoy performances by the Vancouver- and Victoria-based symphony orchestras, choirs, and opera companies, as well as by such prominent dance companies as Ballet B.C. and the Judith Marcuse Dance Company.

Sports: Fans can cheer National Hockey League action with the Vancouver Canucks, football with the B.C. Lions Football Team, basketball with the Vancouver Grizzlies, baseball with the Vancouver Canadians and soccer with the Vancouver 86ers. There is also plenty of minor league hockey, intercollegiate basketball, volleyball and World Cup downhill skiing.

Historic Sites and Landmarks

Barkerville Historic Park is a restored village from the Cariboo gold rush of the 1800s. Open year-round, it comes alive in summer with re-enactments of gold-rush life.

Doukhobor Heritage Village in Castlegar offers a glimpse of the culture of the Doukhobor immigrants who settled this area in 1908. The tomb of their leader Peter Verigin is nearby.

Gold Rush days recreated at historic Barkerville

Fort Langley National Historic Site is the official birthplace of British Columbia. Founded in 1827, the fort was the site of the proclamation of the colony of British Columbia in 1858.

Fort Steele, near Cranbrook, grew during the 1864 Kootenay Gold Rush. Sixty restored buildings allow visitors to experience life in a turn-of-the-century town.

Fort St. James National Historic Park recreates the atmosphere of a frontier trading post. The fort was founded in 1806 by Simon Fraser.

Provincial Legislature, in Victoria, was designed by Francis Rattenbury and completed in 1897. It overlooks Victoria's beautiful inner harbour.

West Coast Trail was established along the southwestern coast of Vancouver Island in 1907 to help shipwrecked sailors reach coastal communities. Now it is an internationally famous hiking trail.

Other Interesting Places to Visit

Botanical Beach, on the west coast of Vancouver Island, is famous for its tidal pools and huge variety of marine life, including chitons, sea robins, urchins and sea anemones.

Chinatown in Vancouver is a vibrant, 100-year-old community with many intriguing shops and restaurants.

Fisgard Lighthouse National Historical Site is at the entrance to Esquimalt Harbour. Built in 1860, the lighthouse was operated for 68 years.

Ninstints, the abandoned Haida village on Anthony Island in the Queen Charlotte Islands is a UNESCO World Heritage Site. It contains the largest number of original-standing totem poles in the world.

O'Keefe Historic Ranch was one of the earliest cattle ranches developed in the Okanagan. Today it includes a furnished log house, a working blacksmith's shop and St. Ann's, the oldest Catholic church in the interior.

Sasquatch Provincial Park is named for the huge ape-like creature that is said to roam the densely wooded shores of Harrison Lake. The lake itself is famous for its hot springs.

Stanley Park in Vancouver is one of the largest inner-city parks in North America. It is a mix of forests, manicured lawns and attractions such as the zoo, the aquarium and the seawall walkway.

Important Dates

Thousands of years before specific events can be dated, the ancestors of today's Native people had established themselves in the lands now known as British Columbia.

1774	Spanish expedition under Juan José Pérez Hernández reaches the Queen Charlotte Islands and anchors later in Nootka Sound.
1778	Captain James Cook lands at Nootka Sound.
1792-1794	Captain George Vancouver surveys the coastline.
1793	Alexander Mackenzie reaches the Pacific coast by travelling overland from Lake Athabasca.
1805	Simon Fraser builds the first of several trading posts in the central interior.
1807-1812	David Thompson explores and maps much of the Columbia River area.
1808	Fraser reaches the Pacific Ocean by travelling down the Fraser River.
1827	The Hudson's Bay Company (HBC) completes Fort Langley.
1835-1838	Smallpox epidemics sweep the northwest coast and many Native people die.
1843	Construction of the HBC's Fort Victoria begins.
1846	The Oregon Boundary Treaty establishes the 49th parallel as the land border between American and British territory west of the Rocky Mountains.
1849	Vancouver Island becomes a Crown colony.
1858	The Fraser River Gold Rush begins; the B.C. mainland becomes a Crown colony.
1859	New Westminster becomes the mainland capital.
1861	Mining boom begins in the Cariboo; construction begins on the Cariboo Wagon Road.
1862	Smallpox epidemic devastates the Native population.
1866	B.C. mainland and Vancouver Island are united.
1868	Victoria is chosen as the capital of the United Colony of British Columbia.
1871	British Columbia joins Confederation.
1877	Coal miners strike on Vancouver Island.
1880	Canadian Pacific Railway (CPR) construction begins.
1885	CPR is completed; the "last spike" is pounded in at Craigellachie.
1886	Vancouver is selected as the terminus of CPR; Yoho and Glacier are established as the first national parks.
1888	Stanley Park in Vancouver officially opens.
1907	Anti-Oriental riots break out in Vancouver.
1911	Strathcona Park becomes the first provincial B.C. park.
1912	Coal miners on Vancouver Island begin a two-year strike.
1913	Hell's Gate landslides block the Fraser River and affect salmon spawning.
1914	Sikh passengers on the *Komagata Maru* are not allowed to disembark in Vancouver; the First World War begins; the

Grand Trunk Railway (now CNR) completes its line into Prince Rupert.

1917 B.C. women gain the provincial vote.

1919 The Winnipeg General Strike is followed by sympathy strikes in B.C.

1929 The Great Depression begins.

1938 Jobless men riot in Vancouver.

1939 World War II begins.

1942 Japanese British Columbians are evacuated from the west coast and interned.

1943 The Alaska Highway is completed.

1947 Chinese and East Indians are allowed to vote in federal and provincial elections.

1949 Native people are allowed to vote in provincial elections; Japanese are allowed to return to the west coast and to vote in provincial and federal elections.

1952 W.A.C. Bennett leads Social Credit Party to its first B.C. victory.

1954 Vancouver hosts the British Empire Games.

1960 Native people are allowed to vote in federal elections.

1962 The B.C. portion of the Trans-Canada Highway is completed.

1964 The Columbia River Treaty is signed by the United States and Canada; joint development of hydroelectric power follows.

1972 The New Democratic Party (NDP) comes to power for the first time in B.C.; Dave Barrett becomes premier.

1975 Social Credit leader Bill Bennett becomes premier.

1986 Expo 86 World's Fair takes place in Vancouver; Social Credit leader Bill Vander Zalm becomes premier.

1988 The federal government officially apologizes to Japanese British Columbians interned during World War II.

1990 The provincial government agrees to participate in Native land claims negotiations.

1991 Social Credit leader Rita Johnston becomes the first woman premier; the NDP under Mike Harcourt is elected.

1994 The Commonwealth Games are held in Victoria.

1996 The provincial and federal governments and the Nishga tribal council sign the first major Native land claims agreement in principle.

1996 The NDP is re-elected for a second term for the first time in B.C. history, with Glen Clark as premier.

B.C. Place during Expo 86

Sir Matthew Begbie

W.A.C. Bennett

Earle Birney

Frank Calder

Important People

Bryan Adams (1959-), born in Ontario; husky-voiced singer, songwriter, rock star; achieved international fame with such albums as *Cuts Like a Knife* and *Waking Up the Neighbors*; also performs in concerts for social and political causes

David Barrett (1930-), born in Vancouver; social worker, politician; NDP leader, 1970-83; as premier, 1972-75, instituted many social reforms; federal MP, 1988-93

Robert Bateman (1930-), born in Ontario; artist, teacher; has achieved international fame with finely detailed, realistic wildlife paintings

Sir Matthew Baillie Begbie (1819-1894), born at sea to British parents; first B.C. judge; sent from England to preserve law and order during the gold rush; upheld the rights of Native people and Chinese residents; was also the province's first chief justice

William Andrew Cecil Bennett (1900-1979); politician; came to Kelowna in 1930; leader of the new Social Credit Party; premier, 1952-72, during an era of explosive growth; succeeded as party leader by his son, who was premier, 1975-86

Thomas Berger (1933-), born in Victoria; lawyer, judge, politician, civil libertarian; known for his strong support of aboriginal land claims and for heading the inquiry that recommended against building a pipeline through the Mackenzie Valley

Earle Birney (1904-1995), born in Calgary; writer; published more than 20 volumes of poetry, work was translated into a dozen languages; gave more than 1500 poetry readings in 30 countries; won two Governor General's awards

Pavel Bure (1971-), born in Moscow; hockey player; became famous at age 21 as right-winger for the Canucks

Frank Calder (1915-), born at Nass Harbour; served as MLA for 26 years; was the first Native person to be elected to a provincial legislature; appointed Minister of the Crown in Canada (1972-73); known for the 1973 Calder case, a landmark decision on the Nishga land claims in the Supreme Court of Canada

Kim Campbell (1947-), born in Port Alberni; politician; MLA, 1986-88, MP, 1988-93; held several cabinet posts before becoming the first woman and the first British Columbian to serve as prime minister of Canada (June-October 1993)

Emily Carr (1871-1945), born in Victoria; painter, writer;

travelled to remote parts of the west coast to paint the wild forests, Native villages and totem poles; now recognized as one of Canada's greatest artists; wrote *Klee Wyck* (Governor General's Award), *The Book of Small, The House of All Sorts*

Brent Carver (1951-), born in Cranbrook; actor, comic, singer; known for his one-man shows and roles in rock operas; won Tony Award for his performance in *Kiss of the Spider Woman*

Amor De Cosmos (1825-1897), born William Alexander Smith in Nova Scotia; journalist, politician, premier, 1872-74; arrived in Victoria in 1858, founded the *British Colonist* newspaper; represented Victoria at four levels of government; strong supporter of Confederation

Robert Davidson (1946-), born in Alaska into Haida Eagle clan; great-grandson of master carver Charles Edenshaw; sculptor, printmaker, jeweller; uses traditional Haida shapes and symbols in a modern way

Sir James Douglas (1803-1877), born in British Guiana (now Guyana); trader, governor; founded Fort Victoria in 1843 while chief factor of Hudson's Bay Company; named governor of Vancouver Island in 1851 and of British Columbia in 1858; often called "the Father of British Columbia"

Robert Dunsmuir (1825-1889), Scottish-born coal baron; came to B.C. in 1851; discovered a rich coal seam north of Nanaimo in 1869, opened his own mine and was soon known as the coal king of B.C.; disliked by miners because of his disregard for safety and ruthless anti-union stands. His son **James Dunsmuir** (1851-1920) ruled the family business empire for many years and served briefly as premier and later as lieutenant-governor

Arthur Erickson (1924-), born in Vancouver; architect; designed many of Canada's greatest public buildings, including the Museum of Anthropology at UBC, Simon Fraser University and Roy Thomson Hall in Toronto; also designed the Canadian Embassy in Washington, D.C.

Judith Forst (1943-), born in New Westminster, one of the world's top mezzo-sopranos; has sung with famous opera companies all over the world; named Canadian Woman of the Year, 1978

Seraphim ("Joe") Fortes (?-1922), born in Barbados, came to Vancouver in 1885; as lifeguard at English Bay performed more than 100 rescues and taught thousands of Vancouver children to swim; children's drinking fountain at English Bay erected in his honour in 1927

Terry Fox (1958-1981), born in Manitoba, raised in Port

Kim Campbell

Emily Carr

Amor De Cosmos

Judith Forst

Chief Dan George

Nancy Greene Raine

Rick Hansen

Harry Jerome

Coquitlam; athlete; in 1980 on an artificial right leg ran across Canada to raise money for cancer research; his "Marathon of Hope" raised $25 million, and fund-raising runs are still held each year in his name

Chief Dan George (1899-1981), born on Burrard Reserve; actor, writer; chief of Squamish Band, 1951-63; began acting at age 60 and became famous in movies such as *Little Big Man;* wrote two volumes of prose poems; respected as a wise and gentle Native elder

Dorothy Grant (1955-), born in Alaska into Haida Raven clan; fashion designer; uses Native designs in high fashion clothes ("wearable art"); her designs are in art collections around the world

Nancy Greene Raine (1943-), raised in Rossland; athlete; member of national ski team, 1959-68; won the 1967 and 1968 World Cups and gold and silver medals at 1968 Olympics; won the Lou Marsh Trophy for Athlete of the Year (1967, 1968); named B.C. Female of the Half-Century

Helena Gutteridge (1879-1960), suffragist, union official, politician; played a leading role in B.C. women's fight for the vote; in 1937, became the first woman elected to Vancouver City Council

Roderick Haig-Brown (1908-1976); conservationist, writer; his love of fishing and his concern for the environment are subjects for many of his 25 books; won Governor General's Award for *Saltwater Summer*

Rick Hansen (1957-), born in Port Alberni; athlete; won 19 international wheelchair marathons and was world champion three times; on his 1985-87 "Man in Motion Tour," wheeled 40 000 kilometres (25 000 miles) and raised $20 million for spinal cord research and wheelchair sports

Bruce Hutchison (1901-1992), raised in Victoria; journalist, author; considered one of Canada's best writers about the West; his best-known book is probably *The Unknown Country;* won three Governor General's awards

Harry Jerome (1940-1982), raised in Vancouver; athlete; one of the greatest sprinters Canada has produced; held world records in the 1960s and won a bronze medal at the 1964 Olympics; statue erected in Stanley Park in his honour

Joy Kogawa (1935-), born in Vancouver; writer; during Second World War was sent to internment camp for Japanese Canadians in Slocan; her novel *Obasan* tells the story of this experience

Kwah (1755?-1840), born near Fort St. James; Carrier chief; provided food and guidance to Simon Fraser and European fur traders; said to have saved the life of James Douglas

David See-Chai Lam (1923-), born in Hong Kong; philanthropist; moved to Vancouver in 1967 and was successful in real estate; made important gifts to B.C. educational and cultural institutions; lieutenant-governor from 1988 to 1995

Dorothy Livesay (1909-), born in Manitoba, lives on Galiano Island; poet, reporter, teacher; has won many poetry prizes, including Governor General's Award for *Day and Night,* a book of poems on social themes

Sir Richard McBride (1870-1917), born in New Westminster; politician; elected to the B.C. Legislature in 1898; premier from 1903 to 1915, during a period of industrial expansion and prosperity; after resigning, become agent-general for B.C. in London, England

Helen Gregory MacGill (1864-1947), feminist, reformer, judge; first woman to graduate from the University of Toronto; moved to Vancouver in 1903; worked for 40 years to improve the lot of women and children; became B.C.'s first woman judge in 1917

H.R. MacMillan (1885-1976), forester, lumber executive; began a small timber export business in 1919, which expanded into a world leader and merged with another company to form MacMillan Bloedel, the largest lumber producer in Canada

Maquinna (?-c.1795), Nootka chief; was the main chief at Nootka Sound when Captain James Cook and other European explorers started visiting the area; an important middleman in the maritime fur trade, he managed to keep his people on friendly terms with both the Spanish and the British

Mungo Martin (1879-1962), born in Fort Rupert; Kwakiutl painter, carver, singer, songwriter; did much to rekindle pride in Native achievements and to preserve his people's culture by recording ancient songs; carved many totem poles

Margaret ("Ma") Murray (1888-1982), well-known, witty, outspoken publisher of *Bridge River-Lillooet News;* received Order of Canada, 1971

Wayne Ngan (1937-), born in China, lives on Hornby Island; artist; award-winning potter; a master of raku firing and salt glazes; uses elements of Chinese, Japanese and Korean ceramics

David See-Chai Lam

Dorothy Livesay

Sir Richard McBride

H.R. MacMillan

Maquinna

"Ma" Murray

Michael Smith

David Suzuki

Patricia Kathleen (P.K.) Page (1916-), born in England; writer, artist; moved to Victoria in 1964; won Governor General's Award for her poetry book *The Metal and the Flower;* her paintings and drawings are widely exhibited

Thomas Dufferin ("Duff") Pattullo (1873-1956), Ontario-born politician; came west in 1897; as Liberal premier (1933-41), started a vast program of public works, including a bridge across the Fraser at New Westminster, to create jobs during the Depression

Francis Rattenbury (1867-1935), born in England; architect; designed the legislative building, the Empress Hotel, and many other B.C. public buildings

William (Bill) Reid (1920-), born in Victoria; artist, sculptor, goldsmith; uses traditional Haida art forms, legends and designs in his own unique style; famous for works such as *The Spirit of Haida Gwaii,* a huge bronze canoe sculpture at the Canadian Embassy in Washington, D.C.; national speaker for Native rights

Alfred Scow (1927-), born in Alert Bay; judge; first Native person to become a lawyer in British Columbia; appointed provincial court judge in 1971; now a B.C. Roving Judge

Jack Shadbolt (1909-), raised in Victoria; artist, writer, teacher; one of Canada's most famous painters; uses primitive and modern styles; has written poetry and books about art

Gordon Shrum (1896-1985), physicist, professor; discovered the "green line" in the northern lights; professor and administrator at UBC for 36 years; first chancellor of Simon Fraser University; helped mastermind the Peace and Columbia rivers hydroelectric power projects

Michael Smith (1932-), born in England; professor, biochemist; came to UBC in 1966; developed ways to alter genes that are being used to fight cancer, create new plants, develop better medicines and build proteins to use in pulp and paper; co-winner of 1993 Nobel Prize for Chemistry

David Suzuki (1936-), born in Vancouver; scientist, educator, environmentalist, writer, broadcaster; widely known as host of CBC's science series *The Nature of Things;* author of many books, including his autobiography, *Metamorphosis: Stages in a Life*

Roy Henry Vickers (1946-), raised in a Nishga village; artist whose work reflects his mixed Tsimshian/Heiltsuk/British heritage; silk screens and wood sculptures known internationally

Ethel Wilson (1888-1980), born in South Africa; writer; moved to

Vancouver at age 10; her love of her adopted homeland showed in all her work; internationally acclaimed for several novels, in particular *Swamp Angel*

George Woodcock (1912-1995); literary journalist, historian, critic, writer; wrote more than 60 books and edited 30 others on subjects ranging from history to literary criticism; included in his works are *British Columbia: A History of the Province* and two volumes of autobiography: *Letter to the Past* and *Beyond the Blue Mountains*

Ethel Wilson

Premiers of British Columbia

John Foster McCreight		1871-1872
Amor de Cosmos		1872-1874
George Anthony Walkem		1874-1876
Andrew Charles Elliott		1876-1878
George Anthony Walkem		1878-1882
Robert Beaven		1882-1883
William Smithe		1883-1887
Alexander E.B. Davie	Conservative	1887-1889
John Robson	Liberal	1889-1892
Theodore Davie		1892-1895
John Herbert Turner		1895-1898
Charles August Semlin	Conservative	1898-1900
Joseph Martin	Liberal	1900
James Dunsmuir		1900-1902
Edward Gawler Prior	Conservative	1902-1903
Richard McBride	Conservative	1903-1915
William J. Bowser	Conservative	1915-1916
Harlan C. Brewster	Liberal	1916-1918
John Oliver	Liberal	1918-1927
John D. MacLean	Liberal	1927-1928
Simon F. Tolmie	Conservative	1928-1933
Thomas Dufferin Pattullo	Liberal	1933-1941
John Hart	Liberal (Coalition Government)	1941-1947
Byron I. Johnson	Liberal (Coalition Government)	1947-1952
W. A. C. Bennett	Social Credit	1952-1972
David Barrett	New Democratic Party	1972-1975
William R. Bennett	Social Credit	1975-1986
Wilhelmus ("Bill") Vander Zalm	Social Credit	1986-1991
Rita Johnston	Social Credit	1991
Michael Harcourt	New Democratic Party	1991-1996
Glen Clark	New Democratic Party	1996-

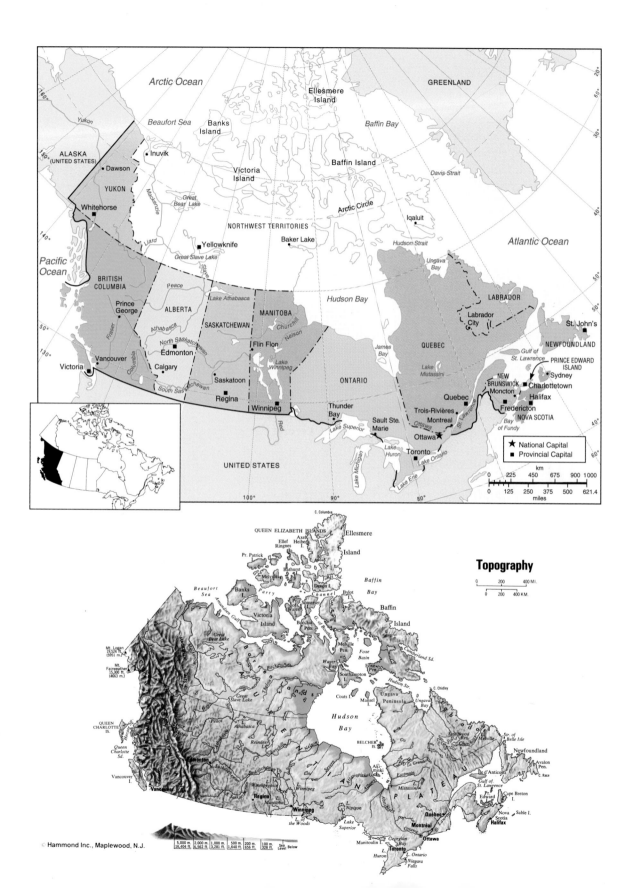

Topography

© Hammond Inc., Maplewood, N.J.

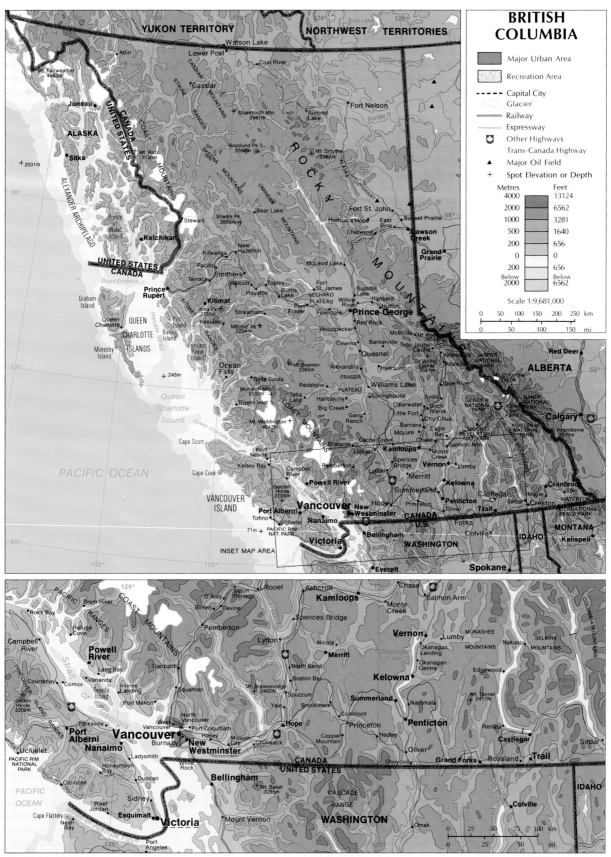

ECONOMY AND AGRICULTURE

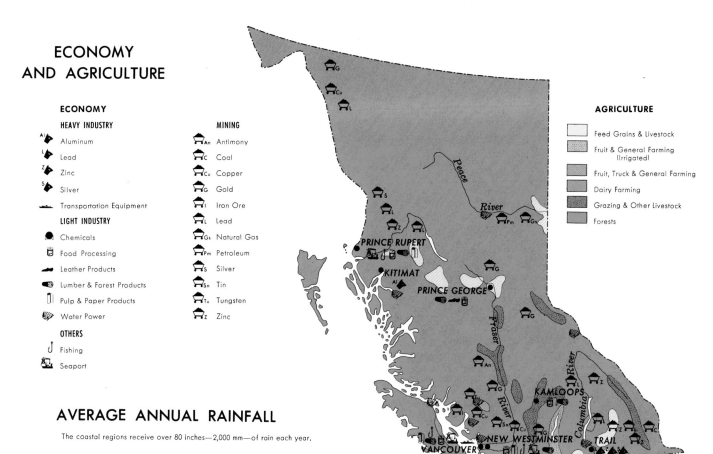

ECONOMY

HEAVY INDUSTRY
- Al — Aluminum
- L — Lead
- Z — Zinc
- S — Silver
- Transportation Equipment

LIGHT INDUSTRY
- Chemicals
- Food Processing
- Leather Products
- Lumber & Forest Products
- Pulp & Paper Products
- Water Power

OTHERS
- Fishing
- Seaport

MINING
- An — Antimony
- C — Coal
- Cu — Copper
- G — Gold
- I — Iron Ore
- L — Lead
- Gs — Natural Gas
- Pm — Petroleum
- S — Silver
- Sn — Tin
- Tu — Tungsten
- Z — Zinc

AGRICULTURE
- Feed Grains & Livestock
- Fruit & General Farming (Irrigated)
- Fruit, Truck & General Farming
- Dairy Farming
- Grazing & Other Livestock
- Forests

AVERAGE ANNUAL RAINFALL

The coastal regions receive over 80 inches—2,000 mm—of rain each year.

Mm		Inches	Mm		Inches	Mm		Inches
250-500	1	10-20	1,000-1,500	3	40-60	over 2,000	5	over 80
500-1,000	2	20-40	1,500-2,000	4	60-80			

Figures within areas are for identification purposes only.

GROWING SEASON

There are more than seven frost-free months each year along the southern coast of British Columbia.

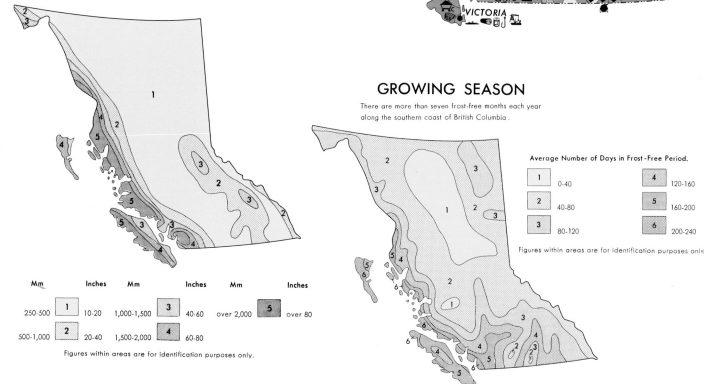

Average Number of Days in Frost-Free Period.

1	0-40		4	120-160
2	40-80		5	160-200
3	80-120		6	200-240

Figures within areas are for identification purposes only.

Index

142

About the Author/Editors

Isabel Nanton is a writer and photographer living in Vancouver. She has written *Adventuring in British Columbia,* now in its fourth printing, and also teaches travel writing at UBC's Continuing Education Dept.

Nancy Flight, West Coast Editorial Associates (WCEA), has worked in book publishing since 1972, editing both trade books and textbooks at all levels.

Barbara Tomlin, WCEA, has been a freelance editor since 1978. She also has taught university English and workshops in editing and proofreading.

Yvonne Van Ruskenveld, WCEA, has been a freelance editor and writer for business, government, non-profit and academic clients since 1987.

Lois Richardson, WCEA, has worked in publishing since 1975 as a journalist and magazine editor. She is the author of two non-fiction books.

MUSHROOM
Yum   SERVES 2 TO 4

Our house is obsessed with mushrooms. Although you can find this style of mushroom yum (salad) in Thailand, I think it's better to make in the States because there are so many different types of mushrooms at the grocery store. Use your favorites or whatever is on hand (my favorites are enoki mushrooms or baby oyster mushrooms).

The reason this mouthwatering salad works so well is that the mild mushrooms have a nice meaty flavor and a texture that soaks up the spicy and sour dressing like a sponge, creating a bright, bold, and savory combination that makes up the best Thai salads. I like to blanch the mushrooms first to get them nice and tender, then toss everything together in a bowl. It's best served chilled.

2 tablespoons fish sauce

½ teaspoon grated lime zest

1 tablespoon fresh lime juice

1 tablespoon light brown sugar

1 teaspoon Roasted Chile Powder (page 226)

2 cloves garlic, grated or finely minced

Kosher salt

¾ pound mixed mushrooms (enoki, oyster, button, shiitake), stems removed or trimmed, cut or torn into bite-size pieces

1 celery stalk, thinly sliced

¼ cup chopped celery leaves

¼ large yellow onion, thinly sliced crosswise

1 cup halved cherry tomatoes

2 tablespoons fresh mint leaves

◆ In a large bowl, whisk together the fish sauce, lime zest, lime juice, brown sugar, chile powder, and garlic.

◆ Fill a large pot halfway with water and add a couple big pinches of salt. Bring the water to a boil, then add the mushrooms. Blanch the mushrooms for 2 minutes, then drain and rinse under cold water.

◆ Transfer the mushrooms to the large bowl and add the celery, celery leaves, onion, tomatoes, and mint. Toss to coat in the dressing.

◆ Serve immediately or chill in the fridge to eat later.

Thai
STEAK SALAD

SERVES 2 TO 4

Whenever they have a date night at home, John and Chrissy love to order delivery from their favorite steakhouse. Have you ever seen a 2-pound dry-aged wagyu rib eye delivered by Postmates? I have.

I use leftovers to make my famous beef salad, called yum nuea in Thai. I've been making this recipe since Chrissy was in diapers, though back then I used cheaper cuts like flank steak or chuck roast, which can be just as tasty. I even used to send it with her and Tina for their school potlucks.

The beef should be well marbled and on the rare side, since the lime juice in the dressing will "cook" the steak a little more. Usually I just cut up steak straight from the fridge to make salad—dinner in ten minutes or less.

I tossed together a giant platter of this yum nuea when Chrissy was a guest on Ellen's show, as a snack for all the people working backstage. They loved it so much, they sent me a beautiful thank-you note, which is more than I can say for Chrissy's elementary school class!

3 tablespoons fresh lime juice (1 to 2 limes)

2 tablespoons fish sauce, plus more to taste

2 tablespoons Toasted Rice Powder, store-bought or homemade (page 226)

½ teaspoon Roasted Chile Powder (page 226), plus more for garnish

1 pound leftover steak (such as Soy-Garlic Pepper Steak, page 81), cold is fine, sliced against the grain into bite-size pieces

2 plum tomatoes, cut into wedges

2 Persian (mini) cucumbers or ½ hothouse cucumber, peeled, halved lengthwise, and thinly sliced

½ medium red onion, halved and sliced

4 scallions, thinly sliced

¼ cup chopped fresh cilantro leaves

Handful of fresh mint leaves

FOR SERVING

Cooked sticky rice (see page 228) or jasmine rice

Romaine lettuce leaves

Cucumber slices

Basil, cilantro, and/or mint leaves

◆ In a large bowl, whisk together the lime juice, fish sauce, rice powder, and chile powder until combined. Add the steak, tomatoes, cucumbers, and onion and gently toss.

◆ When ready to serve, fold in the scallions, cilantro, and mint leaves (don't do this ahead, because you want the leaves to stay fresh and crisp). Transfer the steak salad to a plate and sprinkle with a pinch of chile powder. Serve with rice, lettuce, cucumber, and herbs.

Naked
SHRIMP SALAD

SERVES 2 TO 4

I'm not sure why this dish is called naked shrimp. Maybe because the raw shrimp don't have shells, and the shells are like their clothes? But if I leave the tails on my shrimp . . . is that like being naked with socks on?

Called pla goong in Thai, this dish is somewhere between a salad and a ceviche: barely cooked shrimp dressed in a chile jam, lime juice, and fish sauce that cures the shrimp and gives it a sour-savory-sweet flavor. I like to build them out into a salad by adding shredded cabbage and carrots, sliced onion, and a shower of fresh herbs.

1 pound peeled large shrimp, tails left on

1 tablespoon light soy sauce

¼ cup fresh lime juice (about 2 limes)

2 tablespoons fish sauce

1 tablespoon light brown sugar

½ teaspoon Roasted Chile Powder (page 226)

2 tablespoons Sweet Chile Jam, store-bought or homemade (page 244)

2 thinly sliced bird's eye or serrano chiles

1 tablespoon vegetable oil

2 cups thinly sliced green cabbage
(from about ¼ head cabbage)

¼ cup grated carrot

¼ medium red onion, thinly sliced

½ cup chopped fresh cilantro leaves

½ cup chopped fresh mint leaves

◆ In a medium bowl, toss the shrimp with the soy sauce and set aside for 10 minutes.

◆ Meanwhile, in a large bowl, whisk together the lime juice, fish sauce, brown sugar, chile powder, chile jam, and sliced chiles. Taste and adjust as needed; the dressing should be sour and savory, with a balance of sweetness and heat.

◆ Heat a skillet over medium heat until you can feel the heat when waving your hand over it. Swirl in the oil. Working in batches, sear the shrimp until they're whitish-pink on the outside but still uncooked inside, 10 to 20 seconds on each side. Transfer to a plate and let cool slightly.

◆ Using a paring knife, butterfly each shrimp by cutting down the back, about halfway through, removing the vein in the process. Add the shrimp to the large bowl with the dressing and toss. The lime juice will continue to "cook" the shrimp like a ceviche.

◆ Add the cabbage, carrot, onion, cilantro, and mint, reserving a little of the herbs for garnish. Toss again, transfer to a plate, and top with the herbs. Serve immediately.

Shrimp and Bacon
GLASS NOODLE SALAD

SERVES 4

This is one of my favorite dishes to make in the summer when it's too hot to cook. Chewy glass noodles—they're called that because they turn clear when you cook them—are tossed with a spicy-sour dressing and a colorful mix of red onion, celery, and tomato. The salad is so light and healthy—and especially delicious eaten straight from the refrigerator. For this recipe I've added some shrimp, crispy bacon, and mushrooms, but you can also substitute cooked ground pork, chicken, or seared tofu.

6 ounces glass noodles (bean thread noodles)

½ pound large shrimp, peeled and deveined

Kosher salt

Ground white pepper

8 (6 ounces) slices bacon, thinly sliced crosswise

1 cup button or oyster mushrooms, sliced and stems trimmed

3 cloves garlic, minced

2 tablespoons light soy sauce

3 tablespoons fish sauce

¼ cup lime juice (from 2 limes)

2 tablespoons light brown sugar

2 fresh bird's eye chiles or 1 serrano chile, finely chopped

3 scallions, green parts only, thinly sliced

½ small red onion, thinly sliced

3 small thin celery stalks with leaves, thinly sliced (about ¾ cup)

1 plum tomato, cut into wedges

¼ cup unsalted roasted peanuts, roughly chopped

¼ cup fresh cilantro leaves, roughly chopped

Lettuce leaves, for serving

◆ Place the noodles in a large bowl and cover with room temperature water. Let sit for 10 to 15 minutes, until the noodles are soft and pliable. Drain and set aside.

◆ In a small bowl, season the shrimp with a pinch of salt and white pepper and set aside.

◆ In a skillet or wok over medium heat, add the bacon and cook until browned and crispy, about 4 minutes, stirring occasionally. Add the mushrooms and cook until just tender but not browned, about 2 minutes. Add the garlic and shrimp, cooking until the shrimp have just turned opaque, about 1 minute. Remove the bacon-mushroom-shrimp mixture from the skillet and set aside, then wipe out any remaining oil.

◆ With the skillet still over medium heat, add 1 cup of water and bring to a boil. Add the noodles to the pan, cooking 1 to 2 minutes, until they are stretchy and tender. Drain and rinse under cool water. (If you prefer shorter noodles, use scissors to cut them in thirds.)

♦ In a large bowl, whisk together the soy sauce, fish sauce, lime juice, sugar, and chiles. Add the noodles, scallions, red onion, celery, tomato, and half of the cilantro. Toss to mix. Gently fold in the bacon-mushroom-shrimp mixture and roasted peanuts until everything is combined. Refrigerate until chilled before serving.

♦ To serve, arrange the lettuce leaves on a serving platter and top with the noodle salad. Garnish with the remaining cilantro.

Tangy
CUCUMBER SALAD

SERVES 4

If you've eaten at a Thai restaurant in America, you've probably seen this perfect and simple cucumber salad. It's a little sweet, a little sour, crunchy, and refreshing. Most famously, it goes with chicken satay, but in Thailand they like to eat it with all kinds of rich foods: creamy curries, barbecued meats, fried things. Thai people don't stand for boring salads, so even this one, which takes only a few minutes, has lots of flavor. At home, I think of it like a magic trick: You have grilled pork and rice leftovers in the fridge, but what else do you eat with it? Poof! Instant meal.

⅓ cup sugar

⅓ cup distilled white vinegar

Kosher salt

3 Persian (mini) cucumbers, halved lengthwise and thinly sliced crosswise (about 2 cups)

1 large shallot or ½ medium red onion, halved lengthwise and thinly sliced

2 small sweet red bell peppers, halved lengthwise and thinly sliced

3 fresh bird's eye chiles (very hot) or 1 serrano chile (less hot), thinly sliced crosswise into rings

Handful of fresh cilantro leaves (optional)

◆ In a small saucepan, combine the sugar, vinegar, 1 tablespoon water, and a pinch of salt. Bring to a gentle boil over medium-high heat, stirring until the sugar dissolves. Remove from the heat and let it cool completely.

◆ In a medium bowl, combine the cucumbers, shallot, bell peppers, and chiles. Add the cooled syrup and toss. Refrigerate for up to an hour, or let it sit on the counter for 10 to 15 minutes before serving (don't wait too long or the cucumber will lose its crunch).

◆ Sprinkle with cilantro leaves before serving, if desired.

GREEN PAPAYA SALAD
(Som Tum)   SERVES 4

Som tum, or green papaya salad, is the one dish that I could eat every single day. I make it early in the morning for breakfast. I make it late at night when I want something spicy to wake me up. I make it when I'm bored in the afternoon. My large wooden mortar and pestle, which I use especially for papaya salad and which I bought in Thailand many years ago, is basically my third child. I've trained Chrissy so well that when she hears the plunk-plunk-plunk of me pounding the chiles, her mouth starts to water.

Although I've written down my recipe for you, think of it like a rough guideline. The important thing to know about papaya salad is that there is no right or wrong way to do it. Everything can and should be adjusted to your taste. Maybe you want to add a little more lime or sugar or fish sauce. Maybe you want to add a whole lot more chiles. What you should end up with is a salad that has the right balance of salty, sweet, sour, and spicy for your taste buds. Once you get really good at this process, I guarantee you can make amazing papaya salad in less than three minutes (pounding included). Have someone time you.

The other thing is the green papaya part. Having lived for many years in cities without Asian grocery stores, I've made papaya salad without green papaya many times. I've made it with cucumber, cabbage, and even bean sprouts instead, although the best substitute out there is fresh green beans. Add some cooked shrimp or dried shrimp if you like, or not. Add peanuts, or don't. Eat it with sticky rice or pork rinds or roasted chicken (or all them), or just eat it by itself and feel the burn.

1 lime, halved

1 serrano chile (pretty hot) or
   3 bird's eye chiles (really hot)

1 teaspoon Roasted Chile Powder (optional;
   page 226)

4 cloves garlic, peeled

2 tablespoons light brown sugar

12 cherry tomatoes, halved, or 2 small plum
   tomatoes, cut into wedges

3 tablespoons fish sauce, plus more to taste

1 pound green papaya or 1 pound green beans
   (or a mixture of the two)

3 tablespoons chopped unsalted roasted
   peanuts (optional)

Cooked sticky rice (see page 228) or jasmine
   rice, for serving (optional)

recipe continues ➞

◆ Peel half of the lime and separate the sections. Place the lime sections in a large mortar along with the chile, chile powder (if using), garlic, and brown sugar. Crush with the pestle until the chile is mashed and bruised and the sugar dissolves. Add the tomatoes and pound a few times to bruise them. (You can also accomplish this with a big mixing bowl and a round-ended cocktail muddler or rolling pin. Or you can chop the garlic and chiles first and just mix and mash everything in the bowl.) Squeeze the juice from the remaining lime half (about 1 tablespoon) into the mortar and stir in the fish sauce.

◆ If using green papaya, peel and seed it, then shred with the shredding disc of a food processor or on a mandoline or box grater. If using green beans, trim the ends and then cut them into 2-inch lengths. You should have about 4 cups of papaya or beans. Add the papaya or green beans to the mortar and mash and toss lightly.

◆ Divide the salad among the bowls. Top with the peanuts, if desired. Serve with rice on the side, if using.

---

mortar + pestle 101

I have two types of Thai mortars and pestles in my kitchen. The first has a smaller round bowl and is usually made out of stone; in Thailand it's used for grinding spices and pounding things like curry pastes. You can find this type of mortar and pestle in most kitchens. The second Thai kind is much taller, deeper, and narrower (between 1 and 2 feet tall) and is usually made out of wood, ceramic, or plastic. The main purpose of these is for pounding Thai salads, like som tum, almost like a big mixing bowl. All the papaya salad vendors in Thailand have these. They are available for cheap at Thai markets or online, but if you don't have one, a tall, narrow bowl and a muddler will work instead.

Yai's (GRANDMA'S) specialties

JOK MOO
(Pork and Ginger Rice Porridge) SERVES 8

Breakfast. Comfort. Soothing. Famous. These are some words that describe this jok moo, a Thai rice porridge recipe I learned from my mother and that Tina and Chrissy learned from me. You might remember it from Chrissy's first cookbook, and since then it's become kind of a big deal. Chrissy and I have prepared it for all kinds of famous chefs and celebrities, and it has become one of our better-known Teigen family recipes.

Jok is one of the most popular breakfasts across Thailand. There's usually some kind of protein—a raw egg mixed in at the end is very good—as well as a sharp herb or pickle that contrasts with the silky flavor of the stewed rice broth. My version is on the simple side: garlicky, peppery pork meatballs (moo [not oink] is Thai for pork) and a handful of julienned fresh ginger, scallions, and cilantro. Miles and Luna scrape their bowls clean whenever I make it.

Slow-cooking jok is my therapy—mellow, relaxing, and a great release for stress. Also way cheaper than a therapist. If you're not a morning person (*ahem,* Chrissy) but want breakfast ready when you wake up, the best shortcut is to boil the rice the night before, since the porridge only gets thicker and more flavorful the next day.

1½ cups jasmine rice

2 chicken bouillon cubes

1 pound ground pork

4 cloves garlic, minced

1 tablespoon minced cilantro stems

2 tablespoons light soy sauce

½ teaspoon ground white pepper

3-inch piece fresh ginger, peeled and thinly julienned (see Note on page 176)

Kosher salt

¼ cup chopped fresh cilantro leaves

4 scallions, thinly sliced

FOR SERVING
Fried Garlic (page 236)
Spicy Chile Crisp (page 231)

◆ Rinse the rice well under cold water, then drain and transfer to a large pot. Add 12 cups water and the bouillon cubes. Bring to a boil, reduce the heat to a simmer, and cook, uncovered, until the rice is soft and broken down into a porridge, about 45 minutes.

◆ While the porridge is cooking, in a medium bowl, combine the ground pork, garlic, cilantro stems, soy sauce, and white pepper.

◆ When the rice is at a porridge-like consistency, take a marble-size pinch of the pork and drop it into the pot, repeating for all the pork mixture. Add the ginger and simmer until the pork "dumplings" are cooked through, 5 to 6 minutes. Thin the jok with water as you like and season to taste with salt. Stir in the cilantro and scallions.

◆ Divide the porridge among the bowls and garnish with fried garlic and spicy chile crisp.

Scalloped **POTATOES**

SERVES 16 TO 20

Okay, you've probably heard of these potatoes because they're one of Chrissy's top all-time comfort foods and she has to go and tell evvvvverybody about them. But I'm officially taking them back for my cookbook. I'll bet you didn't know that this dish was the first American food I ever learned how to cook. I remember when I first moved here, Ron bought those instant scalloped potatoes that came in a box. *Americans really love potatoes,* I thought. I made it for dinner one night and told myself, *I bet I can make this better!* (I've thought this about many foods, from tuna tartare, page 107, to my take on spicy spaghetti, page 183). Then I figured out the recipe myself just by tasting. Ham, bacon, onion, butter, milk, and lots of spuds.

Over the years, I would make these potatoes for any big family dinner or holiday, and every time I could never make enough. Eventually I started making the dish on regular nights, not just on special occasions. But everyone always wanted leftovers, so I had to make it in larger and larger batches—now I go through ten pounds of potatoes to make just one batch!

Obviously, you don't have to make as much as I do (but it's not a bad idea). This recipe can be scaled down or up as needed, and you can swap in cooked sausage or even use sweet potatoes if you like. As long as you end up with creamy and gooey sliced potatoes, you will be happy. We like to eat them hot, warm, room temp, or stone-cold, served with other foods or just on their own—eat, reheat, repeat!

recipe continues ➝

5 pounds russet potatoes (not red or new
  potatoes)

1 large yellow onion, finely chopped

1¼ pounds ham, cut into ½-inch cubes

12 slices bacon (not thick-cut), sliced
  crosswise

1 stick (4 ounces) unsalted butter

2 tablespoons garlic salt

½ teaspoon freshly ground black pepper

1½ cups all-purpose flour

5½ cups whole milk

♦ Preheat the oven to 375°F.

♦ Peel the potatoes (or leave the skins if you like), halve them lengthwise,
and slice them crosswise into thin half-moons. Rinse well with cold water
and drain in a colander. Place the potatoes in a large bowl and toss them
with the onion and the ham.

♦ In a large saucepan, cook half the bacon over medium-low heat, stirring
occasionally, until the fat is rendered and the bacon is crisp, 8 to 10 minutes.
Remove the bacon from the pan and set aside. Add the butter and cook,
stirring, until melted, making sure it doesn't burn. Add the garlic salt and
pepper, then whisk in the flour and cook, stirring and working out the
lumps, until smooth. Whisk in the milk until smooth (this takes a little
work). Increase the heat to high and bring to a boil. Cook, whisking, until
thickened, about 5 minutes. Remove from the heat.

♦ Arrange half the potato mixture in the bottom of a 9 by 13-inch baking
dish and spread into an even layer. Cover it with half the sauce and the
cooked bacon. Repeat with the remaining potatoes and sauce. Arrange the
uncooked bacon squares on top of the sauce. Transfer to the oven and bake,
uncovered, until the bacon appears crispy and rendered, 30 to 35 minutes.
Reduce the oven temperature to 350°F, cover the baking dish loosely with
foil, and cook until bubbling, 1 hour 30 minutes longer.

♦ Remove from the oven and place on a trivet. Remove the foil and let cool a
bit before serving.

Thai
GLAZED RIBS

SERVES 4

Let's get this out of the way first. The Thai style of making pork ribs is not smoking or grilling but deep-frying, which gets them tender and perfectly chewy and crispy in a fraction of the time. I know ribs don't sound like a quick lunch, but I cook these for Luna all the time and it's one of her absolute favorites.

For Chrissy's second book, we made these ribs with a quick dry rub and a spicy dipping sauce, but—Pepper being Pepper—I have many variations up my sleeve, one of which is to toss the warm freshly fried ribs in a special sweet-sticky fish sauce-and-tamarind glaze that coats them like barbecue sauce. No dipping required. Here I use a rack of baby backs cut into individual ribs, but if you want smaller bite-size riblets (like they prefer in Thailand), you can also cut each rib in half crosswise (ask your butcher or use a meat cleaver).

Trust me when I say this is the easiest rib recipe you will ever cook. Chrissy will tell you about the one time I almost burned down the house frying these, but never mind that nonsense. Just be sure to turn off the stove when you're done!

FOR THE TAMARIND GLAZE

2 tablespoons fish sauce

2 tablespoons tamarind paste

3 tablespoons light brown sugar or honey

1 tablespoon fresh lime juice

1 tablespoon Roasted Chile Powder (page 226)

1 tablespoon Toasted Rice Powder, store-bought or homemade (page 226)

1 teaspoon finely minced cilantro stems

12 grape or cherry tomatoes, halved

FOR THE RIBS

1 rack baby back pork ribs (12 to 14 ribs), cut into individual ribs

¼ cup light soy sauce

1 tablespoon garlic powder

½ teaspoon ground white pepper

Vegetable oil, for deep-frying

Fresh cilantro leaves, for serving

note
For the leftover glaze, you can serve extra on the side, or store in the fridge for up to 1 week.

recipe continues →

♦ **make the tamarind glaze** In a small bowl, whisk together the fish sauce, tamarind paste, brown sugar, lime juice, chile powder, rice powder, and cilantro stems until the sugar is dissolved. Squeeze in the pulp of the tomatoes (discard the skins) and stir together.

♦ **make the ribs** Place the ribs in a large bowl and add the soy sauce, garlic powder, and white pepper. Toss to coat. Let stand at room temperature until you're ready to deep-fry.

♦ Fill a wok, large heavy pot, or deep skillet with at least 2 inches of oil, making sure to leave a few inches of clearance from the rim. Heat the oil over medium heat to 370°F (use a deep-fry thermometer or test the oil by throwing in a little piece of bread or a grain of rice; if it sizzles immediately but doesn't burn, the oil is ready).

♦ Set a rack in a sheet pan or line a plate with paper towels and have near the stove. When the oil is hot, fry the ribs in batches of 4 or 5 until they're just cooked and well browned on all sides, using a frying spider or slotted spoon to turn them occasionally, 3 to 4 minutes. Adjust the heat as needed to keep the oil at 370°F as you're frying. Transfer the ribs to the wire rack or paper towels to drain and cool (slightly not too much, though).

♦ Place the warm ribs in a large bowl, spoon on as much of the tamarind glaze as you'd like, and toss to coat (see Note).

♦ Transfer to a plate, garnish with cilantro leaves, and serve immediately.

---
note
Throughout the cookbook, I like to use the minced cilantro stems as well as cilantro leaves. The stems are an easy substitute for fresh cilantro root, an ingredient that is common in Thailand but hard to find in the US. Similar to the root, using the crunchy stems of cilantro adds a zestier, earthier flavor that deepens the taste of dressings, sauces, and marinades. And nothing goes to waste!

MILES'S TOFU
Soup SERVES 4 TO 6

This savory pork and vegetable soup with chunks of soft tofu was the first solid food I ever made for Miles, who since has grown into one of the world's hungriest and best-eating toddlers. I'd like to think Yai (grandma) had something to do with that. :-) Even though this soup is light and mild, it's not just for babies. In Thailand, it's common to have a bowl of clear brothy soup as a side dish, especially if you're eating a bold and spicy stir-fry or curry. This is also a great soup to make for someone who is under the weather or, much more likely in our house, hungover! I always have a big pot of it ready in the morning after the Oscars party.

1 pound ground pork

4 cloves garlic, finely minced

¼ teaspoon ground white pepper

2 tablespoons light soy sauce

8 cups low-sodium chicken broth

1 medium carrot, sliced into ½-inch coins

¼ head napa cabbage, cored and roughly chopped (about 2 cups)

8 ounces bok choy, roughly chopped (tough stems trimmed)

2 celery stalks with leaves, chopped

10 ounces medium-firm tofu, drained and cubed

¼ teaspoon kosher salt

1 tablespoon fish sauce or light soy sauce, plus more to taste

FOR SERVING

Cooked jasmine rice

Fried Garlic (page 236)

Chopped fresh cilantro leaves

◆ In a medium bowl, mix together the ground pork, garlic, white pepper, and soy sauce until combined.

◆ In a large pot, bring the chicken broth to a boil. Reduce the heat to a simmer and add the carrot. Drop spoonfuls (about 1 tablespoon) of the pork mixture into the broth to make little meatballs. They won't be perfectly round—that's okay. Let the meatballs cook for 4 to 5 minutes, skimming away any fat that bubbles to the surface. Add the cabbage, bok choy, and celery and cook until the bok choy has turned bright green, 2 to 3 minutes. Add the tofu and cook for another minute, then remove from the heat. Season with the salt and fish sauce, tasting and adding more if needed.

◆ Serve the soup with rice, either mixed in or on the side. Garnish with fried garlic and cilantro.

Garlic-Stuffed
FISH   SERVES 4

Another one of the family's most requested foods, the recipe for this oven-roasted fish changes ever so slightly based on what mood we're in. The constant is a really big handful of garlic (25 cloves!) mashed down with olive oil and salt in my trusty mortar and pestle, which then gets rubbed all over the inside and outside of a whole fish (usually soft and buttery branzino, my favorite). Then come the herbs and citrus, stuffed inside. Sometimes I'll use thyme, rosemary, and lemon if everyone is in an Italian mood. Otherwise I'll make it Thai-style, which is what I do here, and stuff the fish with lemongrass (which I grow in the backyard), limes, ginger, and cilantro. Experiment as much as you like.

Rubbing the branzino all over with garlicky olive oil is what keeps the fish moist and the skin extra crispy. If there's anyone in your life who isn't excited to eat a whole fish, this is the way to convince them. We eat this so often at home, each family member has their own favorite part. John and Luna like the tender fillets, Chrissy likes the skin, and Miles would eat a whole fish if we let him (seriously, you wouldn't believe how this boy loves fish). Me? I go straight for the head, which has all the crispy and juicy bits if you're willing to dig them out. The best!

¾ cup extra-virgin olive oil

25 cloves garlic

1 teaspoon Roasted Chile Powder (page 226)

Kosher salt

1 teaspoon freshly ground black pepper

2 whole branzino (about 2½ pounds total), cleaned

2 small limes, thinly sliced

2-inch piece fresh ginger, peeled, sliced, and smashed with the butt of a knife

2 stalks lemongrass, green tops removed and bottoms smashed with a heavy pan

Handful of fresh cilantro leaves, plus more for serving

Lime wedges, for serving (optional)

♦ Preheat the oven to 425°F. Line a large sheet pan with foil.

♦ In a mortar (or a food processor), combine the oil, garlic, chile powder, 2 teaspoons salt, and the pepper. Mash with a pestle (or pulse) just until the garlic becomes a paste. Transfer the oil mixture to a small bowl, making sure to scrape out all the garlic bits.

♦ Use a sharp knife to make three long cuts on a diagonal, 3 inches long, on one side of both the fish, cutting all the way to the bones. Arrange the fish cut side up on the lined sheet pan, making sure to leave a little space between them.

♦ Spoon about half the oil mixture into the cavities of both fish and all over the outsides, making sure to rub all over and get into all the cuts and crevices. Stuff both fish with the limes, ginger, and lemongrass, making sure to distribute them evenly along the length of the cavity. Dip the cilantro in the remaining oil mixture and stuff that in there, too. Drizzle any remaining oil over the top of the fish. Sprinkle each fish with a pinch of salt.

♦ Cover both fish loosely with foil and bake for 6 minutes, then rotate the pan 180 degrees and bake for another 6 minutes. Remove the foil from the fish, increase the oven temperature to 450°F (or use your oven's broil setting), and leave the oven door slightly ajar (to make sure your broiler stays on). Cook the fish, uncovered, until the skin gets crispy, 3 to 5 minutes, rotating the pan halfway through so the fish brown evenly. Once the skin is golden brown and slightly puffy, remove from the oven and let cool slightly. I like to spoon the hot oil on the sheet pan over the fish while they cool.

♦ Place a spoon in the center of one of the fish and gently peel the fillets off the bones, working from the center of the fish outward. Repeat with the other fish. Garnish both with fresh cilantro and serve with lime wedges, if you like.

--- *note* ---

I like to buy peeled garlic if I can find them, but if not, I'll put the unpeeled cloves in a screw-top jar with a lid and shake it really hard until the skins come off.

Soy-Garlic PEPPER STEAK

 that's me!

SERVES 4

Everyone has (or should have) a basic steak marinade on hand for weeknight emergency dinner situations. This is mine. I'm using steak as the star in this case, but this marinade can also be used with any meat or grill-friendly vegetables like eggplant and zucchini.

5 tablespoons light soy sauce

6 cloves garlic, smashed and peeled

1 tablespoon freshly ground black pepper

3 tablespoons extra-virgin olive oil

2 pounds skirt, hanger, or flank steak

Vegetable oil, for the grill

Kosher salt (optional)

♦ In a large bowl, whisk the soy sauce, garlic, pepper, and olive oil to combine. Add the steak to the bowl and toss to coat evenly, then let marinate at room temperature for 30 minutes to 1 hour (see Note).

♦ Meanwhile, preheat a grill to high heat (or preheat the broiler with the rack as close to the heat source as possible).

♦ Once the grill is ready, brush the grill grates with a little vegetable oil. Remove the steak from the marinade, shake off any excess, and pat dry with a paper towel. Grill the steak over direct heat until you see grill marks, about 4 minutes per side for medium. (Or broil until charred, about 3 minutes per side.) Let the meat rest for 5 minutes before slicing against the grain. Sprinkle with a pinch of salt before serving if you like.

note
You can also massage the meat with the marinade to speed things up a little (trust me!) or marinate it overnight in the fridge. Just let it come to room temperature an hour or so before cooking.

Luna's
BROCCOLI BEEF

SERVES 2 TO 4

As soon as Luna was old enough to chew solid food, I was making her this very basic but very delicious stir-fry, which delivers a shocking amount of rich beefy flavor despite its short ingredient list. The secret is the oyster sauce, which adds serious umami, so much so that you won't even miss the beef if you leave it out. Sometimes I'll make stir-fried broccoli for the kids and it disappears just as fast.

I call this Luna's Broccoli Beef because it's one of her favorite foods, but that is a gene she obviously inherited from John, who might love broccoli more than she does. No matter what age you are, there's a lesson here. Boiled broccoli? Nobody wants seconds. Stir-fried broccoli? You can't make enough of it. A little garlic, oyster sauce, and a hot wok go a long way.

1 pound skirt, hanger, or flank steak, sliced against the grain into ½ by 2-inch strips

2 tablespoons light soy sauce

Ground white pepper

1 pound broccoli (about 2 heads), florets cut into bite-size pieces and stems peeled and thinly sliced

1 teaspoon cornstarch (optional—it helps make the sauce thicker)

3 tablespoons vegetable oil

6 cloves garlic, smashed and peeled

3 tablespoons oyster sauce

Cooked jasmine rice, for serving

◆ In a large bowl, combine the steak, soy sauce, and a pinch of white pepper and toss to coat. Let marinate at room temperature for 20 minutes while you blanch the broccoli.

◆ Fill another large bowl with ice water and set it next to the stove. Bring a medium pot of water to a boil. Add the broccoli and cook until it turns bright green, about 1 minute. Transfer to the bowl of ice water to cool, then drain.

◆ If using the cornstarch, in a small bowl stir it together with 1 tablespoon water to make a slurry and set aside.

◆ In a wok or large skillet, heat the oil over medium-high heat until shimmering-hot. Add the garlic and cook until fragrant, about 15 seconds. Add the steak and stir-fry until it is mostly cooked, about 3 minutes. Add the drained broccoli, oyster sauce, and cornstarch slurry (if using) and toss to coat. Continue to cook, stirring, until a sauce forms and the broccoli is warmed through, 1 to 2 minutes. Serve with the cooked rice.

EAT YOUR
veggies

Hot Basil
EGGPLANT
SERVES 2 TO 4

This is one of my favorite ways to eat the long, skinny purple eggplants that people call Chinese eggplants. Most of the time, Thai cooks will deep-fry the eggplant before they stir-fry it, which, even for me, is a little too much frying. My trick is to salt the raw eggplant slices and let them sit to draw out their water, then microwave them until they're tender. It's lighter and faster than deep-frying, but you still end up with the creamy, silky texture of really good eggplant. The ground pork or tofu are optional, but I like them because they help turn a veggie stir-fry into a meal that will fill your tummy when scooped over rice.

3 medium Chinese eggplants (about 2 pounds)

Kosher salt

Ground white pepper

2 tablespoons vegetable oil

6 cloves garlic, mashed or minced

2 fresh bird's eye chiles or 1 serrano chile, minced

8 ounces ground pork or roughly chopped firm tofu

2 fresh red chiles, such as Fresnos, thinly sliced (or substitute red bell pepper)

1 teaspoon sugar

1 tablespoon oyster sauce

1 tablespoon Thai soybean paste, or 2 teaspoons brown miso paste mixed with 1 teaspoon water

1 cup packed fresh basil leaves

Cooked jasmine rice, for serving

◆ Cut the eggplants crosswise into ½-inch-thick slices and transfer to a medium bowl. Sprinkle the slices with salt and white pepper, tossing to coat. Let sit for 30 minutes.

◆ Working in batches, if necessary, arrange the eggplant slices on a microwave-safe plate in a single layer and microwave on high for 3 minutes, until the eggplant is tender and slightly wilted. Pat the slices dry with a dish towel or paper towel and set aside.

◆ In a wok or large skillet, heat the oil over medium-high heat until shimmering-hot. Add the garlic and chiles and cook until fragrant, less than 1 minute. Add the pork and cook, stirring, until browned, 2 to 3 minutes. Add the eggplant slices and red chiles, and cook until tender and lightly browned, 2 to 3 minutes. Stir in the sugar, oyster sauce, and soybean paste, tossing to coat. Once a thick sauce has formed, after about 1 minute, remove the pan from the heat and stir in the basil leaves.

◆ Serve with jasmine rice.

Easy Wok-Fried
GREENS
SERVES 2 TO 4

Sometimes you just need a plate of sautéed leaves in your life. For this purpose, a big spacious wok is the best tool ever, turning greens that were tough and stemmy magically and suddenly tender and a bit crunchy, soaking up just enough salty sauce. Because you know how we cook at home, of course there have to be garlic and chiles in there as well. Everything else is up to you. If you don't have oyster sauce, use a splash more soy or fish sauce. Black pepper or white pepper is fine. If you don't have any leafy greens, you can use the weeds growing on the hills behind your house. Just kidding (kind of).

2 tablespoons oyster sauce

1 teaspoon fish sauce or light soy sauce

1 teaspoon light brown sugar (optional)

2 tablespoons vegetable oil

4 cloves garlic, mashed or minced

½ teaspoon Roasted Chile Powder (page 226)

6 cups loosely packed leafy greens (kale, spinach, bok choy, Swiss chard, broccoli rabe, stems thinly sliced and leaves roughly chopped

Ground white pepper

◆ In a small bowl, whisk together the oyster sauce, fish sauce, 2 tablespoons water, and the brown sugar (if using). Set aside.

◆ In a wok or large skillet, heat the oil over medium-high heat until shimmering-hot. Add the garlic and chile powder and cook until fragrant, about 1 minute. If using greens with thick stems, add those to the pan first, cooking for 1 to 2 minutes before tossing in the leaves. Otherwise, add the greens and then the reserved sauce. Cook, stirring frequently and adding a tablespoon of water at a time if the pan looks dry, until the leaves are wilted and the stalks are tender, 3 to 5 minutes (the time will vary depending on the type of greens you're using—spinach wilts almost immediately, while broccoli rabe and Swiss chard take a bit longer). Remove from the heat and sprinkle with a pinch of white pepper.

◆ Serve immediately.

Veggie
SUMMER ROLLS

MAKES 12 ROLLS

When we made shrimp summer rolls for Chrissy's first book, they were a big hit. The delicate rice paper filled with herbs and noodles is so light and delicious, you could probably eat six of them and not have to take a nap. So many people asked us how to make them without the shrimp, so I figured I would share my special savory mushroom filling in case you want to go meatless.

FOR THE MUSHROOM FILLING

3 tablespoons vegetable oil

2 tablespoons minced garlic

1¼ pounds mixed mushrooms (oyster, shiitake, button, enoki, cremini), stemmed and thinly sliced

3 tablespoons light soy sauce

1 large carrot, grated

1 cup bean sprouts

¼ teaspoon ground white pepper

FOR THE DIPPING SAUCE

½ cup packed fresh basil leaves

1 clove garlic, minced

Zest of 1 lime

2 tablespoons fresh lime juice

1 tablespoon light soy sauce

1 tablespoon sugar

2 fresh bird's eye chiles or 1 serrano chile, minced

FOR THE ROLLS

6 romaine lettuce leaves

12 large or 24 small basil leaves

12 large or 24 small mint leaves

1 avocado, thinly sliced

12 (8-inch) round rice paper wrappers (see Note)

♦ **make the mushroom filling** In a wok or large skillet, heat the oil over medium-high heat until shimmering-hot. Add the garlic and cook until fragrant, about 15 seconds. Add the mushrooms and cook, stirring occasionally, until soft and slightly browned, 4 to 5 minutes. Stir in the light soy sauce and carrot, cooking until the carrot is soft, about 2 minutes. Add the bean sprouts and cook until they just start to wilt, about 1 minute. Remove from the heat and season with the white pepper. Set aside.

♦ **make the dipping sauce** In a small blender or food processor (or in a mortar), combine the basil, garlic, lime zest, lime juice, soy sauce, 2 tablespoons water, the sugar, and chiles and blend (or mash with a pestle) until a smooth sauce forms. Let sit for 5 minutes for the flavors to meld before serving. (Or, finely chop the basil and whisk with the remaining ingredients until the sugar dissolves.)

◆ *make the rolls*   Rinse the lettuce leaves and pat dry. Remove and discard the center ribs, then slice the leaves crosswise in half so you end up with 24 pieces that are each about 3 inches long.

◆ Set the lettuce, herbs, avocado, and the mushroom filling on your work surface. Fill a shallow bowl with lukewarm water to soak the rice papers. Lay a damp kitchen towel on your workspace. One at a time, dunk a rice paper into the water to soften, then lay it flat on the damp towel.

◆ For assembly, place about ¼ cup of the mushroom filling about one-third up from the bottom of the rice paper wrapper in a straight line. Top with a few leaves of mint and basil, then avocado and lettuce leaves. Roll it up like a burrito by pulling up the bottom, tucking in the sides, then rolling to the end. The rice paper will stick together, sealing it shut. Repeat with the remaining rice papers.

◆ Serve immediately with the dipping sauce.

note ———
You can find the rice paper wrappers in most supermarkets in the Asian food aisle.

BALDESSARI

Pad Thai
BRUSSELS SPROUTS

Pad Thai without noodles? I know it seems crazy. Pad means "noodle" in Thai after all. But after years of people sliding into my DMs for a pad Thai recipe, I've realized what stresses out most non-Thai people is finding the right kind of rice noodles (tip: you want dried thin, flat rice noodles, usually labeled rice sticks). No need to worry, Pepper is here for you.

If you find yourself in such a situation, or you're just looking for a lower-carb alternative to stir-fried noodles, using roasted Brussels sprouts produces that same chewy-tender texture with a different but equally delicious method. The secret is to halve the sprouts and roast them first, so they become crispy and browned. Then toss the sprouts with a sweet-tangy "pad Thai" glaze at the end and garnish with the usual toppings you would find at a street vendor stall in Bangkok: bean sprouts, crushed peanuts, chile powder, and scallions. You could even toss in some dried shrimp if you like. You'll never look at Brussels sprouts the same way again.

½ cup packed light brown sugar

1 teaspoon kosher salt

½ teaspoon ground white pepper

3 cloves garlic, minced

2 tablespoons finely minced cilantro stems, plus cilantro leaves for garnish

¼ cup plus 2 tablespoons fish sauce

2 tablespoons fresh lime juice

2 pounds Brussels sprouts, stem ends trimmed, halved

2 tablespoons vegetable oil

1 cup bean sprouts

3 scallions, thinly sliced

½ cup finely chopped salted roasted peanuts

1 teaspoon Roasted Chile Powder (page 226), or to taste

Lime wedges, for serving

♦ Preheat the oven to 425°F.

♦ In a small saucepan, combine the brown sugar and ½ cup water and stir over medium-low heat until the sauce becomes as thick as caramel and develops a deep amber color, about 15 minutes.

♦ Remove from the heat and let it cool slightly, then stir in the salt, white pepper, garlic, cilantro stems, fish sauce, and lime juice. Return the mixture to low heat and warm through, stirring until a smooth sauce forms, about 4 minutes. Remove the pad Thai caramel from the heat and set aside.

◆ Toss the Brussels sprouts with the oil and arrange them on a sheet pan cut side down. Roast, stirring every 10 minutes or so, until the sprouts are tender, golden brown, and charred in spots, 25 to 30 minutes.

◆ Remove the Brussels sprouts from the oven and transfer to a large bowl. While they're still hot, add the pad Thai caramel and toss to combine. When the glazed sprouts have cooled slightly, add the bean sprouts, scallions, peanuts, and chile powder, then toss once more. Transfer to a serving plate and garnish with cilantro leaves. Serve with lime wedges.

TOMATO-BACON SWEET CORN
with Avocado SERVES 4

Most people in Thailand think of corn as a dessert topping, sprinkled onto tapioca pudding or mixed into shaved ice. But once I moved to the US, I started to appreciate sweet corn in a savory way: slathered with warm butter and a sprinkle of garlic salt. I even bought a set of those corn-shaped pronged holders that you poke into the ends to hold the cob!

Corn cut straight from the cob is great for this summery pan-roasted salad, but I've also used good-quality frozen corn (the super sweet kind) many times. Tangy cherry tomatoes and creamy avocado—like corn, two ingredients that are at their best in the summer and early fall—with the cooked corn and bacon-shallot mixture is a combination that pops with flavor. It's just so good and a healthy, balanced meal on its own.

I season the salad with a simple mixture of lime and fish juice, but you can also try it with your favorite salad dressing—anything tangy and bright works well. And, of course, you can leave out the bacon if you want to go meatless, but I really love the smokiness it adds here. America taught me to appreciate bacon as much as it did corn.

4 ounces bacon (4 to 6 slices), chopped

2 shallots, finely chopped

3 cups corn kernels, fresh (about 3 ears of corn) or frozen

1 cup halved cherry tomatoes

2 fresh bird's eye chiles or 1 serrano, minced

2 teaspoons fish sauce

1 avocado, chopped

½ cup chopped fresh cilantro leaves

1 lime, halved

Kosher salt and freshly ground black pepper

♦ In a wok or large skillet set over medium-high heat, cook the bacon until it is very crisp and the fat has rendered, about 10 minutes. Remove the crispy bacon from the pan and drain; set aside. Pour out the bacon fat from the pan until about 2 tablespoons remain. Return the pan to heat, add the shallots to the bacon fat, and cook until they have softened, about 3 minutes. Add the corn and continue cooking, stirring occasionally, until the corn begins to brown, about 6 more minutes. Stir in the tomatoes and chiles, remove the pan from the heat, and set aside to cool for a few minutes. Transfer to a large bowl.

♦ Add the crispy bacon, fish sauce, avocado, cilantro, and squeeze the lime over the corn mixture. Gently toss to combine. Taste and season with salt and pepper. Serve warm or at room temperature.

Pepper's Detox
CABBAGE SOUP

SERVES 12

The cabbage soup diet has been around since the 1980s and was a popular fad where you ate almost entirely cabbage soup (and other vegetables) for a week and lost a few pounds, enough to fit into a new dress for an awards show after indulging in too many Quarter Pounders (*ahem* not mentioning any names).

I've seen many cabbage soup recipes on the Internet, and as someone who ate my share of something-from-nothing soups, I knew I could do better. Cooked cucumber and radishes add a delicious flavor and keep the texture interesting. Seasonings are your friend, too—I like to finish the soup with soy or fish sauce, lime juice or vinegar, chile powder, and chopped fresh herbs. I promise you won't get bored with it, no matter how many bowls you eat.

Cooking spray or vegetable oil

4 cloves garlic, finely chopped

1 red onion, finely chopped

1-inch piece fresh ginger, peeled and grated

6 ounces mixed mushrooms, stemmed and sliced

½ head green cabbage, cored and thinly sliced crosswise (about 4 cups)

1 large carrot, halved lengthwise and sliced crosswise

½ pound green beans, trimmed and cut into 1-inch pieces (about 1 cup)

1 small cucumber, halved lengthwise and thinly sliced crosswise

6 small radishes, thinly sliced

1 (14.5-ounce) can diced tomatoes

8 cups chicken or vegetable broth

1 tablespoon light soy sauce, plus more to taste

1 tablespoon apple cider vinegar

1 teaspoon freshly ground black pepper

½ teaspoon Roasted Chile Powder (optional; page 226)

¼ cup chopped fresh cilantro leaves

4 scallions, finely chopped (about ¼ cup)

◆ Coat the bottom of a soup pot or large saucepan with cooking spray or a small amount of oil and heat over medium-high heat. When the oil is hot but not smoking, add the garlic, onion, and ginger and cook, stirring often, until the onion is translucent and fragrant, 1 to 2 minutes. Add the mushrooms and cook, stirring occasionally, until they have softened slightly, 3 to 4 minutes. Add the cabbage, carrot, green beans, cucumber, radishes, tomatoes, chicken broth, soy sauce, vinegar, black pepper, and chile powder (if using), stirring to combine.

◆ Bring to a boil, then reduce the heat to a simmer and cook until the vegetables are tender but still have some texture, 30 to 40 minutes. Taste and season with more soy sauce if needed. Remove from the heat.

◆ Stir in the cilantro and scallions just before serving.

FEELING
fancy

Garlic Lover's
SPICY CLAMS

Here is the story behind this recipe: Chrissy and John took me to the best Italian restaurant in Beverly Hills for dinner one night (Chrissy says not to tell you which one, so they all think I'm talking about them). I was in the mood for spicy clams, like I usually am, but all that was on the menu was spaghetti with clams and I didn't want pasta. So Chrissy asked them if they could cook me a big bowl of just clams, no spaghetti, extra-extra-spicy (naturally). And they did it. Still one of my favorite restaurant meals to this day.

These clams aren't exactly the same ones I had that night, but they're what I dream about when I have that spicy clam craving, which as you know, is all the time. A good amount of butter is important here, because it mixes with the clam juice and spicy curry paste and beer (yes, beer) to create a brothy sauce that will stick to your spoon. If you want to soak up this rich, heavenly liquid, I recommend you make my very easy garlic toast, because if there is one flavor I love almost as much as chile peppers, it's garlic.

FOR THE CLAMS

1 stick (4 ounces) unsalted butter

8 cloves garlic, minced or mashed

2 fresh bird's eye chiles or 1 serrano chile, minced

1 tablespoon Thai red curry paste

3 pounds Manila clams or other small clams (like littlenecks)

1 cup lager beer (drink the rest while cooking)

2 teaspoons sugar

½ teaspoon ground white pepper, plus more to taste

½ cup packed fresh basil leaves

¼ cup packed fresh cilantro leaves

Kosher salt (optional)

FOR THE GARLIC TOAST

4 thick (1-inch) slices sourdough bread

4 cloves garlic, halved

Olive oil

Kosher salt

Lemon wedges, for serving

◆ **make the clams** In a large saucepan or skillet, melt the butter over medium-high heat and swirl it around the pan. Once the butter starts to sizzle, add the garlic, chiles, and curry paste and cook until fragrant, about 1 minute. Add the clams, beer, sugar, and white pepper. Stir, reduce the heat to medium, cover, and cook the clams until they have

all fully opened, about 4 minutes—discard any that remain shut. Remove the pan from the heat and stir the basil and cilantro. Taste the broth and season with salt or more white pepper as needed.

♦ *make the garlic toast* While the clams are steaming, toast the bread slices in a toaster or toaster oven until golden brown. Rub one side of each with a few cut cloves garlic, then drizzle or brush with oil. Sprinkle them with a little salt, if you like.

♦ Divide the clams and broth among the bowls and serve immediately with lemon wedges to squeeze over the top and garlic toast on the side.

LARB BURGERS

SERVES 4

I love making larb at home. Chrissy loves making burgers. So one day we made larb burgers, of course. Why it took so long for us to play match-maker I don't know, but I'm happy we did.

In Thailand, larb is usually a salad made with minced meat punched up with fish sauce and lime and tossed with handfuls of fresh herbs. But there is also larb tod, a kind of larb that is shaped into patties and fried, which is the inspiration for these juicy seasoned beef patties. A bright and crisp slaw made from cabbage and mint, crunchy fried onions, and a soy-garlic mayo ties everything together. At first we tried making buns out of sticky rice, but we liked grocery-store hamburger buns better. Chrissy says you can only mess with the burger experience so much.

FOR THE SOY-GARLIC MAYO
½ cup mayonnaise

2 teaspoons light soy sauce

1 clove garlic, grated on a mandoline

FOR THE MINT-CABBAGE SLAW
1½ cups thinly sliced green cabbage (about ¼ small head cabbage)

12 fresh mint leaves, torn in half

¼ cup chopped fresh cilantro leaves

1 tablespoon fresh lime juice

Kosher salt and freshly ground black pepper

FOR THE LARB PATTIES
1½ pounds ground beef (80/20)

3 tablespoons fish sauce

2 teaspoons grated lime zest

1 tablespoon fresh lime juice

1 medium shallot, minced

2 teaspoons minced peeled fresh ginger

1 tablespoon plus 1 teaspoon Toasted Rice Powder, store-bought or homemade (page 226)

1 teaspoon Roasted Chile Powder (page 226)

1 teaspoon vegetable oil

FOR ASSEMBLY
4 hamburger buns

½ cup crispy fried onions (French's or your favorite kind)

◆ **make the soy-garlic mayo** In a small bowl, combine the mayo, soy sauce, and garlic.

◆ **make the mint-cabbage slaw** In a large bowl, toss the cabbage, mint, cilantro, and lime juice. Season with salt and pepper, to taste.

♦ **make the larb patties**   In a large bowl, mix the ground beef, fish sauce, lime zest, lime juice, shallot, ginger, rice powder, and chile powder until combined. Divide the meat into 4 equal portions and shape into ¾-inch-thick patties—the mixture will be a little wet.

♦ In a large skillet, heat the oil over medium-high heat until shimmering-hot. Working in batches, if needed, add the patties and cook until both sides are well browned and the juices run clear, 2 to 3 minutes on each side.

♦ **assemble the burgers**   Toast a burger bun cut side down on the pan used to cook the patties for 1 to 2 minutes over medium-low heat, until warmed through and lightly browned. Brush 2 tablespoons of soy-garlic mayo onto the toasted sides of the bun. Set the larb patty on the bottom bun and top with the fried onions, mint-cabbage slaw, and the top bun. Repeat for the remaining burgers and serve immediately.

Fancy
TUNA TARTARE

SERVES 4 TO 6

Chrissy and John loooooove restaurants, which means I've been lucky enough to dine at many amazing places all over the world. But to be honest, deep down, nothing ever beats home cooking for me. Even when I eat a dish that tastes so amazing, I'm already thinking about how to put my own spin on it. Usually that means more chile peppers.

Tuna tartare, for example—as much as I love to order it at restaurants, the whole time I'm eating it, I'm thinking, *I wonder how I can make this better*.

The most important part of the tartare is the tuna. That's why they call it tuna tartare. Don't make it unless you can find good, fresh fish at the market. If there's a person behind the counter to help you pick the fish, that's even better. Ask for sushi-grade tuna, and a fatty (flavorful) cut if available. Keep it very chilled until you're ready to use it. Once you've done that, everything will fall into place. You can use shallot or red onion, dried chiles or fresh, and whatever fresh herbs you have in the fridge. Just before serving, I drizzle a little olive oil—it makes the whole dish feel extra luxurious.

1 pound sushi-grade raw tuna fillet, cut into ½-inch cubes

1 medium shallot, finely diced

3 tablespoons fish sauce

2 tablespoons Toasted Rice Powder, store-bought or homemade (page 226)

½ teaspoon Roasted Chile Powder (page 226)

2 tablespoons fresh lime juice

1 tablespoon chopped fresh mint, plus sprigs for garnish

1 tablespoon chopped fresh cilantro leaves, plus sprigs for garnish

Kosher salt

Olive oil, for drizzling

Sliced raw vegetables (cucumber, romaine lettuce, cabbage), your favorite crackers, or toasted seaweed sheets, for serving

◆ Place the tuna in a food processor and pulse until finely minced, about 5 seconds. Set aside.

◆ In a large bowl, stir together the shallot, fish sauce, rice powder, chile powder, and lime juice. Gently fold in the tuna, mint, and cilantro until well mixed. Taste and season with a pinch of salt, if needed.

◆ To plate, divide the tuna tartare onto salad plates and drizzle lightly with olive oil. Garnish with the herbs and a pinch more salt, if you like. Arrange the vegetables and crackers around the tartare and serve.

ROASTED RACK OF LAMB
with Mint Pesto SERVES 6

I had never even heard of lamb when I was growing up in Thailand, but surprise, surprise, these days it is one of my favorite things to cook. Chrissy, John, and I—we all love it. When we cook lamb, we keep the marinade basic, but we always use plenty of garlic because it goes so well with the flavor of the meat. I use a rack of lamb, which has cute little bones attached to the lamb chops, but I love to cook leg of lamb or other less fancy cuts, too. Just make sure you don't overcook them: medium-rare or medium at most is the standard in our house.

At home Chrissy likes her lamb with a spicy Thai dipping sauce like nam jim jaew (Red Hot Pepper Sauce, page 238), but when we order lamb at nice restaurants it always comes with some kind of herb-y sauce that I put on everything. So bright and flavorful. This is my own version of that sauce, a spin on pesto made with fresh cilantro and basil, lemon zest, and a little salty kick from the anchovy paste. You'll end up with enough pesto for the lamb plus some extra, which is the best for spooning over warm rice and roasted veggies.

FOR THE LAMB

12 cloves garlic, minced

2 tablespoons light soy sauce

½ teaspoon kosher salt

1 teaspoon freshly ground black pepper

2 tablespoons roughly chopped fresh rosemary

2 racks of lamb (about 1½ pounds each)

2 tablespoons vegetable oil

FOR THE PESTO

½ cup pine nuts or walnuts

2 cups packed fresh cilantro leaves

1 cup packed fresh mint leaves

3 cloves garlic, peeled

½ teaspoon kosher salt

½ teaspoon freshly ground black pepper

1 tablespoon anchovy paste

Grated zest of 1 lemon

2 tablespoons fresh lemon juice

¼ cup freshly grated good-quality Parmesan cheese

¾ cup olive oil, plus more if needed

♦ Preheat the oven to 400°F.

♦ *make the lamb* In a small bowl, stir together the garlic, soy sauce, salt, pepper, and rosemary until a sauce forms, then rub it all over the lamb. Place the lamb in a shallow dish or resealable plastic bag and marinate at room temperature for 30 minutes.

♦ In a large ovenproof skillet, heat the vegetable oil over high heat until shimmering-hot. Add the racks of lamb and cook fat side down, turning, until both sides are browned, 5 to 6 minutes total. Arrange the racks bone side down in the skillet and transfer the pan to the oven (you can also transfer the racks to a roasting pan if you prefer). Roast, uncovered, until an instant-read thermometer registers 125°F (for medium-rare), about 20 minutes. (Cook to 135°F if you prefer medium lamb.)

♦ *make the pesto* In a small dry skillet or saucepan, toast the pine nuts over medium-low heat, stirring often, until golden brown in spots, 3 to 4 minutes. Transfer the pine nuts to a bowl (so they don't keep toasting in the hot pan) and let them cool slightly.

♦ Once the pine nuts are cooled, transfer them to a blender or food processor and add the cilantro, mint, garlic, salt, pepper, anchovy paste, lemon zest, lemon juice, Parmesan, and olive oil. Blend or pulse until the herbs and nuts are finely chopped, adding more olive oil to help it along if needed.

♦ Transfer the lamb to a cutting board, loosely cover it with a sheet of foil, and let it rest for 10 minutes. Use a large knife to slice the racks into single chops by cutting between the bones. Arrange the chops on a serving platter and spoon the pesto generously over the top. Serve with the remaining pesto on the side.

Stir-Fried
CURRY CRAB

SERVES 2 TO 4

When we lived in Snohomish, Washington, around when Chrissy was in middle school, Ron had a fishing boat that we'd use to go crabbing, which is extremely popular around Puget Sound when Dungeness crab season arrives in the spring. We'd take the girls out on the water and spend the whole day, rain or shine, catching crabs and salmon and whatever else wandered into the traps. Sometimes we'd drive the boat all the way to Canada!

Whenever we caught crabs, I was ready. I'd chop up some of them raw and pickle them in fish sauce and garlic to put in papaya salad later, which is what people do in Thailand with the small river crabs. Sometimes I'd bring a portable stove with me and boil the crabs right there on the boat, then finish them off with hot sauce before we got back to shore.

But the best crab dish of all, and the one I always looked forward to making the most, is curry crab, a traditional Thai dish made by stir-frying the whole crab in a hot wok, then tossing it in a creamy yellow sauce seasoned with garlic, ginger, and curry powder. Once all the crabmeat is picked out, smart people know to spoon rice into the empty crab shells to soak up every drop of that delicious savory sauce.

Finding a whole crab can be tricky depending on where you live, so I consider this a special-occasion kind of dish. But if you love crab (and crabbing) as much as I do, you have to try it at least once. Thai-style involves cracking the crab into pieces (you can ask the fishmonger to do this when you buy the crab) and sucking out the tender meat after you've cooked it in the curry sauce. Don't be afraid of getting your fingers a little dirty, though if you just got a manicure, maybe wear a pair of those clear plastic gloves.

recipe continues ➡

2 large live Dungeness crabs (about 2 pounds total)

2 large eggs, lightly beaten

½ cup half-and-half

2 tablespoons Madras curry powder

1 tablespoon plus 1 teaspoon fish sauce

1 tablespoon Sweet Chile Jam, store-bought or homemade (page 244)

1 tablespoon oyster sauce

1 teaspoon light brown sugar

3 tablespoons vegetable oil

½ medium yellow onion, halved and sliced

6 cloves garlic, finely minced (about 2 tablespoons)

2 teaspoons minced peeled fresh ginger

2 large celery stalks, thinly sliced (about 1 cup), plus the celery leaves, chopped

2 fresh red chiles, such as Fresnos, thinly sliced (or substitute red bell pepper)

2 scallions, cut into 1½-inch sections

FOR SERVING

Cilantro sprigs (optional)

Cooked jasmine rice

Lime wedges

Spicy Chile Crisp (page 231)

◆ Place the crabs in the freezer for 2 hours, or until they stop moving. Remove the legs and claws and crack them with a rolling pin. Remove the top of the shell, scoop out the insides with a spoon or your fingers and discard, then rinse the body clean. Chop the crab body and top shells into quarters.

◆ In a medium bowl, whisk together the eggs, half-and-half, curry powder, fish sauce, chile jam, oyster sauce, and brown sugar until combined.

◆ In a wok or large skillet, heat the oil over medium-high heat until shimmering-hot. Add the onion, garlic, and ginger and cook until soft, 3 to 4 minutes. Add the sliced celery stalks and chiles and cook, stirring, for 1 minute. Add the crab and cook, stirring, until the meat becomes slightly firm and opaque, 3 to 5 minutes. Reduce the heat to medium-low and add the egg mixture, stirring constantly and scraping the edges of the pan. Once the eggs have thickened but are still runny (like a very soft scramble), fold in the scallions and celery leaves and cook for another minute, until the egg is almost dry.

◆ Garnish with a few cilantro sprigs, if you like, and serve over rice, with lime wedges and chile crisp on the side.

Sticky Caramelized
SHRIMP LETTUCE WRAPS

The absolute star of this dish is Vietnamese fish sauce caramel, a deeply flavorful sauce that is basically what it sounds like: fish sauce and brown sugar cooked down until you have a caramelized sweet-and-sticky glaze that goes perfectly with all different kinds of seafood, especially big plump shrimp. This recipe was such a hit the first time I made it, we ended up eating the shrimp straight out of the pan!

For this book, I wanted to take these crispy caramelized shrimp to another level—sort of Vietnamese meets Thai meets P.F. Chang's takeout—so we wrapped them in lettuce leaves along with quick-pickled radishes and carrots and tossed them with some garlic, chile powder, scallions, and crushed peanuts. WOW. We went from eating out of the pan to fighting over the last lettuce cup.

A note about the shrimp: I've called for peeled here, but since the shells will soften after they're cooked in the caramel, you can also use the shell-on kind and eat them whole if you're into that.

FOR THE PICKLES

¼ cup hot water

1 tablespoon sugar

Kosher salt

¼ cup apple cider vinegar

1 medium carrot, julienned

4 medium red radishes, julienned

FOR THE SHRIMP

1 tablespoon vegetable oil

6 cloves garlic, minced

½ teaspoon Roasted Chile Powder (page 226)

1 pound peeled and deveined large shrimp

Kosher salt

¼ cup packed light brown sugar

1 teaspoon fresh lime juice, lemon juice, or white vinegar

3 tablespoons fish sauce

2 teaspoons light soy sauce

¼ teaspoon freshly ground black pepper

2 scallions, thinly sliced

¼ cup unsalted roasted peanuts, chopped

FOR THE LETTUCE WRAPS

12 Bibb or Boston lettuce leaves

½ English cucumber, peeled and cut into 2-inch matchsticks

Cilantro leaves

2 cups cooked jasmine rice, warmed (optional)

recipe continues ⟶

♦ *make the pickles*   In a medium bowl, combine the water, sugar, and a pinch of salt and stir until the sugar is dissolved. Add the vinegar, carrot, and radishes and toss to combine. Transfer to the fridge to chill for at least 20 minutes while you cook the shrimp.

♦ *cook the shrimp*   In a wok or large skillet, heat the oil over medium-high heat until shimmering-hot. Add the garlic and chile powder and cook, stirring, until fragrant, less than 1 minute. Add the shrimp in an even layer and season with a pinch of salt. Cook, turning once, until the shrimp are lightly browned and almost cooked through, but still slightly translucent, 2 to 3 minutes total. Transfer the shrimp to a plate and wipe out the wok with a paper towel.

♦ Place a measuring cup with ¼ cup water next to your cooktop. Set the wok over medium heat and add the brown sugar, lime juice (this helps keep the sugar from crystallizing), and 2 tablespoons water. Cook, stirring often, until the sugar turns into an amber-colored caramel (it should be as thick as honey), 6 to 7 minutes. Remove from the heat, then stir in the fish sauce, soy sauce, and remaining 2 tablespoons water. Once a smooth sticky sauce forms (about as thick as honey), after 30 seconds or so, add the cooked shrimp, pepper, scallions, and peanuts and toss to coat. Return to medium heat and continue cooking until the shrimp finish cooking and are evenly coated, less than 1 minute. Remove the pan from the heat and let the shrimp cool in the wok before transferring them and the sauce to a bowl.

♦ *assemble the lettuce wraps*   Remove the pickles from the fridge and arrange the lettuce leaves, cucumber, and cilantro on a serving platter. To serve, spoon some of the shrimp onto a lettuce leaf along with some rice (if using) and top with a few pickles, cucumber, and a sprig of cilantro. Roll up and eat immediately.

BACK HOME in Korat

PAD KORAT

SERVES 2 TO 4

My hometown of Korat is about three hours east of Bangkok. Some people call it "the gateway to Isaan" because it's one of the biggest cities in the northeastern part of Thailand. Farming is popular there, so all around you'll see lush green fields where they grow rice. Even my grandpa was a rice farmer. The famous noodle dish in Bangkok is pad Thai, of course, but in Korat we have our own style, pad Korat—it's a little more on the spicy, savory, and saucy side. I cooked pad Korat all the time for the kids growing up. If there was meat or seafood tossed in, that meant Daddy had some money, but if it was getting near the end of month, sometimes it would be made with just vegetables. Either way, it reminds me of home.

These days, I cook Korat noodles for Chrissy, Luna, and Miles at least twice a week and my claim to fame is that I can make it with just about anything we have in the fridge—chicken, beef, tofu, eggs, vegetables. All I need are some pad Thai rice noodles and my cupboard of sauces. The possibilities are endless. Instead of soaking the dried noodles beforehand, I add them to the wok with the sauce, so they soak up all the sweet and savory goodness in the pan. At the very end I toss in scallions and bean sprouts so they stay fresh and crunchy, then serve the noodles with lime wedges and chile powder so everyone can tweak the spicy-sour flavor to their own taste.

3 tablespoons vegetable oil

4 cloves garlic, minced

2 tablespoons minced shallot

1 teaspoon Roasted Chile Powder
(page 226)

½ pound boneless, skinless chicken thighs
(2 to 3 thighs), cut into bite-size pieces
(see Note)

2 tablespoons oyster sauce

2 tablespoons fish sauce

2 tablespoons Thai soybean paste,
or 4 teaspoons brown miso paste
mixed with 2 teaspoons water

1 tablespoon light brown sugar

3 tablespoons apple cider vinegar (or the brine
from any jar of pickled vegetables)

8 ounces dried vermicelli (thin rice stick
noodles)

2 large eggs, lightly beaten

1½ cups bean sprouts

4 scallions, green parts only, cut into 1-inch
pieces

FOR SERVING

Lime wedges

Fish sauce

Roasted Chile Powder (page 226)

♦ In a wok or large skillet, heat the oil over medium-high heat until shimmering-hot. Add the garlic, shallot, and chile powder and cook until fragrant, about 1 minute. Add the chicken and toss, cooking until browned all over but not cooked through, about 2 minutes. Add the oyster sauce, fish sauce, soybean paste, brown sugar, vinegar, and 1 cup water, mixing until combined. Add the dried noodles. Cook, stirring, until the noodles have softened and absorbed the water, 2 to 3 minutes (you can always add more water if the noodles look too dry). Once the noodles have soaked up the sauce, push them to the side of the pan and add the beaten eggs. Swirl the pan in a circle to spread out the eggs, letting them sit undisturbed for 1 minute, then stir and mix them into the chicken and noodles until they're mostly cooked but slightly wet (like a soft scramble), about 1 minute. Add the bean sprouts and scallions, toss again to mix, and then remove the pan from the heat, letting the bean sprouts and scallions wilt in the residual heat.

♦ To serve, place the noodles in a serving bowl or divide among the plates. Serve with lime wedges, fish sauce, and chile powder, so everyone can season their noodles as desired.

note

Instead of chicken you can also use an equal amount of beef, extra-firm tofu, mushrooms, or hearty vegetables like broccoli, carrots, or snow peas.

---

note

If you have a lot of hungry people in your house, you can easily double this recipe. Sometimes I use up to two pounds of dried noodles—my big wok gets so full I have to have Chrissy hold it while I stir!—and it disappears in no time anyway. In my experience, you can never have too much.

Thai
BBQ PORK

SERVES 4

Another Thai grilling classic, moo yang is usually made with fatty cuts of pork neck that are tenderized in a salty-sweet sauce and then grilled over hot coals until smoky and charred.

My take is simpler but still captures that special Thai roadside barbecue taste. First, I tenderize thin pork chops by poking them all over with a fork, then I marinate them in a mixture of honey, oyster sauce, and other spices (they need at least 2 hours to tenderize and soak in the flavor). Finally, I sear them under the broiler so they develop a brown crust while staying plump and juicy inside. Pick up the thinnest chops you can find—that's very important, as they need to cook through under the broiler.

4 thin-cut (¾-inch-thick) bone-in pork chops or pork shoulder steaks (about 2 pounds total)

3 tablespoons light soy sauce

2 tablespoons oyster sauce

2 tablespoons light brown sugar

2 tablespoons finely chopped cilantro stems

1 tablespoon honey

1 tablespoon whole milk

2 teaspoons ground white pepper

2 teaspoons kosher salt

Vegetable oil, for the pan

FOR SERVING

2 tablespoons packed fresh cilantro leaves

Red Hot Pepper Sauce (page 238), for dipping

◆ Use a fork to poke the pork all over (while thinking about your ex-lovers) so it can absorb the marinade. In a large shallow bowl or resealable plastic bag, combine the soy sauce, oyster sauce, brown sugar, cilantro stems, honey, milk, white pepper, and salt. Add the pork, seal the bag (remove as much air as possible before sealing), and massage the marinade into the pork. Marinate in the fridge for at least 2 hours or overnight.

◆ Position a rack 4 inches from the heating element and preheat the broiler.

◆ Line a sheet pan with foil and brush with oil. Remove the chops from the marinade, letting any excess drip off and brushing off any pieces of cilantro, and arrange them on the sheet pan so they don't touch. Broil until well browned and charred in spots, about 4 minutes, then flip them over and continue cooking until the chops are browned and firm to the touch, about 4 minutes more. Remove from the oven and rest for at least 5 minutes before removing the meat from the bone and thinly slicing.

◆ Serve garnished with cilantro leaves, with hot pepper dipping sauce alongside.

Turkey
GRAPOW

SERVES 2 TO 4

Growing up, my mother worked at a school cafeteria in Korat, cooking food that all the little kids would eat at lunchtime, like grilled pork and papaya salad. Pad grapow, a spicy and savory stir-fry made with ground meat and chopped green beans, was a favorite. For a couple baht (that's Thai money) you could get a big plate with rice and a runny fried egg. When I got married, grapow was the only Thai dish that Ron would eat. But he really loved it, so I would cook it all the time.

You can make grapow with any kind of meat—I like to use turkey or chicken, which go well with the salty garlic-chile sauce. The important part is the sweet flavor of the basil added at the end (that's what grapow means—basil). If you can find Thai basil leaves, that's great, but don't worry if you have only regular basil. That's all I had during the years in Utah and Idaho when I didn't live close to a Thai grocery store. Grapow still tasted delicious!

1 pound ground turkey or chicken (not extra lean)

2 tablespoons oyster sauce

1½ tablespoons light soy sauce

8 cloves garlic, peeled

5 fresh bird's eye chiles (very hot) or 1 serrano chile (less hot)

3 tablespoons vegetable oil

½ large yellow onion, thinly sliced

¼ pound green beans, trimmed and sliced into 1-inch pieces (about ½ cup)

1 tablespoon fish sauce, plus more to taste

2 teaspoons sugar, plus more to taste

2 cups loosely packed basil leaves

2 small sweet red peppers, thinly sliced

Ground white pepper

FOR SERVING

4 cups cooked jasmine rice

4 Puffy Fried Eggs (optional; page 235)

Spicy Garlic-Lime Fish Sauce (page 243)

◆ In a medium bowl, combine the ground turkey, oyster sauce, and soy sauce and mix thoroughly until combined. Set aside.

◆ In a mini food processor, combine the garlic and chiles and pulse until finely minced. (Alternatively, use a mortar and pestle.)

◆ In a wok or a large skillet, heat the oil over medium-high heat until shimmering-hot. Add the garlic-chile paste and cook until the garlic is fragrant, less than 1 minute. Add the meat and cook, stirring often, until browned, about 3 minutes. Stir in the onion,

green beans, fish sauce, and sugar. Continue cooking, stirring often, until the onion and green beans have softened slightly, about 2 minutes.

♦ Remove from the heat and stir in the basil and sweet peppers; the basil leaves will wilt in the residual heat of the pan. Season with a pinch of white pepper and add more fish sauce or sugar to taste.

♦ To serve, divide the rice evenly among individual bowls or plates and cover with the grapow. Top with fried eggs, if you like. Serve immediately with the garlic-lime fish sauce at the table.

Fried Curry
MEATBALLS

SERVES 4

Growing up in Korat, my grandma would make these little meatballs for lunch. She squished them into small patties and fried them until browned and crisp. Each morning she would pack them with sticky rice and pickles in our little lunch pails and off we would go to school.

These are special thanks to the baking soda and cornstarch, which help make the inside extra bouncy and fluffy once you cook them. There's crunch and texture from the green beans and shredded coconut—if it seems weird, trust me—and a fragrant pop from the lime zest and curry paste. There are a lot of flavors going on, but it all comes together to create a meatball experience like no other. Even IKEA's famous Swedish meatballs can't touch these.

Usually I serve these an appetizer, but you can eat them with rice and salad to make a meal.

1 large egg

1 pound ground pork

2 tablespoons fish sauce

2 tablespoons Thai red curry paste

1 teaspoon baking soda

1 teaspoon light brown sugar

1 tablespoon minced cilantro stems, plus cilantro leaves for garnish

Grated zest of 1 lime

½ pound green beans, trimmed and thinly sliced crosswise (about 1 cup)

¼ cup unsweetened shredded coconut

¼ cup cornstarch

Kosher salt and ground white pepper

Vegetable oil, for deep-frying

Tangy Cucumber Salad (page 59), for serving

◆ In a large bowl, lightly beat the egg. Add the ground pork, fish sauce, curry paste, baking soda, brown sugar, and 2 tablespoons cold water and mix to combine. Add the cilantro stems, lime zest, green beans, coconut, and cornstarch, mixing until combined. Season with a pinch of salt and white pepper. If you like, microwave a teaspoon of the meatball mixture for 20 seconds or so until cooked, then taste and season with more salt and pepper if needed.

◆ Using your hands, shape the mixture into small meatballs, about 2 heaping tablespoons each. Flatten the balls into patties ¾ inch thick and place them on a plate.

◆ Pour at least 2 inches oil into a wok, large heavy pot, or deep skillet, making sure to leave a few inches of clearance from the rim. Heat the oil over medium heat to 370°F

(use a deep-fry thermometer or test the oil by throwing in a little piece of bread or a grain of rice; if it sizzles immediately but doesn't burn, you're ready).

♦ Set a wire rack in a sheet pan or line a plate with paper towels and have nearby. Working in batches to not overcrowd the pan, fry the meatballs until they're crispy and golden brown on all sides, turning as needed, about 3 minutes. Adjust the heat as needed to keep the oil at 370°F as you're frying. Drain the meatballs on the wire rack or paper towels until slightly cooled.

♦ Garnish with cilantro leaves and serve with the cucumber salad.

Roasted Lemongrass
CHICKEN   SERVES 4

Gai yang (gai = chicken; yang = grilled) is popular at street food stalls and restaurants all over Thailand but especially in my hometown of Korat. Each region has its own cooking method, but the general recipe involves splitting the chicken in half so it cooks evenly and marinating it for a few hours with Thai seasonings like pepper, garlic, cilantro stems, and fish sauce. I like to stir in some half-and-half or coconut milk, too, which makes the meat extra juicy and helps the skin get nice and brown. Traditionally, gai yang is grilled over charcoal, but if you don't feel like setting up a grill, roasting the chicken in the oven is just as flavorful—and it's the way I make it most often. A simple roast chicken, papaya salad, sticky rice, and spicy dipping sauce—that's all you need for an extremely easy, extremely Thai meal.

12 cloves garlic, peeled

¼ cup thinly sliced cilantro stems

4 stalks lemongrass, tender bottom sections only, thinly sliced

1 large shallot, roughly chopped

¼ cup half-and-half or full-fat coconut milk

2 tablespoons Thai sweet dark soy sauce, store-bought or homemade (page 232)

2 tablespoons oyster sauce

2 teaspoons light soy sauce

1 teaspoon ground white pepper

1 whole chicken (about 4 pounds), spatchcocked (ask your butcher to do this, or see Note)

FOR SERVING

Thai sweet chili sauce

Red Hot Pepper Sauce (page 238)

Cooked sticky rice (see page 228)

Green Papaya Salad (page 60)

◆ In a blender or food processor, combine the garlic, cilantro stems, lemongrass, shallot, half-and-half, dark soy sauce, oyster sauce, light soy sauce, and white pepper and blend until a smooth and thick sauce forms (add a little water to help it along, if needed).

◆ Place the chicken in a large shallow dish or resealable plastic bag and pour the marinade mixture over the top, rubbing it into every nook and cranny. Cover and refrigerate for at least 3 hours or overnight.

recipe continues →

♦ When ready to cook, remove the chicken from the fridge at least 30 minutes prior so it has time to come to room temperature (it will cook more evenly this way).

♦ Preheat the oven to 350°F.

♦ Arrange a wire rack over a foil-lined sheet pan. Coat the rack with cooking spray or rub with a little oil to make cleanup easier. Remove the chicken from the marinade, letting any excess drip off, and place the chicken breast side down on the rack.

♦ Roast for 50 minutes, rotating the pan front to back and flipping the chicken halfway through. Increase the temperature to 425°F and roast until the skin is golden brown and an instant-read thermometer inserted into the thickest part of the thigh registers 165°F, 10 to 15 minutes.

♦ Remove the chicken from the oven and set aside to rest for at least 5 minutes before carving. Serve with sweet chili sauce and hot pepper sauce for dipping and with sticky rice and papaya salad on the side.

───────────────────── *note* ─────────────────────

To spatchcock a chicken yourself, set the chicken breast-side down and use a sharp pair of kitchen shears to cut along both sides of the chicken's backbone, separating it from the ribs. Remove the backbone (save it in a freezer bag if you like making homemade chicken stock), then turn the chicken over so the breast is facing up. Splay the legs and breasts until they lie flat, and give the bird a firm press in the center of the breast; you will hear a crack, then it should lie flat on its own.

MOO PING

Everybody knows chicken satay in the US, but in Thailand moo ping (grilled pork skewers) are the more famous street food. You will find moo ping vendors on every almost corner in Bangkok with their little charcoal grills lined with wooden skewers that you can buy for a dollar or two as a snack on the way home from work. The smell is so amazing, it's like free advertising. Many Thai people name their dogs Moo Ping, because stray dogs always hang out around pork skewer stands, hoping that some friendly customer will buy them a round.

Whenever I miss the very specific scent of Thai street food, grilling moo ping at home takes me back. Every vendor has their own secret technique or marinade, closely guarded with their life. You don't want to know what I had to do to get this recipe! Just kidding, I know someone who knows someone. Coconut milk in the marinade keeps the pork tender and juicy and helps create a nicely browned crust on the grill. Make sure to brush on a little extra as it cooks—the way we would do it back home was to tie a strip of pandan leaf to a chopstick and use it like a paintbrush.

Be sure to allow yourself enough time to let the pork marinate—overnight is best, but a few hours is okay, too.

2 pounds boneless pork shoulder, cut into strips 3 inches long and ½ inch thick (you should end up with about 40 pieces, see Note)

1 tablespoon ground coriander

1 teaspoon ground white pepper

1 teaspoon grated lime zest, plus 1 lime cut into wedges for serving

1 tablespoon finely minced cilantro stems, plus leaves for serving

8 cloves garlic, grated or finely minced

2 tablespoons light brown sugar

2 tablespoons fish sauce

1 tablespoon cornstarch

2 teaspoons vegetable oil

Kosher salt

1 (13.5-ounce) can full-fat coconut milk

EQUIPMENT

20 bamboo skewers (look for the 10-inch-long ones)

Vegetable oil, for grilling

note
To make the pork easier to slice, freeze it for 15 to 30 minutes before cutting.

recipe continues ⟶

♦ In a large bowl, combine the pork, coriander, white pepper, lime zest, cilantro stems, garlic, brown sugar, fish sauce, cornstarch, oil, 1 teaspoon salt, and 1 cup of the coconut milk. Cover and marinate in the fridge for at least 4 hours (overnight is best for extra tender pork). Refrigerate the remaining coconut milk.

♦ About 30 minutes before you're ready to grill, remove the pork from the fridge and soak the bamboo skewers in water so they don't burn.

♦ Season the reserved coconut milk with 1 teaspoon salt and set aside until you're ready to cook the pork.

♦ Thread one piece of pork onto a skewer, then thread it back through the meat to secure it, bunching the meat tightly together like an accordion. Thread a second piece of pork onto the skewer the same way, making sure the meat is tightly bunched and there are a few inches of skewer at the bottom to act as a handle. Repeat the skewering process with the remaining skewers and pork.

♦ Prepare a grill (charcoal or gas) for direct high heat or heat a grill pan over high heat. Brush the grill grates with oil. Cook the skewers, turning them and brushing with the reserved coconut milk frequently, until the meat is lightly charred and the pork is cooked through, 8 to 10 minutes. Let the skewers cool slightly.

♦ Serve garnished with cilantro leaves, with lime wedges for squeezing over the top.

Crispy
PORK BELLY

SERVES 6 TO 8

Crispy pork belly (moo grob) is pure and simple golden-brown delicious-ness, the best snack ever with sticky rice and your favorite dipping sauce. For Thai people, moo grob is like our bacon, only way thicker and juicier.

Some people fry their pork belly, but I've found you can get each piece extra crispy in the oven (or in an air fryer). The secret is to poke little holes in the fatty skin (not into the meat, just through the skin and fat) with a knife or fork. Poke, poke, poke, and poke some more—sometimes I poke it all morning. This helps the fat render so the skin will be nice and crackly. Then you rub the outside with salt to draw out the moisture, which will help the skin brown. I recommend making more crispy pork than you think you need, because it can be added to so many things.

2 pounds skin-on boneless pork belly

1 tablespoon distilled white vinegar

2 teaspoons kosher salt

♦ Preheat the oven to 300°F (or set an air fryer to 325°F).

♦ Poke the rind side of the pork belly all over with a knife. You can't poke too much, so really go nuts (this will help the fat render and make the skin crispy). Use the knife to carefully slice the skin side of the pork belly crosswise every 2 inches or so, cutting halfway down but not all the way through.

♦ Rub the vinegar all over the pork, getting into every crack and crevice, then sprinkle with the salt and do the same, rubbing to make sure the pork is evenly coated with salt. Let sit, uncovered, for at least 30 minutes, then pat the pork skin dry with a paper towel.

♦ Wrap the bottom half of the pork belly tightly in foil, leaving the skin exposed. Place skin-side up in the oven on a sheet pan or on the air fryer rack and cook until the pork is tender and yields easily to a knife, about 1 hour (or 45 minutes if using an air fryer). Remove and let it cool slightly.

♦ Leave the oven on and increase the temperature to 450°F (or set air fryer to 450°F).

♦ Return the pork to the oven (or air fryer) and cook until the skin is golden brown and slightly puffy, 10 to 15 minutes. Remove from the oven and let cool at least 10 minutes before cutting into ½-inch-thick slices, then cutting each slice into 1-inch-wide chunks. Serve warm or at room temperature. Store in a covered container in the fridge up to a week.

Sour
SAUSAGE
MAKES ABOUT 4 POUNDS

If you follow me on Instagram, you might have seen me on one of my famous sausage-making days. In Isaan, the region of Thailand where I'm from, one of the most popular foods is called sai krok isaan, which is a garlicky sausage that gets fermented for a few days so it develops a tart flavor, almost like lime juice but much more subtle and slightly funky. I know it might sound strange, but trust me—or just ask one of the many people I've hooked on my sausage over the years.

What helps the sausage become sour is rice and salt. As you let it sit out, the salt cures the sausage and the starch in the rice develops a pleasant tangy flavor, like sourdough. I always make sure to hang the sausage links in a place that gets some sunlight and a little airflow. But be careful, because sometimes the pork fat will drip! I used to hang them over the light fixtures in our kitchen, but now Chrissy makes me hang them in my bedroom (I don't mind, because I tell her I love sleeping with the sausage in my bed . . . ha!).

After three days, the sausage will have a lovely balanced tangy flavor, but if you prefer it really sour, let it go for five days. To stop the fermentation, just toss it in the fridge. Although the sausage is fermented, it is still raw, so it's important that you cook it all the way through before serving. On the grill is my favorite method, but you can also brown it in a skillet with a little water to keep the pan from scorching. In Thailand, we eat sour sausage like a taco filling, tucked into a crunchy cabbage leaf and topped with a little fresh ginger, peanuts, and chile peppers.

25 cloves garlic, peeled

2½ pounds ground pork

3 tablespoons kosher salt

2 tablespoons oyster sauce

1 tablespoon freshly ground black pepper

3 cups cooked jasmine rice

FOR SERVING

Green cabbage, cut into eighths, leaves separated

Sliced cucumber

4-inch piece fresh ginger, peeled and cut into thin matchsticks

Unsalted roasted peanuts

Fresh bird's eye chiles, halved (optional)

EQUIPMENT

Natural hog casings (ask your butcher for some or buy them online; one package is plenty)

Sausage stuffer (see Note)

Cheesecloth (optional)

◆ In a mini food processor or mortar, process/pound the garlic until minced/mashed. Transfer to a large bowl and add the ground pork, salt, oyster sauce, and pepper. Use your hands to mix thoroughly until combined, then add the rice and continue mixing until everything is incorporated. Microwave a small pinch of the sausage for a few seconds until cooked and taste for seasoning. Adjust the salt and pepper in the bowl of pork mixture as needed.

◆ Prepare the sausage casings according to package directions (some kinds have to be rinsed and soaked before using). Carefully thread the casing onto the end of your sausage stuffer (if you don't have a stuffer, see Note on page 140) and tie a simple overhand knot on the other end. Stuff the sausage mixture into the casing, using your index finger and thumb to push the sausage toward the knotted end. Once all the mixture has been stuffed, use your hands to evenly distribute the pork in the casings by using your hands. Trim any excess casing and tie off the other end.

◆ To form sausage links, measure 2 inches down and squeeze and twist the long part of the sausage three times. Repeat this process, moving your way down the entire length of the stuffed casing and twisting a new link every 2 inches.

◆ Arrange the stuffed links on a wire rack set over a sheet pan. Use a toothpick to poke holes all over the casing on both sides. If desired, drape a sheet of cheesecloth over the sausages and place them somewhere warmish, ideally between 60°F and 70°F, but away from direct sunlight and air drafts. Let the sausages ferment at room temperature for up to 3 days (or 5 days if you like them really tangy), checking them each day to make sure no mold forms (if you see any discoloration, cut out the link and discard it).

◆ After they have fermented, your sausage can be refrigerated for a few days or stored in a resealable plastic bag for up to 1 month in the freezer.

◆ To cook the sausages, preheat a grill to medium heat, brush the grates with oil, and grill the sausages until cooked through, turning occasionally, about 10 minutes. You can also add the sausage and a small amount of water (enough to barely cover) to a large skillet, bring the water to a boil, reduce the heat, and simmer, covered, for 10 minutes. Uncover and continue cooking, turning occasionally, until the water has evaporated and the sausages are browned on both sides.

◆ Serve the sausages with cabbage leaves, ginger, peanuts, and chiles.

note

If you don't have a sausage stuffer on hand, that's okay. For many years, before I bought my fancy sausage grinder, I stuffed sour sausages by hand using a funnel or the cut-off neck of a 2-liter soda bottle. Stretch the sausage casing over the tip of the funnel or the mouth of the bottle and use the handle of a wooden spoon to push the stuffing all the way down.

KHAO MAN GAI
(Poached Chicken with Chicken Fat Rice)

SERVES 4 TO 6

Khao man gai is the Thai version of Hainan chicken rice, which is a dish made with tender poached chicken and fragrant rice cooked in chicken fat. It's one of the ultimate comfort foods in Thailand, so simple but so delicious. Whenever Thai people go out to eat and can't decide what they want to order, they say, *Well, I can always get chicken and rice.*

Since the chicken is the star of this dish, you want to make sure you don't overcook it. Don't let the chicken sit in water at a full boil or it will get tough! If done right, even the breast meat will be as soft as silk. As the chicken cooks in the broth, skim the fat off the top and save it for toasting the rice, which will add another level of chicken-ness to your chicken experience.

The greatest part of this dish, in my opinion, is the special Thai dipping sauce—salty, tangy, and zesty with just a touch of sweetness from the dark soy sauce.

FOR THE CHICKEN

1 small whole chicken (about 2½ pounds), cut into quarters

2-inch piece fresh ginger, peeled and thinly sliced

4 scallions, crushed with the butt of a knife

1½ tablespoons kosher salt

FOR THE RICE

2 tablespoons chicken fat or vegetable oil

8 cloves garlic, mashed or minced

2-inch piece fresh ginger, peeled and thinly sliced

Kosher salt

2 cups jasmine rice, rinsed and drained

FOR THE KHAO MAN GAI SAUCE

¼ cup Thai sweet dark soy sauce, store-bought or homemade (page 232)

¼ cup Thai soybean paste or brown miso paste

1 teaspoon light brown sugar

2 tablespoons apple cider vinegar

1 tablespoon fresh lime juice

2 tablespoons minced peeled fresh ginger

2 tablespoons minced garlic

2 fresh bird's eye chiles or 1 serrano chile, thinly sliced

FOR SERVING

Fresh cilantro leaves

Cucumber slices, scored lengthwise with a fork

recipe continues ⟶

♦ **cook the chicken**   In a large pot, combine the chicken, ginger, scallions, salt, and water to cover. Bring to a near boil, then immediately reduce the heat to a gentle simmer and cook until the chicken is cooked through but tender, about 30 minutes. Remove from the heat. Skim off any fat that has floated to the top and reserve for making the rice. Let the chicken sit in the broth until you're ready to serve.

♦ **make the rice**   In a large saucepan, heat the reserved chicken fat over medium-high heat until shimmering-hot. Add the garlic, ginger, and a pinch of salt, and cook until fragrant, less than 1 minute. Add the rice and stir to coat in the chicken fat. Once the rice starts to smell nutty, 2 to 3 minutes, add 2½ cups for the chicken broth from the pot (make sure to reserve ¼ cup of the broth of making the khao man gai sauce). Reduce the heat to a simmer, then cover and cook until all (or most of) the broth has been absorbed, 15 to 20 minutes. Remove from the heat, cover, and let sit for at least 10 minutes before fluffing with a fork.

♦ **make the khao man gai sauce**   In a blender, combine the soy sauce, soybean paste, brown sugar, vinegar, lime juice, ginger, garlic, chiles, and 3 tablespoons of the reserved chicken broth. Process until smooth, adding a little more chicken broth as needed to form a sauce. Serve immediately or refrigerate until ready to use.

♦ Remove the chicken from the broth and carve: Remove the legs by cutting through the thigh joints, then separate the thighs from the drumsticks. Carve the breast meat from the bone and slice each breast crosswise into 6 pieces.

♦ **to serve**   Spoon the rice into a small bowl and arrange pieces of chicken over the top; garnish with cilantro leaves and cucumber slices. Serve with the khao man gai sauce. If you want, you can also serve the leftover broth on the side for sipping.

TOM ZAPP
(Isaan Hot and Sour Soup)

SERVES 4

Tom zapp is a traditional family meal served in Isaan, the northeastern part of Thailand where I'm from. It's eaten like hot pot there—you throw whatever you want (beef, seafood, pork) into a big clay pot and simmer it until everything is cooked and the flavors come together and smell amazing. In our family, there were always plenty of vegetables, too, because they didn't cost much and filled up the bellies of my four siblings and me.

What really makes tom zapp stand out? It's the nutty toasted rice powder, lots of fresh herbs, and a bold sour flavor, which comes from lime juice and tamarind. Isaan people love that sourness.

2 stalks fresh lemongrass

2-inch piece fresh galangal or ginger, thinly sliced

1 pound beef skirt steak or chuck steak, sliced against the grain into bite-size pieces

1 tablespoon grated lime zest (from 2 limes)

1 medium shallot, finely chopped

2 tablespoons tamarind paste

1 teaspoon (or cube) beef or chicken bouillon

1 teaspoon kosher salt

½ yellow onion, thinly sliced

1 cup chopped green cabbage

2 scallions, cut into 1-inch pieces

1 (2-ounce) package dried bean thread noodles or rice vermicelli (optional)

2 tablespoons Toasted Rice Powder, store-bought or homemade (page 226)

2 tablespoons fish sauce, plus more to taste

½ teaspoon Roasted Chile Powder (page 226)

¼ cup roughly chopped fresh dill

¼ cup fresh Thai basil leaves

¼ cup fresh cilantro leaves

Lime wedges, for serving

recipe continues ➡

♦ Cut the tops from the lemongrass and remove the tough outer husk, leaving about three-quarters of the stalk. Using the butt of a knife or other heavy object, lightly pound the lemongrass stalks and the galangal or ginger slices until smashed. Cut the lemongrass into 4-inch sections.

♦ In a medium pot, combine the lemongrass, galangal, skirt steak, lime zest, shallot, tamarind paste, beef bouillon, salt, and 7 cups water. Stir to dissolve the tamarind paste and bring to a boil over medium-high heat, stirring occasionally. Reduce the heat, cover, and simmer for 30 minutes.

♦ Uncover and add the onion, cabbage, scallions, and bean thread noodles (if using). Simmer until the cabbage is crisp-tender and the noodles are cooked, 3 to 5 minutes. Add the rice powder, fish sauce, and chile powder. Remove from the heat, then stir in the dill, basil, and cilantro. Taste and season with more fish sauce if needed. Serve with lime wedges.

HOMESTYLE KHAO TOD
(Crispy Rice Salad)

SERVES 4

Khao tod, also known as crispy rice salad, is one of my favorite dishes from Korat. My mom would make it as a treat for me and my siblings on the weekend, and we'd pile spoonfuls into cabbage leaves and eat them like tiny tacos. I still make it all the time for Chrissy. With every bite, you get crunchy bits of fried rice, tangy lime, refreshing herbs, the snap of raw ginger, a touch of heat from the chiles and the roasted peanuts.

Most of the work is rolling the seasoned rice into balls and frying them. I like my rice extra crunchy so I flatten the balls into discs to get more crispy edges. Traditionally it is made with naem, which is a fermented Thai sausage, but I use Spam (yes, I love Spam!) cooked until tender with garlic and lime juice to give it a savory-tangy taste. But if you don't like Spam, you can also substitute cooked ground pork, or crumbled Thai Sour Sausage (page 138).

1 cup diced Spam Less Sodium

2 cloves garlic, minced

2 teaspoons fresh lemon juice

Vegetable oil, for shallow-frying

1 large egg

2 tablespoons Thai red curry paste

Grated zest of 1 lime

¼ cup all-purpose flour

4 cups cooked jasmine rice (preferably cold)

8 small dried red chiles, such as chile de árbol (optional)

½ cup unsalted roasted peanuts

6 tablespoons fresh lime juice (2 to 3 limes)

6 tablespoons fish sauce

1 tablespoon sugar

2 teaspoons Roasted Chile Powder (page 226) or 4 thinly sliced fresh bird's eye chiles, to taste

2 small to medium shallots, or ½ medium red onion, halved lengthwise and thinly sliced (about ⅔ cup)

2-inch piece fresh ginger, peeled and cut into thin matchsticks

½ cup chopped fresh cilantro leaves

8 scallions, finely chopped

◆ In a small saucepan, combine the Spam, garlic, lemon juice, and water to cover. Bring to a simmer over medium-low heat and cook for 5 minutes to heat the Spam through and reduce some of its saltiness. Remove from the heat, drain off the water, and set aside.

◆ Pour about 1 inch of oil into a wok, large heavy pot, or skillet. Heat the oil over medium-high heat to 370°F (test the oil by throwing in a grain of rice; if it sizzles immediately and doesn't burn, you're ready).

♦ Meanwhile, in a medium bowl, whisk together the egg, curry paste, and lime zest. Add the flour and rice and mix thoroughly. Shape the mixture into about 16 rounds the size of a golf ball, then gently flatten them into 1-inch-thick patties.

♦ Line a plate with paper towels and set aside. Add the dried chiles, if using, and the peanuts to the oil and fry just enough to darken them slightly, 1 to 2 minutes. Use a slotted spoon to transfer them to the paper towels.

♦ Line another plate with paper towels. Working in batches, add the rice cakes to the oil and fry until crispy and golden brown on both sides, about 3 minutes per side. Transfer the rice cakes to the paper towels.

♦ In a large bowl, whisk together the lime juice, fish sauce, sugar, and chile powder. Crumble the crispy rice cakes into different sizes in the bowl. Add the shallots, ginger, cilantro, scallions, peanuts and chiles, and the reserved Spam. Toss until evenly mixed and serve.

QUEEN OF *leftovers*

Fridge-Cleaning
FRIED RICE SERVES 4

On Monday nights, we clean out the fridge. The easiest and tastiest way to clear out everything is to turn it into a belly-filling pan of fried rice. Nothing goes to waste! The exact recipe below is not so important—what is key is the order in which you add everything to the wok: 1) Garlic goes in first. 2) Add the onion and whatever leftover meat or vegetable additions you want—if they're already cooked, all you need to do is heat them up; otherwise cook them until they're tender. 3) Add the egg and cook and stir it a little bit so it firms up. 4) Add as much rice and seasonings as you want. 5) At the end, add fresh vegetables or herbs that don't need to be in the wok very long, like tomatoes and scallions. That's it! Remember to keep the wok hot and always be stirring.

3 tablespoons vegetable oil

6 cloves garlic, roughly chopped

½ medium yellow onion, thinly sliced

1½ cups sliced rotisserie chicken, steak, shrimp, cooked sausage, or other leftover meat

1 cup cooked or roasted vegetables, cut into bite-size pieces (broccoli, greens, carrots, etc.)

2 large eggs, lightly beaten

4 cups cooked white rice (preferably day-old)

1½ tablespoons light soy sauce

1½ tablespoons oyster sauce

2 teaspoons sugar

1 plum tomato, roughly chopped

4 scallions, cut into 1-inch sections

Ground white pepper

FOR SERVING

Fresh cilantro leaves

Lime wedges

Spicy Garlic-Lime Fish Sauce (page 243)

Sriracha sauce

◆ In a wok or large skillet, heat the oil over medium-high heat until shimmering-hot. Add the garlic and cook until fragrant, less than 1 minute. Add the onion, leftover meat, and cooked vegetables and cook, stirring, until the onion is slightly softened, about 3 minutes. Stir in the eggs, cooking until just set, less than 1 minute. Then pile the rice on top along with the soy sauce, oyster sauce, and sugar, tossing to combine.

◆ Cook, undisturbed, until the rice crisps and browns, 2 to 3 minutes. Add the tomato and scallions and cook, stirring, until warmed through. Remove from the heat and season with a pinch of white pepper.

◆ Serve with cilantro leaves, lime wedges, fish sauce, and Sriracha.

PAD MAMA

SERVES 4

The one instant noodle brand that everyone knows in Thailand is Mama. It's like our Top Ramen. We love it so much we use it in all sorts of dishes, the most famous being pad Mama, or stir-fried instant noodles. Growing up, we never had much money, so we would stretch one packet of noodles with lots of vegetables to feed me and my four siblings. I've made it with all kinds of instant noodles—but if you want the most classic Thai taste, get the tom yum–flavored ones. Look for them at any Asian market.

I keep the seasoning on the lighter side since I use the seasoning packets (I call them surprise packets) at the end of cooking. This is one of Chrissy's favorite afternoon snacks. So much flavor from a little packet of noodles.

3 (2-ounce) packages Thai instant noodles (preferably Mama brand)

2 tablespoons vegetable oil

1 tablespoon minced garlic

½ pound ground pork

1 tablespoon oyster sauce

2 tablespoons light soy sauce or fish sauce

1 teaspoon sugar

½ medium yellow onion, sliced into half-moons

½ cup roughly chopped Chinese broccoli, bok choy, or cabbage

½ medium carrot, julienned

1 plum tomato, cut into small wedges

½ cup bean sprouts

2 scallions, green parts, cut into 1-inch pieces

Ground white pepper

Fresh cilantro leaves

◆ Bring a medium pot of water to a boil. Unwrap the instant noodles (reserve the seasoning packets) and break the blocks into quarters as you add them to the pot. Cook, stirring, just long enough for them to soften and loosen, about 1 minute. Drain immediately, shaking off as much water as you can.

◆ In a wok or large skillet, heat the oil over medium-high heat until shimmering-hot. Add the garlic and cook until fragrant, about 30 seconds. Add the pork and cook until browned, about 3 minutes. Stir in the oyster sauce, soy sauce, and sugar. Add the onion, broccoli, and carrot and cook until the vegetables brighten in color, about 2 minutes. Add the drained noodles and the tomato. Continue cooking, stirring until the noodles have absorbed some of the sauce, about 3 minutes. Stir in the bean sprouts and scallions, then remove from the heat. Season with a pinch of white pepper and the reserved seasoning packets (use as much as you like) and garnish with cilantro. Serve immediately.

Fried
CHICKEN LARB

SERVES 2 TO 4

Thai people like to make larb (a very popular chopped meat salad) out of just about anything. Some protein, some herbs, some seasoning. Toss them together and that's larb. So easy! This version is inspired by the amazing fried chicken we tried at KFC in Thailand, which was seasoned with traditional larb flavors like lime, fish sauce, rice powder, and chile powder—it was way better than the Colonel's. When we got home, I decided to make my own fried chicken larb. You can use leftover homemade fried chicken (like John's special fried chicken from Chrissy's first book, *Cravings*), or there's no shame in picking up your favorite fast-food or deli counter tenders.

FOR THE DRESSING

2 tablespoons fresh lime juice

1 tablespoon fish sauce

1 teaspoon light brown sugar

1 tablespoon Toasted Rice Powder, store-bought or homemade (page 226)

1 teaspoon Roasted Chile Powder (page 226)

FOR THE LARB

6 fried chicken tenders (about 12 ounces), sliced, or 3 heaping cups of chopped fried chicken

1 medium shallot or ½ red onion, halved and thinly sliced (about ½ cup)

4 scallions, thinly sliced (about ¼ cup)

¼ cup packed cilantro leaves

¼ cup torn mint leaves

FOR SERVING

Cooked sticky rice (see page 228) or jasmine rice

♦ *make the dressing*   In a small bowl, whisk together the lime juice, fish sauce, brown sugar, rice powder, and chile powder until combined. Set aside.

♦ *make the larb*   Preheat the oven to 400°F.

♦ Spread the chicken on a sheet pan and bake until heated through, 10 to 15 minutes.

♦ In a large bowl, combine the warm chicken, shallot, scallions, cilantro, and mint, then slowly pour the dressing over the top while tossing. Mix gently but thoroughly. Taste and adjust any seasonings as needed. The larb should be tangy, salty, and a little spicy (like me).

♦ Serve immediately with rice.

Thai Stuffed
OMELET

SERVES 2

I think of this as the Thai version of a fully loaded Denver omelet. It's stuffed with ground pork and tomato paste and seasoned with soy sauce and garlic. We like it for any meal, not just breakfast. Cooking a fancy omelet can be intimidating for a lot of people (myself included), but it's important to remember that this is Thai-style and not French-style. A Thai-style omelet is made in a wok to get the eggs crispy and browned around the edges—which is exactly what you want! The sloped edges of a wok also help you easily flip the omelet. If you want to eat this omelet with toast and hash browns, I won't stop you, but my favorite way to eat it is with a side of rice and a few splashes of chile vinegar and fish sauce. It's a great way to use up any vegetables that are lying around your kitchen, too.

FOR THE FILLING

1 tablespoon vegetable oil

6 ounces ground pork

¼ small yellow onion, diced

4 cloves garlic, minced

¼ cup thinly sliced (crosswise) green beans

¼ cup fresh or frozen corn kernels

1 tablespoon oyster sauce

1 tablespoon light soy sauce

1 small plum tomato, diced

1 tablespoon tomato paste

2 scallions, thinly sliced

FOR THE OMELET

4 large eggs

1 teaspoon fish sauce

½ teaspoon sugar

Ground white pepper

1 tablespoon unsalted butter

FOR SERVING

Cilantro leaves

Cooked jasmine rice

Spicy Garlic-Lime Fish Sauce (page 243)

Pickled Chile Vinegar (page 239)

◆ **make the filling** In a wok or large skillet, heat the oil over medium-high heat until shimmering-hot. Add the pork, onion, and garlic and cook, stirring, until the pork is mostly cooked and the onion is softened, 2 to 3 minutes. Add the green beans, corn, oyster sauce, soy sauce, tomato, and tomato paste and cook until most of the liquid has evaporated and a thick sauce starts to form, 2 to 3 minutes. Remove from the heat and stir in the scallions. Taste and season with more soy sauce, if needed.

◆ **make the omelet** In a small bowl, stir together the eggs, fish sauce, sugar, and white pepper. Wipe out the wok or skillet, set the pan over medium-low heat, and add the

butter. Once the butter is melted and sizzling, pour in the egg mixture. Let the egg sit in the center of the pan for a moment, then tilt it to spread it around the pan to make a very thin omelet. Cook until the egg is just set in the center, 2 to 3 minutes, then remove from the heat.

◆ Spoon the pork filling into the center of the omelet. Use your spatula or hands to fold the ends of the omelet in, then fold the sides over, burrito-style, to form a square. Flip the omelet over onto a serving plate so that the fold is underneath.

◆ *to serve*   Garnish with cilantro leaves and serve with rice, season to taste with the spicy garlic fish sauce and pickled chile vinegar.

PEPPER'S NOODLE BAR
(Build-Your-Own Noodle Soup)

SERVES 6 TO 8

Noodle bar—Chrissy came up with the name—is a family tradition in our house for quick and easy weeknight dinners. The first part I make is the chicken broth, seasoned with garlic, ginger, cilantro stems, and soy sauce. Then I cook some noodles (we use rice noodles often, but any kind of soup noodle will work) and green leafy vegetables, and finally I poach some chicken or pork in the broth and chop it up. If you can find frozen fish balls at the store, use those, too. They have a bouncy texture that goes so well with the chewy noodles. Finally, I spread out all kinds of different seasonings and toppings on the table—this is the most important part for real Thai-style noodle soup.

When we're ready to eat, everyone grabs a bowl and goes through the line: noodles, broth, vegetables, meat, and whatever toppings they want to mix and match. It's like having a street noodle stand set up in the kitchen!

FOR THE BROTH

10 cups low-sodium chicken broth

¼ cup light soy sauce

10 cloves garlic, smashed

2 tablespoons minced cilantro stems

2-inch piece fresh ginger, peeled and thinly sliced

½ yellow onion, roughly chopped

2 small celery stalks (leaves reserved), roughly chopped

1 teaspoon ground white pepper

1 teaspoon kosher salt

FOR THE PROTEIN

8 ounces boneless, skinless chicken thighs or beef tenderloin

1 pound ground pork

1 teaspoon kosher salt

8 ounces store-bought frozen fish balls, thawed, or cubes of extra-firm tofu

FOR THE VEGETABLES

Kosher salt

½ pound Chinese broccoli, leaves roughly chopped and stems thinly sliced (or regular broccoli, cut into small florets)

¾ pound baby bok choy, root ends trimmed, quartered lengthwise

3 cups bean sprouts (you can also use sliced mushrooms, baby corn, cherry tomatoes . . . anything really)

FOR THE NOODLES

1 pound rice noodles, egg noodles, or glass noodles

FOR SERVING

6 scallions, green parts only, thinly sliced

½ cup roughly chopped fresh cilantro leaves

¼ cup roughly chopped celery leaves

Granulated sugar

Roasted Chile Powder (page 226)

Pickled Chile Vinegar (page 239) or brine from any jar of pickled food

Fried Garlic and Garlic Oil (page 236)

Crushed pork rinds

Fish sauce

Lime wedges

♦ **make the broth**   In a large pot, bring the chicken broth, soy sauce, garlic, cilantro stems, ginger, onion, celery, white pepper, and salt to a boil over high heat. Reduce to medium-low and simmer for 20 minutes while preparing the rest of the ingredients.

♦ **prepare the protein**   If using beef tenderloin, place it in the freezer for 15 to 20 minutes until firm. Meanwhile, in a medium bowl, season the ground pork with the salt. Mix until combined. Using a spoon or your hands, shape the mixture into meatballs, about 2 tablespoons each.

♦ Add the meatballs to the simmering chicken broth and simmer until the meatballs are cooked through, 8 to 9 minutes. Use a slotted spoon to transfer them to a bowl and set aside. Add the fish balls to the broth, cooking according to package directions or until warmed through. Remove and set aside. If using chicken thighs, add the pieces to the broth and poach until cooked through, about 10 minutes. Remove the chicken and let cool lightly, then cut into bite-size pieces and set aside. If using beef tenderloin, remove it from the freezer, slice it into ¼-inch-thick strips, and poach it in the simmering broth until cooked through, about 3 minutes, then transfer it to a bowl and set aside.

♦ **blanch the veggies**   Fill another large pot two-thirds full with water, add a few big pinches of salt, and bring to a boil. Working in batches, if needed, blanch the broccoli and bok choy until they are bright green and tender, about 2 minutes. Use a slotted spoon or small sieve to transfer them to a colander and rinse under cold water to stop cooking. Blanch the bean sprouts for 30 seconds, then drain and rinse with cold water. Set aside.

♦ **cook the noodles**   In the boiling water used to blanch the veggies, cook the noodles according to package directions. Drain the noodles and set aside.

♦ **to serve**   Skim away any foam or fat from the top of the broth, then strain (this is optional). Divide the noodles into bowls and add broth, protein, and veggies. Top with any or all garnishes and seasonings.

MISO EGG DROP
Soup SERVES 2 TO 4

I could probably eat miso soup every day and never get tired of it—it's so comforting, so soothing. The best part is that since miso paste packs so much flavor, you don't need many other ingredients to give this soup its deep and savory taste. Just remember to use a quality miso paste—either the sweeter white or the saltier dark variety will work, depending on your taste.

Miso soup is perfect as a snack or light lunch, but it also makes a wonderful quick breakfast, especially on a cold morning (soup for breakfast is a favorite in Thailand, so if you don't know, try it). I always stir in soft tofu, scallions, and dried seaweed—I use the kind that comes in those little snack packages that we buy for Miles and Luna. Beyond those essentials, I'll add a handful of spinach and crack in some eggs to cook in the broth for an egg drop soup-like effect if I'm craving something heartier. This recipe checks all my morning meal boxes: nutritious, filling, and on the table in less time than it takes Chrissy to check her Twitter mentions.

4 cups low-sodium chicken stock or vegetable stock

¼ cup brown miso paste

1 cup diced soft tofu

1 cup packed baby spinach leaves

3 large eggs, well beaten

6 scallions, thinly sliced

2 (⅓-ounce) packages toasted nori snacks, cut into thin strips

♦ In a medium saucepan, bring the chicken stock to a boil. Reduce the heat to a simmer and stir in the miso paste until dissolved. Add the tofu and spinach and cook until the spinach is wilted and the tofu is warmed through, about 1 minute.

♦ Slowly stir in the beaten eggs. As you add it, the egg will ribbon and begin to cook. Once the egg is opaque, add the scallions and nori and remove the pan from the heat. Divide into bowls and serve.

Nam Prik Moo
SLOPPY JOES

SERVES 6

This recipe is based on a northern Thai dish called nam prik ong, which is a spicy ground pork and tomato dip that is so delicious when scooped up with a handful of sticky rice (see page 228), cabbage, and sliced cucumber. It looks a lot like sloppy Joe filling. Maybe you can see where this is going . . .

The first time I made these sandwiches they were a huge family hit—they took John right back to his childhood Manwich days—and I knew I was onto something. I use crispy fried onions from the can (the ones that go on green bean casserole) and fresh cilantro for toppings, but I'll also serve the cabbage and sliced cucumber on the side. That way, whatever sloppiness drips onto the plate can be scooped up with those crunchy veggies.

2 tablespoons vegetable oil

8 cloves garlic, minced

2 medium shallots, halved and thinly sliced

1 pound ground pork

8 ounces cherry tomatoes, halved

½ green bell pepper, diced

¼ cup tomato paste

2 tablespoons whole milk or full-fat coconut milk

1 tablespoon fish sauce

1 tablespoon brown miso paste

¼ teaspoon Roasted Chile Powder (page 226)

½ teaspoon freshly ground black pepper

1 tablespoon light brown sugar

FOR SERVING

6 warm potato buns

¾ cup crispy fried onions (like French's)

¾ cup roughly chopped fresh cilantro leaves

◆ In a wok or medium skillet, heat the oil over medium-high heat until shimmering-hot. Add the garlic and shallots and cook, stirring often, until they're fragrant and softened, about 2 minutes. Add the ground pork and sauté until mostly cooked, breaking the meat up with a spatula and stirring it around, 2 to 3 minutes. Add the tomatoes and bell pepper and cook until the tomatoes soften and give up their liquid, 2 to 3 minutes longer.

◆ Stir in the tomato paste, milk, fish sauce, miso paste, chile powder, pepper, and brown sugar. Continue cooking and stirring until a thick sauce starts to form, about 5 minutes, then remove from the heat.

◆ To serve, spoon between ¾ and 1 cup (depending on how sloppy you like it) of the pork sauce onto each of the bottom buns and top with the fried onions and cilantro. Add the top buns and serve immediately.

I LOVE MY wok

Sweet and Sour
STIR-FRY
SERVES 2 TO 4

I know what you're thinking, but this dish isn't the Chinese takeout classic (sorry to P.F. Chang's). Thai-style sweet and sour is sharper and more pungent, which in this case means fish sauce and extra vinegar mixed in with the usual sweet red glaze. Some people might look at the ingredient list and say, *Ketchup??* That's not Thai. Wrong! Thai ketchup is the best. My favorite part of this dish, though, are the juicy and sweet vegetables that work in perfect harmony with the addictive, tangy sauce. If you've never tried stir-fried cucumber before, prepare to be converted.

FOR THE SWEET AND SOUR SAUCE

2 tablespoons Thai sweet chili sauce

2 tablespoons tomato paste

2 tablespoons ketchup

1 tablespoon oyster sauce

1 tablespoon apple cider vinegar

1 tablespoon light soy sauce

2 teaspoons fish sauce

1 teaspoon light brown sugar

½ teaspoon sesame oil

¼ teaspoon ground white pepper

FOR THE STIR-FRY

12 ounces boneless, skinless chicken breast or thigh, cut into bite-size pieces

2 teaspoons light soy sauce

1 teaspoon dry sherry

¼ teaspoon ground white pepper

2 teaspoons cornstarch

2 tablespoons vegetable oil

2 cloves garlic, minced

1 small yellow onion, cut into ¼-inch slices

2 fresh red chiles, such as Fresnos, thinly sliced (or substitute red bell pepper)

½ green bell pepper, cut into bite-size pieces

1 Persian (mini) cucumber, quartered lengthwise and cut into bite-size pieces (about 1 cup)

1 plum tomato, cut into ½-inch wedges, or 1 cup halved cherry tomatoes

1 cup canned pineapple tidbits or fresh pineapple cut into ¾-inch pieces

2 scallions, cut into 1-inch sections

FOR SERVING

Fresh cilantro leaves

Cooked jasmine rice

♦ **make the sweet and sour sauce** In a small bowl, whisk together the sweet chili sauce, tomato paste, ketchup, oyster sauce, vinegar, soy sauce, fish sauce, brown sugar, sesame oil, and white pepper until combined.

♦ **make the stir-fry** In a medium bowl, toss the chicken with the soy sauce, sherry, white pepper, and cornstarch until evenly coated. Let marinate for 10 minutes.

♦ In a wok or large skillet, heat the vegetable oil over medium-high heat until shimmering-hot. Add the garlic and cook until fragrant, less than 1 minute. Add the marinated chicken and cook, stirring, until seared and mostly cooked, 3 to 4 minutes. Add the sweet and sour sauce, onion, red chiles, bell pepper, cucumber, tomato, and pineapple and toss to mix, cooking for about 1 minute, or until everything is warmed through and combined. Add the scallions and toss once more. Continue cooking until the sauce has thickened and the vegetables are just tender, less than 1 minute.

♦ *to serve* Garnish with cilantro leaves and serve with jasmine rice.

Crispy
PORK PRIK KING

SERVES 4

This recipe is just one of the many wonderful ways you can use your leftover stash of Crispy Pork Belly (page 137). Big tender pieces of crispy-cooked pork are stir-fried in the wok with fresh green beans and a big spoonful of spicy curry paste. A handful of fragrant basil leaves over the top gives it a beautiful pop of flavor. Serve with rice for a quick and easy one-pan meal.

2 tablespoons vegetable oil

2 tablespoons Thai red curry paste

4 cloves garlic, minced or crushed

2-inch piece fresh ginger, peeled and finely chopped

1 pound Crispy Pork Belly (page 137), cut into 1 by ½-inch pieces

¾ pound green beans, trimmed and cut into 2-inch pieces (about 1½ cups)

1 tablespoon oyster sauce

1 tablespoon fish sauce, plus more to taste

2 teaspoons light brown sugar, plus more to taste

1 cup packed fresh basil leaves

Cooked jasmine rice, for serving

♦ In a wok or large skillet, heat the oil over medium-high heat until shimmering-hot. Add the curry paste, garlic, and ginger and cook until fragrant, about 1 minute. Add the pork belly and green beans, tossing to coat in the curry paste. Stir in the oyster sauce, fish sauce, 2 tablespoons water, and the brown sugar. Toss to coat, then continue cooking until the liquid has reduced and the green beans are crisp-tender, 2 to 3 minutes.

♦ Remove from the heat and stir in the basil leaves. Taste and adjust the seasoning with more fish sauce or sugar if needed. Serve with rice.

Chicken
CASHEW NUT

SERVES 2 TO 4

Just like sweet and sour, this is another classic Chinese dish that we Thais have put our own stamp on. The twist here is a spoonful of chile jam, which adds a sweet roasted chile flavor and a touch of heat to the traditional savory oyster/soy sauce combination. Make sure to briefly shallow-fry the cashews and dried chiles in oil before you start the stir-frying process. It takes only a minute, and the cashews add a deep roasted flavor.

FOR THE SAUCE

2 tablespoons oyster sauce

2 tablespoons light soy sauce

4 teaspoons Sweet Chile Jam, store-bought or homemade (page 244)

2 teaspoons light brown sugar

½ teaspoon sesame oil

¼ teaspoon ground white pepper

FOR THE STIR-FRY

12 ounces boneless, skinless chicken breast or thigh, cut into bite-size pieces

2 teaspoons light soy sauce

1 teaspoon dry sherry

¼ teaspoon ground white pepper

2 teaspoons cornstarch

2 tablespoons vegetable oil

¾ cup roasted salted cashews

6 small dried red chiles, such as chiles de árbol (optional)

4 cloves garlic, minced

1 small yellow onion, halved and cut into ¼-inch wedges

1 red bell pepper, cut into bite-size pieces

½ green bell pepper, cut into bite-size pieces

3 scallions, cut into 1-inch lengths

FOR SERVING

Roasted Chile Powder (page 226)

Cooked jasmine rice

◆ **make the sauce** In a small bowl, whisk together the oyster sauce, soy sauce, 2 tablespoons water, the chile jam, brown sugar, sesame oil, and white pepper until combined.

◆ **make the stir-fry** In a medium bowl, toss the chicken with the soy sauce, sherry, white pepper, and cornstarch until evenly coated. Let marinate for 10 minutes.

◆ In a wok or large skillet, heat the vegetable oil over medium-high heat until shimmering-hot. Fry the cashews and, if using, the red chiles in the oil, just enough to darken them slightly, 1 to 2 minutes, being careful not to burn them. Use a slotted spoon to remove them from the pan and set aside on a plate lined with paper towels to drain.

♦ Add the garlic and cook until fragrant, less than 1 minute. Add the marinated chicken and cook, stirring, until seared and mostly cooked, 2 to 3 minutes. Add the sauce, onion, and bell peppers, tossing to mix. Continue cooking for about 1 minute, or until everything is heated through and combined. Add the scallions, cashews, and dried chiles and toss once more. Continue cooking until the sauce has thickened, less than 1 minute.

♦ *to serve* Garnish with a sprinkling of roasted chile powder and serve with jasmine rice.

note

Here's how to easily julienne your ginger. Start by peeling it with a spoon (not a knife), then slice the ginger lengthwise into thin planks. Stack the planks on top of one another and slice them lengthwise again to make matchsticks (julienne). If you need minced ginger, you can just slice the matchsticks very thinly crosswise to end up with tiny bits.

Seafood
PAD CHA

SERVES 4 TO 6

The two essentials for pad cha are a very hot wok and fresh seafood. The name of this dish literally comes from the loud "cha cha" sound of the ingredients when they hit the sizzling pan. What I love about this super-fast stir-fry is that when you add the chiles, cilantro, lemongrass, and garlic, the most delicious smell explodes from the wok and fills the entire room. The sauce soaks into the seafood, giving it a spicy kick. You can use a blend of seafood, but I've also made this many times with just shrimp or firm white fish fillets cut into bite-size pieces and it's just as wonderful.

3 tablespoons vegetable oil

6 cloves garlic, mashed or minced

4 fresh bird's eye chiles or 2 serrano chiles, minced

2-inch piece ginger, peeled and julienned (see Note)

1 tablespoon minced cilantro stems

2 teaspoons minced lemongrass (tender part of the stalk only)

½ teaspoon freshly ground black pepper

2 pounds mixed seafood (shrimp, fish, mussels, calamari)

2 tablespoons shaoxing wine or dry sherry

1 tablespoon oyster sauce

1 tablespoon light soy sauce

1 tablespoon fish sauce

1 tablespoon sugar

2 teaspoons grated lime zest

2 scallions, cut into 1½-inch lengths

¼ cup packed fresh basil leaves

FOR SERVING

Fresh cilantro leaves

Roasted Chile Powder (optional; page 226)

Cooked jasmine rice

◆ In a wok or large skillet, heat the oil over medium-high heat until shimmering-hot. Add the garlic, chiles, ginger, cilantro stems, lemongrass, and pepper and cook until the aromatics are fragrant and lightly browned, about 1 minute. Add the mixed seafood, sherry, oyster sauce, soy sauce, fish sauce, and sugar, tossing to coat. Continue cooking until the seafood is opaque and just cooked through and most of the liquid has evaporated, 2 to 3 minutes. Stir in the lime zest, scallions, and basil leaves.

◆ Garnish with cilantro leaves and a sprinkle of roasted chile powder. Serve with jasmine rice.

BACON-PINEAPPLE-CURRY
Fried Rice SERVES 4

When I came to the US in the 1980s, Thai restaurants in America were already coming up with dishes that were fancier and more over-the-top than anything I grew up eating back home. Pineapple fried rice is one classic example. Whoever came up with a way to get people to pay more for fried rice by putting it inside a pineapple is a genius! Surprise, surprise, when I first ordered this dish, I realized it tastes just as good as it looks.

There's a lot going on in this recipe, but somehow it all works magically: The pineapple adds a juicy sweetness that goes with the salty bacon. Curry powder provides a beautiful color and a touch of spice. There are cashews and raisins for texture, and bell pepper and green peas for freshness and color. It's a whole balanced meal inside a tropical fruit.

1 large pineapple or 1 cup canned tidbits

½ cup salted roasted cashews

6 slices bacon, diced

1 tablespoon unsalted butter

2 tablespoons minced garlic

12 ounces boneless, skinless chicken thighs, cut into bite-size pieces

½ large yellow onion, diced

2 tablespoons curry powder

3 tablespoons fish sauce, plus more to taste

2 teaspoons sugar

1 cup frozen green peas

½ teaspoon Roasted Chile Powder (page 226)

4 cups cooked jasmine rice

¼ cup golden raisins

2 fresh red chiles, such as Fresnos, thinly sliced (or substitute red bell pepper)

3 scallions, thinly sliced

1 teaspoon ground white pepper

Fresh cilantro leaves, for garnish

Lime wedges, for serving

♦ If using fresh pineapple, slice the pineapple and stem in half lengthwise. (If you're using canned pineapple, skip this whole step.) Use a knife to cut around the perimeter of the pineapple meat to form a bowl shape, then slice into the pineapple crosswise (taking care not to go through the skin on the bottom). To form the bowl, use a spoon to scoop out the slices, carefully carving out any remaining bits left behind. Cut the pineapple meat into bite-size pieces. Measure out 1 cup and set aside. Save the leftover pineapple half for a late-night snack.

♦ In a dry wok or large skillet over medium heat, toast the cashews, stirring frequently, until lightly browned and fragrant, 3 to 5 minutes. Remove the cashews and set aside.

♦ Increase the heat to medium-high, add the bacon and cook for 2 minutes to render the bacon fat and crisp the bacon. Add the butter and garlic and cook until the butter is melted and the garlic is fragrant, less than 1 minute. Add the chicken and onion and cook until the chicken is seared on the outside and the onions have softened, 2 to 3 minutes. Add the curry powder, fish sauce, sugar, peas, and chile powder, tossing to distribute the curry powder. Add the rice, reserved pineapple, raisins, and red chiles. Cook for about 2 minutes, stirring and tossing often until any liquid has evaporated and the rice starts to brown. Add the scallions, toasted cashews, and white pepper, tossing to combine. Taste and season with more fish sauce if needed.

♦ Transfer the mixture to the pineapple bowl (if using) or a serving platter. Garnish with cilantro leaves and serve with lime wedges.

tip

Because pineapples don't ripen properly after they are picked, it's important to find one that is sweet and juicy. A ripe pineapple should feel firm with a little give when you squeeze it, but the easiest way to tell is the smell. Give the bottom of the pineapple a big whiff—if it smells like delicious tropical sunshine, it is ready to go.

STIR-FRIED SPAGHETTI
with Chile Jam and
Sun-Dried Tomatoes

SERVES 2

I'm not exactly sure how this recipe came together. It might have been inspired by a craving Chrissy had for a certain pasta dish from CPK (that's California Pizza Kitchen for those not in the know), or it might have been because I was thinking about how popular spaghetti has become at restaurants in Thailand these days (some places even have green curry spaghetti!). Whatever it was, I ended up raiding the big kitchen pantry at the house and came up with this beautiful noodle creation—a little Thai, a little Italian. Thaitalian? I'm a big fan of tangy sun-dried tomatoes and find they're much better when stir-fried until tender and soft. Meanwhile the chile jam provides a sweet-savory flavor that clings to the pasta—another reason to always have a jar in your fridge. Toss with garlic bread crumbs and fresh basil and prepare to be amazed.

2 tablespoons olive oil, plus more for drizzling

4 cloves garlic, thinly sliced

½ cup panko bread crumbs

8 ounces spaghetti

3 tablespoons Sweet Chile Jam, store-bought or homemade (page 244)

¼ cup drained and finely chopped oil-packed sun-dried tomatoes

2 teaspoons fish sauce

½ cup chopped fresh basil leaves

Freshly ground black pepper and kosher salt

Grated Parmesan, for serving (optional)

♦ In a wok or large skillet, heat the oil over medium-high heat until shimmering-hot. Add the garlic and cook until fragrant, about 15 seconds. Stir in the panko and cook until golden, 2 to 3 minutes. Transfer the mixture to a bowl and set aside.

♦ In a large pot of salted boiling water, cook the spaghetti just shy of al dente. Drain well, reserving some of the pasta water (¼ cup should be plenty).

♦ Place the pan used to toast the panko over medium heat. Add the chile jam and sun-dried tomatoes and cook until sizzling and fragrant, about 2 minutes. Add the hot drained pasta, fish sauce, and about 2 tablespoons of the pasta water and toss well. Continue cooking until a thick sauce forms and clings to the noodles. Remove the pan from the heat, add the panko mixture and basil, and toss well. Taste and season with plenty of pepper and a pinch of salt, if needed.

♦ Drizzle the pasta with a little more oil just before serving. Serve with grated Parmesan, if desired.

"Bow-Thai" SEE EW SERVES 4

One question people ask me all the time on Instagram is how to make pad see ew. It's a good question! Whenever we order takeout from one of the many excellent Thai restaurants in LA, we almost always order it, the good kind where the sweet soy has caramelized just right and soaked into the chewy pan-fried noodles. But finding the Thai wide rice noodles can be hard. What to do then?

The solution came to me one day when I was thinking about spaghetti. Dried spaghetti noodles are very popular in Thailand these days, and people use them in all kinds of traditional stir-fry dishes. So why not other kinds of pasta? After a few experiments, I discovered that supermarket bow-tie pasta made a good substitute for pad see ew noodles. The bow-tie shape helps them soak up the sweet dark soy sauce in their little folds and wrinkles, and when cooked al dente they end up perfectly chewy-tender after being cooked in the very hot wok. Even if this "pad see ew" is not exactly the same as takeout, I am proud of my noodle innovation. Feel free to enter my name for the Nobel Prize this year, thank you.

½ pound boneless, skinless chicken thighs or pork shoulder, cut into bite-size pieces

1 teaspoon ground white pepper

1 tablespoon oyster sauce

1 teaspoon sesame oil

1 teaspoon light brown sugar

12 ounces bow-tie pasta

¼ cup vegetable oil

6 cloves garlic, finely chopped

4 large eggs, lightly beaten

½ pound Chinese broccoli or regular broccoli, cut into ½-inch pieces (about 2 cups)

⅓ cup Thai sweet dark soy sauce, store-bought or homemade (page 232)

2 tablespoons light soy sauce

½ cup fresh basil leaves

FOR SERVING

Pickled Chile Vinegar (page 239)

Roasted Chile Powder (page 226)

◆ In a medium bowl, combine the chicken, white pepper, oyster sauce, sesame oil, and brown sugar, tossing to coat. Cover and marinate at room temperature for 30 minutes to 1 hour (or overnight in the fridge).

◆ Meanwhile, bring a large pot of salted water to a boil. Cook the pasta a few minutes less than package directions for al dente, then drain well.

◆ In a wok or large skillet, heat 2 tablespoons oil over medium-high heat until shimmering-hot. Add the garlic and cook until fragrant, about 20 seconds. Stir in the chicken and broccoli and cook, stirring often, about 3 minutes, until the meat is lightly browned and the broccoli is almost tender.

◆ Stir in the eggs and cook until the eggs are dry and lightly browned, about 1 minute. Stir in the pasta, sweet soy sauce, and light soy sauce. Cook, tossing often, until the pasta is warmed through and coated evenly in sauce, about 3 minutes. Stir in the basil and turn off the heat.

◆ Serve immediately with the pickled chile vinegar and chile powder on the side.

CURRIES & stews

Duck Red Curry
WITH SQUASH

SERVES 4

I like to use skin-on duck breasts here, because you can get the skin browned and crispy in the pan first, then use any leftover duck fat to fry the curry paste and bring out its deep aroma and flavor. But another easy option is to use preroasted Chinese duck from any Chinese takeout place and stir it in at the end until warmed through.

2 skin-on duck breasts (about 8 ounces each)

2 tablespoons Thai red curry paste

1 (13.5-ounce) can full-fat coconut milk

2 cups low-sodium chicken broth

½ small kabocha or butternut squash (about 1½ pounds), peeled, seeded, and cut into 1-inch cubes

1 tablespoon light brown sugar

2 tablespoons fish sauce

½ cup packed fresh basil leaves

2 fresh red chiles, such as Fresnos, thinly sliced (or substitute red bell pepper)

Cooked jasmine rice or Buttery Roti Bread (page 222), for serving

◆ Heat a large saucepan or cast-iron skillet over medium heat. Use a knife to score the duck skin five or six times to cut through the layer of fat, then add the duck to the pan, skin side down. Cook without moving the duck until the skin is golden and crisp, about 7 minutes. Remove the duck and set aside. Pour off the remaining fat and reserve for later (it's great for stir-frying), leaving about 3 tablespoons in the pan.

◆ Stir the curry paste into the duck fat and cook until fragrant, less than 1 minute. Add the coconut milk, broth, and squash, stirring to make sure the squash is submerged. Bring to a boil, then reduce to a simmer, cover, and cook, stirring occasionally, until the squash is tender, 20 to 25 minutes.

◆ Meanwhile, slice the duck crosswise against the grain ½ inch thick.

◆ Once the squash has been cooking for 10 to 15 minutes, uncover the pan and stir in the sliced duck, brown sugar, and fish sauce. Continue cooking, uncovered, until the duck is firm but slightly springy, about 5 minutes. Remove the pan from the heat and gently stir in the basil and red chiles. Serve with rice or roti bread.

Roasted Veggie
GREEN CURRY

SERVES 6 TO 8

For me, green curry is all about the vegetables. The fresh green chile flavor of the curry paste is so bright and complex, which complements whatever healthy and vibrant vegetables are hanging out in your fridge's crisper drawer. The twist here is that rather than boiling the veggies in the curry sauce, I put them all on a sheet pan and roast them, which gives them a slightly smoky-caramelized taste that is a perfect match for the zesty curry paste. Since the roasted veggies will be mostly tender when you add them to the curry, you need to simmer them only for a few minutes before finishing off the curry with fresh basil.

1 small peeled sweet potato (about 6 ounces), cut into 1-inch chunks

1 medium Chinese eggplant (about 6 ounces), cut into 1-inch chunks

8 ounces canned baby corn, drained and halved

2 fresh red chiles, such as Fresnos, thinly sliced (or substitute red bell pepper)

1 zucchini (about 6 ounces), halved lengthwise and cut crosswise into half-moons

6 ounces green beans, trimmed and cut into 2-inch pieces

Vegetable oil

2 teaspoons kosher salt, plus more to taste

1 teaspoon ground white pepper

1 (13.5-ounce) can full-fat coconut milk

1 (4-ounce) can Thai green curry paste

2 tablespoons minced cilantro stems

1 tablespoon light soy sauce

2 teaspoons light brown sugar

10 ounces canned bamboo shoots, drained and rinsed

1 cup packed fresh basil leaves

FOR SERVING

Bean sprouts

Cooked jasmine rice or cooked rice vermicelli

◆ Preheat the oven to 425°F.

◆ On two large sheet pans, arrange the sweet potato, eggplant, baby corn, red chiles, zucchini, and green beans in an even layer. Drizzle the vegetables generously with oil and sprinkle with the salt and white pepper, tossing on the pan to coat.

◆ Roast the vegetables until they are browned but still crisp at the center, 20 to 25 minutes, stirring at least once during roasting for even browning.

◆ Meanwhile, in a large saucepan, bring the coconut milk to a boil over medium-high heat. Continue to boil until the coconut milk has reduced and the oil has started to

separate, 2 to 3 minutes. Stir in the curry paste and cilantro stems. Continue cooking until fragrant, about 1 minute. Add the remaining coconut milk, 3 cups water, the soy sauce, and brown sugar. Bring to a boil, then reduce the heat, cover, and simmer while the vegetables finish roasting.

♦ Remove the vegetables from the oven and let them cool slightly. Add the bamboo shoots to the curry along with the roasted vegetables, stirring gently to combine. Continue simmering for a few more minutes, making sure the sweet potatoes and eggplant are tender and the bamboo shoots are warmed through.

♦ Remove from the heat and stir in the basil leaves. Taste and season with salt if needed. Serve the curry topped with bean sprouts and a side of jasmine rice.

Massaman
BEEF CURRY

SERVES 4 TO 6

Slow-cooked and filled with tender beef and potatoes, Massaman is a rich and mild coconut curry that comes from the southern part of Thailand. If you love Indian curries, you will really love this one—warm spices like cardamom, coriander, and clove make it taste fragrant and extra luxurious.

When you have a short attention span like I do, sometimes making curry can be hard, because it takes patience (unlike my papaya salad, which I can make in minutes). My suggestion is to reduce the heat all the way and let the curry cook slowly while you go do your hair or paint your toenails. Multitasking!

One more thought: I use store-bought curry paste for this recipe (and for most of the curries I make), because it saves so much time and the flavor is spot-on. Even in Thailand, very few people make their own curry paste at home. My favorite brands are Maesri and Aroy-D, which come in little cans and can be found at any Asian market.

2 pounds beef brisket or chuck roast, cut into 1½-inch chunks

2 teaspoons kosher salt

3 tablespoons vegetable oil

2 (13.5-ounce) cans full-fat coconut milk

1 (4-ounce) can Massaman curry paste

1 tablespoon light brown sugar

1 tablespoon tomato paste

3 bay leaves

1 pound Yukon Gold or other waxy potatoes, peeled and halved (keep in cold water to prevent browning)

1 small onion, halved and cut into ½-inch wedges

¼ cup salted roasted peanuts

1 tablespoon fresh lime juice, plus more to taste

1 teaspoon fish sauce, plus more to taste

FOR SERVING

½ cup packed fresh cilantro leaves

2 fresh red chiles, such as Fresnos, thinly sliced (or substitute red bell pepper)

Cooked jasmine rice

recipe continues →

♦ Sprinkle the beef evenly with the salt.

♦ In a large pot or wok, heat the oil over medium-high heat until shimmering-hot. Add the beef and cook, stirring constantly, until browned on all sides, about 6 minutes total. Transfer the beef to a plate. Add 1 can of the coconut milk to the pan and bring to a boil. Once the coconut milk has reduced slightly, about 2 minutes, stir in the curry paste and cook until aromatic, about 2 minutes. Return the beef to the pot and add the brown sugar, tomato paste, bay leaves, ¾ cup of water, and the remaining can of coconut milk. Add enough water to cover the beef, reduce the heat to a simmer, cover, and cook, stirring occasionally and adding water if needed, until the beef is tender or near-tender (use a fork to test), about 1 hour.

♦ Uncover and stir in the potatoes, onion, and peanuts. Continue to simmer, uncovered, until the potatoes are soft and tender, about 30 minutes, stirring occasionally. Stir in the lime juice and fish sauce, tasting and adding more if needed.

♦ Divide the curry into bowls and garnish with cilantro leaves and sliced chiles. Serve with rice.

PEPPER-STYLE KHAO SOI
(Curry Noodle Soup)

SERVES 4

When you can't decide if you want a bowl of curry or a bowl of noodles, khao soi is here to comfort you. Although this dish is from northern Thailand and I grew up in northeastern Thailand (very different!), I've learned to make a mean khao soi, because everyone here seems to have a craving for it these days, myself included.

My method for khao soi is not fussy at all: a thick and rich yellow curry made with simmered bone-in chicken (more flavor that way) and a combo of both boiled and crunchy fried noodles, which can be either egg noodles or fettuccine depending on what you have in the cupboard. What makes a big bowl of khao soi shine for me is the toppings: pungent raw shallots, crisp bean sprouts, fresh cilantro, a generous squeeze of lime, and a spoonful of chile oil.

1 cup plus 2 tablespoons vegetable oil

2 tablespoons Thai red curry paste

2 tablespoons curry powder

2 (13.5-ounce) cans full-fat coconut milk

2 cups low-sodium chicken broth

2 pounds bone-in, skin-on chicken thighs, wings, or drumsticks

1 pound Chinese egg noodles or fettuccine

1 tablespoon light brown sugar, plus more to taste

2 tablespoons fish sauce, plus more to taste

FOR SERVING

Thinly sliced shallots or red onion

Bean sprouts

Fresh cilantro leaves

Lime wedges

Spicy Chile Crisp (page 231)

◆ In a large heavy pot, heat 2 tablespoons of the oil over medium-high heat until shimmering-hot. Add the curry paste and curry powder and cook, stirring constantly, until fragrant, about 1 minute. Stir in the coconut milk and chicken broth and bring to a boil. Reduce to a simmer, add the chicken, cover, and cook until fork-tender, 20 to 25 minutes.

recipe continues ⟶

♦ Meanwhile, in a large pot of boiling water, cook the noodles according to package directions. Drain well. Measure out about one-quarter of the cooked noodles, setting the rest aside.

♦ In a medium saucepan, heat the remaining 1 cup oil over medium-high heat until shimmering-hot. Working in batches, if necessary, add the measured-out cooked noodles and fry until golden brown and crisp, about 2 minutes. Drain on a plate lined with paper towels and set aside.

♦ Remove the cooked chicken from the pot and set on a plate. Let it cool slightly, then remove the chicken meat from the bones, slice, and stir back into the pot. Discard the bones. (You can also leave the chicken on the bones if you want.) Season the curry with the brown sugar and fish sauce, tasting and adding more if needed.

♦ To serve, divide the unfried cooked noodles among four bowls and top with the curry. Garnish with shallots, bean sprouts, cilantro leaves, and the fried noodles. Serve with lime wedges and spicy chile crisp.

notes

Five-spice powder is a very fragrant and unique spice blend that originated in China and is used in some Chinese-Thai dishes like moo palo (five-spice pork stew). It is usually made with star anise, cloves, fennel, cinnamon, and peppercorns. Some brands might mix in ginger, coriander, or bay leaf as well. Though no two are exactly alike, any Thai or Chinese brand of five-spice should achieve the right flavor.

In many recipes I use **white pepper** instead of black pepper. What's the difference? White pepper has a citrusy and floral taste and is earthier and less sharp than black pepper, which makes it good for balancing Thai dishes that already have many bold flavors going on. It's not a firm rule, however, and sometimes I like black pepper in dishes that might normally call for white pepper.

Five-Spice
PORK STEW

SERVES 8

This hearty soup/stew was one of my favorite dishes to eat during chilly nights growing up in Thailand. What makes it stand out is the intoxicating aroma of Chinese five-spice powder (see Notes) and sweet dark soy sauce, which adds a deep caramel flavor to the broth. After hunks of pork shoulder are tossed in the sweet spice-infused glaze, they get braised until the meat is soft enough to cut with a spoon. You can also add your favorite leafy greens and simmer them until tender before serving.

10 cloves garlic, peeled

3 tablespoons finely chopped cilantro stems

Kosher salt

2 tablespoons vegetable oil

2 pounds boneless pork shoulder or skinless pork belly, cut into 1½-inch cubes

2 tablespoons light brown sugar

3 tablespoons Thai sweet dark soy sauce, store-bought or homemade (page 232)

2 tablespoons light soy sauce, plus more to taste

4 teaspoons Chinese or Thai five-spice powder (see Note)

½ teaspoon ground white pepper (see Notes)

2 cinnamon sticks

3 whole star anise

3 bay leaves

3 ounces store-bought deep-fried tofu, halved or cut into bite-size pieces

4 soft-boiled eggs, peeled and halved

Fresh cilantro leaves, for garnish

Cooked jasmine rice, for serving

◆ In a mortar, mash the garlic and cilantro stems with the pestle until a smooth paste forms, adding a pinch of salt to help it along. (Or, process in a mini food processor to form a paste.)

◆ In a large pot, heat the oil over medium-high heat until shimmering-hot. Add the garlic paste and cook until fragrant, less than 1 minute. Add the pork and brown on all sides, about 4 minutes. Add the brown sugar, dark soy sauce, light soy sauce, five-spice powder, and white pepper and stir to combine. When the sauce comes to a boil and starts to thicken, add 8 cups water (to cover) and add the cinnamon sticks, star anise, bay leaves, and 1 teaspoon kosher salt.

◆ Bring to a boil, then reduce to a simmer, cover, and cook for 40 minutes. Add the fried tofu and boiled eggs and simmer until the pork is tender (test with a fork), about 20 minutes longer. Taste and season with soy sauce, as needed.

◆ Remove from the heat and cool slightly. Garnish with cilantro and serve with rice.

Spicy Coconut
TOM KHA

SERVES 4

Creamy, coconutty tom kha is the soup that everyone knows from their neighborhood Thai restaurant. If you leave out the coconut milk, you get tom yum, which is the other famous spicy-sour soup that is on all Thai restaurant menus. I know these soups well. I've been making tom yum since I was old enough to cook—it was Chrissy and Tina's version of chicken noodle soup as kids—but there was something that made me raise my eyebrows at tom kha. I love my soup as hot and sour as possible, and pouring in coconut milk seemed like watering (or milking!) down the flavors. But because Chrissy and John love tom kha so much, I figured what the heck, I'll come up with my own recipe that can make everyone happy. Though the coconut adds creaminess, the fragrant and savory flavors shine through in each spoonful. Mission accomplished.

2 stalks lemongrass, tough outer layers removed

2-inch piece fresh galangal or ginger, peeled and thinly sliced

4 cups low-sodium chicken broth

1 (13.5-ounce) can full-fat coconut milk

1½ pounds boneless, skinless chicken thighs, cut into bite-size pieces

8 ounces mixed mushrooms, stemmed and quartered or halved

1 plum tomato, roughly chopped

¼ cup fish sauce, plus more to taste

1 teaspoon light brown sugar, plus more to taste

2 fresh bird's eye chiles or 1 serrano chile, minced

2 scallions, thinly sliced

1 teaspoon Roasted Chile Powder (page 226)

1 tablespoon Sweet Chile Jam, store-bought or homemade (page 244)

1 tablespoon grated lime zest

¼ cup fresh lime juice (about 2 limes), plus more to taste

4 makrut lime leaves, halved diagonally (optional)

FOR SERVING

Fresh cilantro leaves

Lime wedges

Sweet Chile Jam (page 244) or Spicy Chile Crisp (page 231)

◆ Cut the tops off the lemongrass, leaving about three-quarters of the stalk. Using the butt of a knife or other heavy object, lightly pound the lemongrass stalks and galangal slices until smashed. Cut the lemongrass into 4-inch sections.

◆ In a large saucepan, combine the lemongrass, galangal, chicken broth, and coconut milk and bring to a boil. Reduce the heat to a simmer and add the chicken thighs,

mushrooms, tomato, fish sauce, and brown sugar. Simmer, stirring occasionally, until the mushrooms are tender and the chicken is cooked through, 5 to 6 minutes. Remove the pan from heat and stir in the chiles, scallions, chile powder, chile jam, lime zest, lime juice, and lime leaves. Taste and adjust the seasoning with more fish sauce, brown sugar, or lime juice as needed.

♦ At home, we usually leave the lemongrass and galangal in the bowl and eat around them, but you can fish them out before serving if you like. Sprinkle the soup with cilantro leaves just before serving, with lime wedges and sweet chile jam or spicy chile crisp on the side.

Choo Chee
CURRIED SALMON

SERVES 4

Choo chee is the Thai phrase that describes the sound of sizzling, like the noise you hear when you order a plate of fajitas. I've always had a soft spot for choo chee curry—instead of being a soupy curry, it's a thick, creamy sauce that is simmered in the pan until it pops and sizzles and is then poured over any kind of seafood (baked salmon is my favorite). As a bonus, you can make the whole dish using one pan.

4 skin-on salmon fillets (6 to 8 ounces each), any bones removed

1 tablespoon light soy sauce

½ teaspoon garlic powder

¼ teaspoon ground white pepper

4 tablespoons vegetable oil

2 tablespoons Thai red curry paste

5 fresh makrut lime leaves, halved lengthwise (optional)

1½ cups full-fat coconut milk

2 tablespoons fish sauce

2 tablespoons light brown sugar

Grated zest of 2 limes

2 teaspoons fresh lime juice

¼ cup thinly sliced fresh basil leaves

2 fresh red chiles, such as Fresnos, thinly sliced (or substitute red bell pepper)

Cooked jasmine rice, for serving

◆ Rub the salmon all over with the soy sauce and sprinkle with garlic powder and white pepper.

◆ In a large skillet, heat 2 tablespoons of the oil over medium-high heat until shimmering-hot. Add the salmon skin side down and cook until the skin is crisp, about 3 minutes. Reduce the heat to medium, flip the fillets over, and cook until the fish is firm and flakes easily with a fork, 2 to 4 minutes. Remove the salmon from the pan.

◆ Wipe out the pan with a paper towel. Add the remaining oil and heat over medium heat until shimmering-hot. Add the curry paste and lime leaves and cook, stirring, for 1 to 2 minutes, until fragrant. Add 1 cup of the coconut milk and bring to a bubble, then stir in the fish sauce, brown sugar, lime zest, and lime juice. Once the sugar is dissolved, return the salmon to the pan and turn to coat in the sauce (you're just glazing the salmon with the sauce—you're not cooking the salmon any more).

◆ Remove the pan from the heat and transfer to a serving plate. Drizzle each fillet with 1 tablespoon coconut milk, and garnish with basil and chiles. Serve with rice.

A LITTLE
dessert

KANOM KROK
(Thai Coconut Pancakes)

When I was ten years old, my first job was selling kanom krok, which are little half-moon coconut pancakes that are crispy on the outside with a soft and smooth coconut cream topping, and since Thai people love a little savory with their sweet, we often sprinkle on some kernels of sweet corn or finely chopped scallions to add a pop of flavor and color. Popular all over Thailand, I would wake up very early to make the rice flour batter, then cook them outside and sell them to people heading to work—all before I left for school at 7 a.m. I still remember that feeling of counting the little stack of money in my hand and being so excited.

In our family, kanom krok is a tradition that is passed down from mother to daughter. My grandma taught my mom, and my mom taught me. Even before we were allowed to use the stove, my sisters and I would play in the dirt and pretend we were making little mud pie versions of kanom krok. When Chrissy and Tina were little, I taught them how to make the pancakes so they were just the right texture. They were really skilled at it, too! It was the perfect food for us to cook and eat together. When I was working on this book, Luna got to make her first kanom krok, ladling the batter in the hot pan and watching the edges bubble. She was a natural, so it must be in our genes.

note ———

Both the batter and topping can be made in advance and stored in the fridge for up to a day. If the batter has thickened too much, add water until it's thin enough to pour easily.

note ———

To make kanom krok, you need a special pan/griddle, which has several circular cups to cook the batter. I've had my cast-iron kanom krok griddle forever, but you can find them very easily online or at most Thai supermarkets. You can also use a pan designed for Dutch aebleskiver or Japanese takoyaki, or an electric cake pop maker, though the capacity of the cups may vary slightly.

FOR THE BATTER

1 cup rice flour

¼ cup cooked jasmine rice

¼ cup full-fat coconut milk

¼ cup unsweetened shredded coconut

3 tablespoons light brown sugar

½ teaspoon kosher salt

FOR THE TOPPING

1 cup full-fat coconut milk

1 tablespoon tapioca starch or cornstarch

2 tablespoons granulated sugar

¼ teaspoon kosher salt

TO FINISH

Melted coconut oil, for cooking, or vegetable oil

8 scallions, finely chopped

½ cup canned corn kernels, drained

♦ **make the batter** In a blender, combine 2 cups warm water, the rice flour, cooked rice, coconut milk, shredded coconut, brown sugar, and salt and blend until smooth. Set the blender jar aside (you can use it to pour the batter later).

♦ **make the topping** In a small bowl, whisk together the coconut milk, tapioca starch, granulated sugar, and salt until dissolved and no lumps remain.

♦ **to finish** Place a kanom krok pan (see Note below) over medium heat and let it heat up for a few minutes (the pan is ready when a drop of water sizzles immediately). Set a wire rack for the cooked pancakes on your work surface. Have the bowl of topping nearby.

♦ Brush the cups of the pan generously with oil. Use a spatula to give the batter a good stir, then fill each cup about two-thirds full with batter. After the batter has cooked for about 1 minute, give the bowl of topping a good stir and spoon enough topping into the center of each pancake to completely fill the cup. Sprinkle each pancake with a few scallions and corn kernels.

♦ Reduce the heat to medium-low and loosely cover the pan with a lid (any large lid will do) or tent with foil. Cook, covered, until the edges of the pancakes are golden brown and the tops are no longer watery, about 6 minutes (since the pan is nonstick, use a small spoon to check the bottom of the pancakes to see if they're browned). Using a small spoon or butter knife, gently lift the pancakes from the pan and place on the wire rack. Repeat with the remaining batter. Serve the kanom krok warm.

---
note

If you're not able to find a special pan for kanom krok, you can use an oven and a muffin pan to get pretty close to the real deal. Here's how:

Muffin Pan Method

◇ Preheat the oven to 450°F. Place a muffin pan in the oven and heat for 5 minutes.

◇ Carefully remove the muffin pan from the oven and add a few drops of oil to each cup, using a heatproof brush or paper towel to evenly coat the cups. Place the pan back in the oven to heat the oil, 2 minutes.

◇ Remove the pan from the oven and fill each cup about ¾ inch deep with batter; you should hear it sizzle. Gently tilt the pan so the batter spreads evenly. Bake until the batter has formed a skin, 3 to 4 minutes.

◇ Carefully spoon a generous tablespoon of the topping into the center of the mostly cooked batter, filling each cup another ¾ inch or so. Sprinkle each with corn and scallions.

◇ Return the pan to the oven and cook until filling is firm, 12 to 15 minutes. Use a butter knife to carefully loosen the kanom krok from the surface of the pan tray. Repeat with the remaining batter.

◇ Serve the kanom krok warm.

Sweet-Salty COCONUT STICKY RICE WITH MANGO

SERVES 4

Mango sticky rice was always a special treat for me and my siblings when we were growing up. After dinner, my mom would buy it from the street vendors who rode around on bicycles selling it in little banana leaf packages. It was an expensive dessert, so we always shared one among all five of us. Two bites each!

Chrissy and Luna love when I make mango sticky rice, but I always tell them I have to find a really good mango first. That's essential. The little yellow ones are my favorite, but any type of mango will work. What's important is that the mango be very ripe but not mushy.

The coconut sticky rice? That's the easy part. Cook the sticky rice in the microwave and then mix it with the hot, salty-sweet coconut milk. The heat from the coconut milk will help it soak into the rice and make it so creamy and tender. All done. Fresh mangoes are great, but if you don't have any, coconut sticky rice is so good with everything—spicy curries, grilled steak, even fried chicken. There's no such thing as making too much.

½ cup unsweetened shredded coconut

1½ cups Thai sticky rice

1 (13.5-ounce) can full-fat coconut milk

¼ cup sugar

1½ teaspoons kosher salt

2 large ripe mangoes, peeled, pitted, and thinly sliced

Toasted sesame seeds, for garnish (optional)

Mint leaves, for garnish (optional)

◆ In a dry skillet, toast the coconut over medium-low heat, stirring, until lightly browned and fragrant, 4 to 5 minutes. Transfer to a plate to cool (don't leave it in the skillet or it might burn).

◆ Place the sticky rice in a microwave-safe bowl and cover with 1¾ cups warm water. Let soak for at least 10 minutes or up to 1 hour. Cover the bowl with an upside-down plate or plastic wrap and microwave on high for 3 minutes. Carefully stir the rice from top to bottom, then cover and cook the rice for another 3 minutes. Repeat the process, stirring and microwaving 3 minutes at a time, until all the water has been absorbed and the rice has turned translucent (this means it's cooked). Set aside to cool slightly.

◆ In a medium saucepan, bring the coconut milk to a boil over medium heat. Reduce the heat to a simmer, add the sugar and salt, and stir until they dissolve. Remove from the heat, pour the hot coconut milk over the warm sticky rice, and stir to combine. Let sit for 5 minutes so the rice can absorb the coconut milk.

◆ Transfer to a serving bowl and top with the toasted coconut. Serve with sliced mango. If desired, garnish with sesame seeds and fresh mint.

PINEAPPLE SOFT SERVE
with Spicy Candied Coconut   SERVES 6

Ever since Chrissy and John took Luna to Disneyland for her birthday a couple years ago, we've been obsessed with re-creating the famous Dole Whip, a creamy-tangy pineapple soft serve that's sold there. It turns out that there's no secret Disney magic involved (don't tell them I said that!); all you really need is a blender or food processor, frozen pineapple, coconut milk, and a few other basic items. If you're starting with fresh pineapple cubes, just make sure they're frozen solid before you blend—that's what gives the dairy-free soft serve its silky texture.

Of course, I had to add a spicy Pepper Thai twist, too—a crunchy candied coconut topping with a kick of heat.

FOR THE CHILE-COCONUT

¾ cup unsweetened shredded coconut

½ teaspoon Roasted Chile Powder (page 226)

2 teaspoons kosher salt

2 tablespoons agave nectar

FOR THE SOFT SERVE

3 cups frozen pineapple chunks, or fresh pineapple cut into ½-inch chunks and frozen overnight

¾ cup full-fat coconut milk

2 teaspoons fresh lime juice

3 tablespoons agave nectar

¼ teaspoon kosher salt

♦ *make the chile-coconut*   In a dry skillet or saucepan, toast the coconut over medium-low heat, stirring frequently, until the flakes are mostly golden in color. Remove from the heat and immediately add the chile powder, salt, and agave nectar. Stir until the mixture is combined, then let the coconut cool completely before transferring to a bowl.

♦ *make the soft serve*   In a food processor or blender, combine the frozen pineapple, coconut milk, lime juice, agave, and salt and pulse until the pineapple is finely chopped. Then process or blend until smooth and airy, 3 to 4 minutes, stopping to scrape down the sides of the bowl/jar as needed.

♦ Serve immediately. (Or transfer to a resealable top plastic bag and freeze until just firm, about 20 minutes. Trim off the corner of the plastic bag and pipe the mixture into serving bowls, soft serve–style.) Garnish with the candied chile-coconut.

Crispy
FRIED BANANAS

SERVES 6

Back in my hometown there was an old woman who was famous for selling fried bananas, Thai-style—meaning a tempura-like batter with coconut and sesame seeds mixed in. The bananas were crunchy outside and sweet and gooey inside—and came in tiny paper bags. I used to fold one hundred bags for her and she'd pay me one baht for each and give me the bananas that broke. I loved it!

For the cookbook I tried to re-create those famous bananas, but I never got the taste right. Then I had an idea. The children of the old woman were still selling them, so I had one of my cousins ask for the secret recipe. They told me I could share it with you as long as you promise not to move to Korat and open a fried-banana stand!

¾ cup all-purpose flour

¾ cup rice flour

2 tablespoons cornstarch

2 teaspoons baking powder

½ cup sugar

2 teaspoons kosher salt

¾ cup unsweetened shredded coconut

¼ cup sesame seeds

Vegetable oil, for deep-frying

6 large ripe (not brown) bananas, peeled

Vanilla or salted caramel ice cream (or your favorite flavor), for serving

◆ In a large bowl, sift together the all-purpose flour, rice flour, cornstarch, and baking powder. Add the sugar and salt, then gradually pour in 1 cup warm water, mixing until smooth. Add the coconut and sesame seeds and stir the batter to combine.

◆ Set a wire rack in a sheet pan or line a plate with paper towels. Pour at least 2 inches oil into a wok or large heavy pot, leaving a few inches of clearance from the rim. Heat the oil over medium heat to 370°F (use a deep-fry thermometer or test the oil by adding a drop of batter; if it sizzles immediately and doesn't burn, it's ready).

◆ While the oil is heating, halve the bananas crosswise, then slice each half lengthwise. Place next to the fryer along with the batter.

◆ When the oil is hot, working in batches, dip the banana slices in the batter to coat, then add them to the oil (don't worry about dripping batter). Fry until golden brown, flipping once, about 4 minutes total. Use a frying spider or slotted spoon to transfer the bananas to the wire rack or paper towels. Serve warm with a scoop of vanilla or salted caramel ice cream.

Thai Tea
BREAD PUDDING

Creamy and sweet, a good Thai tea is a dessert as much as it is a drink. In Thailand, the famous iced tea vendors line the streets year-round, mixing the spiced orange tea with cream and sugar and then pouring it back and forth between metal cups so it becomes extra frothy. There's nothing more satisfying on a hot day or, if you're in my family, when you're trying to cool down your taste buds after eating some of my extra-spicy Green Papaya Salad (page 60).

I use Thai tea, with its beautiful sunset color (which comes from strong-brewed tea mixed with cream), in the custardy base of this brioche bread pudding, which is sweetened with condensed milk. Try to find real Thai tea mix made with tea leaves (not the presweetened instant stuff), which has a beautiful and unique smell to it. They always sell it at Thai markets, or you can order it for cheap online. And whatever you don't use for the bread pudding, you'll go through quickly making iced tea. This bread pudding is so rich and delicious by itself, but I like to go the extra mile and serve it with an easy orange-vanilla sauce and a spoonful of whipped cream.

3 tablespoons unsalted butter

1 (14- to 16-ounce) loaf brioche or challah bread, cut into 1-inch cubes

3 large eggs

2 large egg yolks

½ cup packed light brown sugar, plus more for sprinkling

½ teaspoon ground cardamom

½ teaspoon ground cloves

1 teaspoon kosher salt

1 (14-ounce) can sweetened condensed milk

1 cup half-and-half

2 cups double-strength brewed Thai tea (see Note)

Orange-Vanilla Rum Sauce (recipe follows), for serving

Sweetened whipped cream, for serving (optional)

Note ———

Loose-leaf Thai tea mix can be found in Asian markets or online; to create a tea concentrate for this recipe, brew using double the amount of tea called for on the package.

recipe continues ➡

♦ Preheat the oven to 325°F. Grease a 9 by 13-inch baking dish with 1 tablespoon of the butter.

♦ Spread the bread cubes onto a sheet pan and bake until dry, tossing halfway through, 10 to 12 minutes. Remove from the oven and set aside to cool.

♦ In a large bowl, whisk together the whole eggs, egg yolks, brown sugar, cardamom, cloves, and salt until smooth. Whisk in the condensed milk, half-and-half, and Thai tea until thoroughly combined.

♦ Add the bread cubes to the mixture, gently folding them with a rubber spatula until the cubes are saturated. Transfer to the prepared baking dish and let sit for 20 minutes to absorb the liquid.

♦ In a saucepan or in the microwave, melt the remaining 2 tablespoons butter and dab over the top of the pudding. Sprinkle with 1 tablespoon or so of brown sugar. Transfer to the oven and bake until the center of the pudding has set and releases no liquid when pressed, 40 to 45 minutes. Cool for at least 20 minutes before serving.

♦ To serve, cut into squares and top with orange-vanilla rum sauce and a dollop of whipped cream, if you like.

ORANGE-VANILLA RUM SAUCE MAKES ABOUT 1¼ CUPS

1 cup half-and-half

¼ cup sugar

1 tablespoon cornstarch

1½ teaspoons vanilla extract

2 tablespoons dark or spiced rum (optional)

Grated zest of 1 orange (about 1 tablespoon)

2 tablespoons unsalted butter

Kosher salt

♦ In a medium saucepan, whisk together the half-and-half, sugar, cornstarch, vanilla, dark rum, and orange zest. Bring to a simmer over medium heat. Whisk in the butter, then cook, stirring constantly, until the sauce is thickened and slightly reduced, about 3 minutes. Remove from the heat and season with salt to taste. Serve warm. Store leftovers in an airtight container in the fridge for up to 5 days.

PUMPKIN CUSTARD
with Walnut-Coconut Crumble

SERVES 6 TO 8

Thai pumpkin custard, or what we call sankaya, is one of my all-time top desserts. It starts with a kabocha squash (which some people call a Japanese pumpkin) that is hollowed out and filled with a lightly sweet custard made from coconut milk and eggs. The whole pumpkin is steamed until the custard is set and the pumpkin is soft enough to pierce with a fork. The savory flavor of the kabocha mellows the sweetness from the custard, so you end up with a dessert that is very balanced. In Thailand, people mostly make it for special occasions like a wedding or when they go to temple, but as long as you have a covered pot big enough to fit a small squash, it's easy to prepare anytime.

But let me also tell you about that crumble. Chrissy and John will eat anything with a crumble topping—cobbler, cake, muffins—so I decided to cobble (get it?) together my own with shredded coconut and walnuts (you can use your favorite nut, too). *So good.* We couldn't believe it. Chrissy was running around the kitchen excited and ended up eating half of it before we sprinkled it over the pumpkin. Crumble and custard—BFFs meant to be.

FOR THE CUSTARD

1 medium kabocha squash (about 2½ pounds)

¾ cup packed light brown sugar

1 cup full-fat coconut milk

½ teaspoon kosher salt

2 teaspoons vanilla extract

½ teaspoon ground nutmeg

6 large eggs

FOR THE WALNUT-COCONUT CRUMBLE

1 cup unsweetened shredded coconut

1 cup chopped walnuts

½ cup packed light brown sugar

¼ cup all-purpose flour

½ teaspoon kosher salt

1 stick (4 ounces) unsalted butter, at room temperature

◆ *make the custard* Wash the squash thoroughly, then cut a circular opening in the top using a serrated bread knife. Scoop out the seeds and fibers and rinse to make sure it's smooth and clean inside.

recipe continues ➡

◆ In a medium bowl, whisk together the brown sugar, coconut milk, salt, vanilla, and nutmeg, making sure there are no lumps in the brown sugar (a fine-mesh sieve is great for straining the mixture). Add the eggs and mix well to combine. Pour the mixture into the hollowed and cleaned squash, filling it to the bottom of the circular opening (if you have any custard left over, pour it into a shallow bowl and top with squash sliced from the "lid," then steam alongside the whole squash).

◆ Arrange a small wire rack or metal trivet inside a large pot or Dutch oven with a lid. Place the squash in a heatproof glass bowl that will fit inside the pot and place the bowl on the rack so it sits above the bottom of the pot. Fill the pot with enough water to come one-quarter of the way up the glass bowl. Place over medium heat. Once the water is at a full boil, reduce the heat to medium-low and cover tightly.

◆ Steam the squash for 1 hour, checking the water level occasionally and replenishing with hot water as needed so it always reaches one-quarter of the way up the sides of the bowl. After 1 hour, the top of the custard should puff up slightly. Pierce the center of the custard with a wooden skewer; if it comes out clean, remove the bowl from the pot. Let the squash cool for at least 45 minutes (the custard will continue to set).

◆ *make the walnut-coconut crumble*   Preheat the oven to 350°F.

◆ In a large bowl, mix the coconut, walnuts, brown sugar, flour, and salt together. Add the butter and stir until combined. Spread the mixture out evenly onto a sheet pan lined with parchment paper and bake until golden brown, 12 to 15 minutes. Let cool completely, then break up the crumble into pieces and transfer to a sealed container.

◆ To serve, cut the cooled squash into wedges (you can also chill the squash in the fridge before slicing if you prefer to eat the custard cold). Place the individual wedges on a plate and sprinkle with the walnut-coconut crumble before serving.

Buttery
ROTI BREAD

MAKES 10 ROTI

At the night markets, I used to love watching the skilled roti vendors flip the dough into the air, stretch it thin, then slap in onto the hot steel griddle on their street car. There are both sweet and savory versions, and every vendor's varies in style, but the result is always flaky, buttery goodness that is crispy on the outside and tender inside.

To make roti at home, start by mixing together a simple dough. Because the griddle is so hot, most vendors use margarine to cook the roti because it doesn't burn as easily as butter. For me, it isn't real roti unless it has that specific margarine flavor. You have to eat them while they're still warm from the griddle, just like on the street.

1 tablespoon sugar, plus more for serving (optional)

½ teaspoon kosher salt

1 large egg

½ cup melted margarine or ghee, plus more as needed

3 cups all-purpose flour, plus more for kneading

Sweetened condensed milk, for serving (optional)

◆ In a large bowl, dissolve the sugar and salt in ¾ cup warm water. Add the egg and 6 tablespoons of the melted margarine, stirring until the egg is lightly beaten. Fold in the flour until a loose dough forms. Knead on a lightly floured surface or in a stand mixer with the dough hook attachment until the dough is shiny and soft, about 10 minutes. The dough should be tacky and slightly wet but not sticking to the surface/bowl or your hand. Rub the inside of the mixer bowl with some margarine. Place the dough ball in the bowl, cover with plastic wrap, and let rest at room temperature for at least 2 hours or in the fridge overnight.

◆ Divide the dough into 10 equal pieces and roll into balls between your hands. Place on a sheet pan or plate and let rest for 30 minutes. On a floured surface, use a rolling pin to flatten the balls into 8- to 10-inch rounds, getting them as thin as possible (about ⅛ inch thick is your goal). Brush each roti with margarine and stack them as you roll, separating them with sheets of parchment paper.

◆ Set up a wire rack or line a plate with paper towels. Heat a large skillet or cast-iron griddle over medium heat. When the skillet is hot, melt a teaspoon or so of margarine in the pan and add a roti, brushing the top with another teaspoon or so of margarine.

Cook until lightly blistered and cooked through, 2 to 3 minutes per side. Transfer to the wire rack or paper towels to cool. Repeat to cook the remaining roti.

◆ Serve hot with Massaman Beef Curry (page 193) for dipping or top to taste with sweetened condensed milk and a sprinkle of sugar for a simple dessert.

pepper's PANTRY

Toasted Rice Powder

MAKES $^1/_3$ CUP

Toasted rice powder adds a very specific nutty flavor to dishes. I use it a lot in my cooking. Don't skip out on it: It is sooooo easy to make, and my oven method is foolproof.

½ cup jasmine rice

♦ Preheat the oven to 400°F.

♦ Spread the rice evenly across a sheet pan and roast, stirring with a wooden spoon halfway through, until the rice is deep golden brown and smells like popcorn, 18 to 20 minutes.

♦ Transfer to the hot toasted rice to a plate and let cool completely. Crush with a mortar and pestle to a powder the consistency of coarse sand (or use a spice grinder or small blender on high speed for 10 to 15 seconds; make sure the blender has no moisture in it). Store the rice powder in an airtight container and it will keep for months in the cupboard.

Roasted Chile Powder

MAKES ABOUT 1 CUP

Roasted chile powder is one of my most essential ingredients because it adds both earthiness and heat. If you can't find dried Thai chiles at the market, any small dried red chile will work.

2 cups dried red chiles, such as Thai, de árbol, or japones

♦ Preheat the oven to 350°F. If you have an oven hood fan, turn it on.

♦ Spread the chiles evenly across a sheet pan and roast for about 6 minutes, checking them halfway through. The chiles are done when they change color from red to a very dark reddish brown. Watch closely near the end to make sure they don't burn.

♦ Transfer chiles to a plate and let cool completely. Place them in a mortar and grind with the pestle until they're the size of red pepper flakes (or use a spice grinder or small blender on high speed for 10 to 15 seconds; make sure the blender is totally dry). Store the chile powder in an airtight container; it keeps for about 3 months or longer if kept in the freezer.

226

TOASTED RICE POWDER

ROASTED CHILE POWDER

TRADITIONAL STICKY RICE (see next page)

Traditional
STICKY RICE

SERVES 6 TO 8

Although you can make sticky rice very quickly in the microwave (see Note), at least once you should make it the traditional way. There's nothing exactly like the chewy and tender texture of real Thai-style sticky rice. Thankfully, all you need is a steamer basket (you can use a basic metal one or find a bamboo steamer online or in a Thai market) and some cheesecloth or a clean dish towel. Back in Korat, my grandparents worked as rice farmers. My grandpa—I remember him being short and skinny and a very hard worker—would farm the rice himself without any modern machinery. He made sure we never spilled a single grain when we were eating because he knew how much work it took to grow. As far as I know, they ate sticky rice at every meal—always in a big bamboo basket in the center of the table so it stayed warm. And we always had to leave a little behind in case our ancestors' spirits happened to visit in the middle of the night and wanted something to eat!

All of which is to say, I really love sticky rice! Give me a little bamboo basket filled with rice and some nam prik pao (page 244) or jaew nam jim (page 238) and I'm happy. Every Asian supermarket and some American supermarkets will carry sticky rice (sometimes labeled glutinous or sweet rice), but for the best taste I suggest trying to find a Thai brand. From there, it's as simple as soak (the rice needs to soak for at least 2 hours), rinse, steam, and serve. One more great thing about sticky rice is that it will stay moist for a long time if you store it correctly. I suggest making a large batch like the recipe below and placing the leftovers in plastic sandwich bags. Keep them in the fridge, and when you're ready to reheat, splash a tiny amount of water on the rice and microwave until soft and warmed through.

4 cups uncooked Thai glutinous (sweet) rice

◆ Place the rice in a bowl and cover with cold water. Swish the rice around until the water becomes cloudy, then drain the rice in a sieve. Return the rice to a bowl and repeat until the water runs clear, not milky. Cover the rice with warm water and let it soak for at least 2 hours or up to 24 hours.

◆ Assemble a steamer: Fill a pot with a few inches of water and bring it to a boil over high heat.

◆ Line a steamer basket with a double layer of damp cheesecloth large enough to hang over the edges of the basket. Drain the soaked rice and transfer to the cheesecloth-lined steamer basket, using your hands to spread the rice into an even layer. Fold the cheesecloth over the rice to form a loose bundle.

◆ When the water in the steamer pot is boiling, reduce the heat to a steady simmer. Place the steamer basket over the pot, making sure the steamer basket isn't touching the water. Cover the pot and steamer with a lid.

◆ Steam for 15 minutes, then uncover the pot and carefully flip the cheesecloth bundle over. Cover again and continue to cook until the rice is tender but still chewy, about 15 more minutes. Remove from the heat and let the rice rest for 10 minutes.

◆ If serving immediately, remove the rice from the cheesecloth and transfer it to a bowl. Cover to keep warm. Divide what you're not eating right away into small resealable plastic bags for individual portions. The wrapped sticky rice will keep for up to 1 week in the fridge; just splash some water on the cold rice and microwave until heated through.

note

To make sticky rice in the microwave: Place the sticky rice in a microwave-safe bowl and cover with 1¾ cups warm water. Let soak for at least 10 minutes or up to 1 hour. Cover the bowl with an upside-down plate or plastic wrap and microwave on high for 3 minutes. Carefully stir the rice from top to bottom, then cover and cook the rice for another 3 minutes. Repeat the process, stirring and microwaving 3 minutes at a time, until all the water has been absorbed and the rice has turned translucent (this means it's cooked). Set aside to cool slightly.

Spicy
CHILE CRISP

MAKES 2½ CUPS

Would it be a true Pepper Thai cookbook without a recipe for spicy chile oil? I don't think so. This is a great all-purpose hot sauce for fried rice, noodles, eggs, or vegetables. The "crisp" part comes from garlic and shallots, which get crispy and crunchy when they're fried in the oil. They crisp as they cool and then get stirred into the spicy chile oil.

¾ cup dried red chiles, such as Thai, de árbol, or japones

4 small shallots, thinly sliced

12 cloves garlic, thinly sliced

1½ cups vegetable oil

2 tablespoons sesame seeds

¼ teaspoon ground white pepper

1 tablespoon sugar, plus more to taste

1 teaspoon kosher salt, plus more to taste

◆ Preheat the oven to 350°F.

◆ Place the chiles on a sheet pan in a single layer and roast for about 5 minutes, shaking the pan halfway through to make sure they don't burn. Remove from the oven and set aside to cool, then transfer to a mortar or blender and grind until you're left with crushed chile flakes.

◆ In a medium saucepan, combine the shallots, garlic, and oil. Cook over medium heat, stirring occasionally, until the garlic and shallots are golden brown, 20 to 25 minutes. Remove from the heat.

◆ In a heatproof medium bowl, combine the chile flakes, sesame seeds, white pepper, sugar, and salt. Set a fine-mesh sieve over the bowl and pour the garlic-shallot mixture into it. Set the sieve of garlic and shallots aside to cool completely so they become crisp.

◆ Once the oil is cooled to room temperature, stir the cooled and crisp shallots and garlic back into the oil. Taste and add more sugar or salt as needed. Transfer to a screw-top jar and refrigerate for up to 1 month. Stir well before using.

Sweet Dark
SOY SAUCE

Dark soy sauce, which has a sweet molasses-like flavor to it, is an important ingredient for stir-fried noodles and other dishes in Thai cooking. But if you don't have an Asian market near by or can't find store-bought dark soy sauce, this easy recipe is a good substitute.

1 cup dark brown sugar   ½ cup light soy sauce

♦ In a small saucepan over high heat, combine the brown sugar with ¼ cup of water. Stir until the sugar is dissolved, then reduce the heat to medium-low. When the sugar syrup starts to look like the color of coffee, 4 to 5 minutes, slowly pour in the soy sauce (so it doesn't bubble up) and stir until combined. Let cool completely; store in the refrigerator for up to 1 month.

Puffy
FRIED EGG

MAKES 1

I'm guessing you have made a fried egg before, but what about Thai-style? We love our eggs extra crispy and browned on the bottoms and all around the edges. The trick is to fry the egg in a good amount of hot oil (plus some butter if you like), then drain on a paper towel right away. I love a runny fried egg over my Turkey Grapow (page 126) or Fridge-Cleaning Fried Rice (page 153).

½ cup vegetable oil

1 large egg

Kosher salt

1 tablespoon unsalted butter (optional)

◆ In a wok or small skillet, heat the oil over medium-high heat until shimmering-hot (make sure the oil is very hot, or the egg white will stick to the bottom of the pan). Crack the egg into the pan (it should start sizzling immediately) and sprinkle with a pinch of salt. Use a spoon or spatula to drizzle the hot oil over the yolk to help it cook. You can also add the butter to the pan and, once it melts, spoon that over as well for extra flavor.

◆ Continue cooking until the edges are browned and crispy and the white surrounding the yolk is cooked but the yolk is still runny, about 2 minutes. If you like your yolk on the cooked side, continue spooning the oil until the yolk is firm, or flip the whole egg over and let it brown and become crispy on the other side. Remove from the pan and serve immediately.

FRIED GARLIC
and Garlic Oil

Fried garlic is a crunchy, savory accent you can add to any dish. The smartest thing to do if you are a #garliclover like me is to make a big batch in advance so you will always have some when the need arises. As a bonus, you will have garlic oil left over, which you can use like regular oil to add a delicious savory flavor to whatever you're cooking.

24 cloves garlic, peeled

Vegetable oil, for deep-frying

Kosher salt

♦ Chop the garlic or pulse in a food processor a few times until finely chopped (but not pureed).

♦ Line a plate with paper towels. Pour 1 inch oil into a large heavy pot and heat to 300°F (you'll know it's ready when a piece of garlic almost immediately begins to gently sizzle when dropped into the oil).

♦ Add half the garlic and fry, stirring with a slotted spoon to help the garlic cook evenly, until it is lightly golden brown (it will darken more as it cools), 3 to 4 minutes. Use the slotted spoon or a spider to remove the garlic and drain on the paper towels. Sprinkle with salt while hot. Repeat with the remaining garlic. Save the oil after it cools and use whenever you want to add a boost of delicious garlic flavor to whatever you're cooking. Fried garlic keeps in an airtight container at room temperature for up to 2 weeks; the garlic oil keeps for 2 months.

PICKLED CHILE VINEGAR
(see page 239)

GARLIC OIL

**RED HOT PEPPER SAUCE
(NAM JIM JAEW)**
(see next page)

FRIED GARLIC

RED HOT PEPPER SAUCE
(Nam Jim Jaew)

MAKES ²/₃ CUP

As made famous in both of Chrissy's books, this is my signature red hot red pepper sauce (or some combination of those words)! Since Chrissy took it from me, I'm going to change it up a little bit and give it right back to you. In Thai, we call this sauce jaew, and everybody makes their version a little differently. It is always spicy and sour with a nutty roasted flavor from rice powder. It is truly the best dipping sauce ever for any kind of roasted or grilled meat.

2 tablespoons Roasted Chile Powder (page 226)

2 tablespoons fresh lime juice

2 tablespoons fish sauce

1 tablespoon Toasted Rice Powder, store-bought or homemade (page 226)

1 tablespoon minced cilantro stems

2 teaspoons light brown sugar

10 grape tomatoes, halved

♦ In a small bowl, whisk together the chile powder, lime juice, fish sauce, rice powder, cilantro stems, and brown sugar. Squeeze in the pulp of the tomatoes (discard the skins) and stir. The sauce keeps in the fridge for 1 week.

Pickled
CHILE VINEGAR

MAKES 1 CUP

This mildly spicy vinegar is found in little seasoning jars on every table of every noodle stand in Thailand. A splash is especially delicious on stir-fried noodle dishes like pad see ew (see "Bow-Thai" See Ew, page 184) and Pad Korat (page 120), but use it anywhere you want the sharp tang of vinegar and fresh chile heat.

1 jalapeño pepper

1 cup distilled white vinegar or apple cider vinegar

◆ Halve the jalapeño lengthwise and remove the seeds, then thinly slice crosswise. Combine the vinegar and jalapeño in a glass jar or other airtight container. For the best flavor, refrigerate overnight before using. The vinegar keeps in the fridge for 2 months.

PAK DONG
(Thai Salt-Pickled Cabbage) MAKES 1 QUART

Once you try the traditional Isaan way of making pickles, it's hard to go back to anything else. The process is so unbelievably simple. Start by rinsing some uncooked rice until you get a few cups of starchy, milky-looking water. Save it! Then take whatever vegetables you want to pickle—I use cabbage, scallions, and garlic in whatever ratio is on hand—and sprinkle them with salt. Then give them a nice firm massage, crunching the veggies between your fingers until they are bruised and moist. This helps draw out the water so the salt can seep in. Next put the vegetables in a jar, cover with the rice water, and let it sit on the counter (or like me, at your bedside) for a few days. The starch in the rice water helps the pickles become tangy and gives them a really complex and delicious flavor to complement their crunch, sort of like a mild version of kimchi (aka Korean spicy fermented cabbage). After a few days, the pickles should be ready. Eat them with everything, as a topping or a side dish.

1 cup jasmine or Thai gelatinous (sweet) rice

1 large bunch of scallions, trimmed and cut crosswise into thirds

12 cloves peeled garlic

1 small head green cabbage, cored and roughly chopped into bite-size pieces

2 teaspoons kosher salt, plus more to taste

2 fresh bird's eye chiles or 1 serrano, roughly chopped

◆ Rinse the rice to remove any dust or particles, then soak it in 4 cups water for a few minutes, stirring to release the starches. Reserving the starchy rice water, drain the rice. (Cook the rice to serve or store.)

◆ Use a heavy object or the butt of a knife to pound the white sections of the scallions and the garlic until they're smashed.

◆ Spread out the cabbage on a sheet pan and sprinkle evenly with the salt. Use your hands to vigorously massage the salt into the cabbage, working for a few minutes until the cabbage starts to release moisture and wilt slightly. Add the scallions and garlic to the sheet pan and continue massaging until the green sections of the scallions are slightly wilted.

◆ Taste a piece of cabbage. It should taste slightly salty but not overpowering. Adjust with more salt as needed; if you add too much, just rinse the cabbage and drain well.

♦ Add the chiles to a clean 1-quart screw-top jar and top with the cabbage mixture, compacting it down firmly. Fill the jar with the reserved starchy rice water until almost at the rim (you want to submerge the cabbage as much as possible). Loosely cover with a lid and let sit at room temperature for at least 3 days and up to 5 days, depending on your sourness preference and the weather (the cabbage will ferment faster when it's hot or humid). Since the fermenting veggies will start to bubble and release gas, "burp" the lid once or twice.

♦ When the cabbage is ready, it will look yellowish-green and slightly translucent. You should not see any mold or unusual dark colors. If it looks or smells off, toss it and try again. Taste a piece using a clean, dry utensil; it should be sour and salty, but more sour than salty. When you're happy with the results, transfer the jar to the fridge and chill before eating. The pickled cabbage can be refrigerated for several months.

Spicy Garlic-Lime
FISH SAUCE

This is another version of my green pepper hot sauce made famous in Chrissy's first book, *Cravings*. It's a little heavier on the lime juice and fish sauce but still balanced. I use it as an all-purpose seasoning kept on the table to adjust any food to my taste—sort of like Pepper's salt and pepper.

½ cup fish sauce

¼ cup fresh lime juice (about 2 limes)

1 tablespoon light brown sugar

12 fresh bird's eye chiles or 4 serrano chiles, thinly sliced or finely chopped

4 cloves garlic, mashed or minced

◆ In a small bowl, whisk together the fish sauce, lime juice, 2 tablespoons water, the brown sugar, chiles, and garlic until the sugar is dissolved. Transfer to a glass jar or other airtight container. For the best flavor, refrigerate for 2 hours before using. The fish sauce will keep in the fridge for 2 weeks.

SWEET CHILE JAM
(Nam Prik Pao)

MAKES ABOUT 2 CUPS

This dark red sticky jam made from dried chiles is a must-have in my pantry. It's jam-packed (get it?) with deep umami flavor and a balanced amount of sweetness and heat. Thai people use it to add a roasted tangy flavor to just about everything, from soups to instant noodles, or sometimes as a dip for pork rinds, shrimp chips, or vegetables.

You can find it sold in Thai markets as nam prik pao, but I think you should try making it yourself—I find the flavor is much deeper and richer.

¼ cup plus 2 tablespoons vegetable oil

12 cloves garlic, sliced

2 medium shallots, roughly chopped

2 tablespoons small dried shrimp

¾ cup dried red chiles, such as Thai, de árbol, or japones

½ cup light brown sugar, plus more to taste

2 tablespoons tamarind paste

2 tablespoons fish sauce

1 teaspoon anchovy paste or shrimp paste

Kosher salt

♦ In a large skillet, heat ¼ cup of the oil over medium-high heat until shimmering-hot. Add the garlic and shallots and fry, stirring occasionally, until lightly browned and crisp, about 2 minutes. Add the dried shrimp and fry until the shrimp turn dark in color and become fragrant, about 2 minutes more. Remove the pan from the heat and let everything cool slightly, then scrape the mixture (along with the oil) into a blender or food processor.

♦ Without wiping it out, return the pan to medium-low heat. Add the red chiles and toast until they darken in color and become brittle, 3 to 4 minutes, making sure they don't burn (when they start to smell roasty-fragrant, you're about there). Immediately transfer the chiles to the blender.

♦ Add the brown sugar, tamarind paste, fish sauce, anchovy paste, and ½ cup warm water to the blender and blend until smooth.

♦ Add the remaining 2 tablespoons oil to the same pan you used to toast the chiles and heat over medium heat. Once the oil is shimmering-hot, add the blended paste to the pan. Cook, stirring occasionally, until the paste has reduced to a thick jam-like consistency with a thin layer of oil on top (you should be able to make a hole in the center of the pan and not have the paste immediately fill it back in), 15 to 20 minutes.

♦ Taste and adjust the seasoning with salt and add more brown sugar, if needed. Remove the pan from the heat and let the jam cool completely. Transfer to a clean glass jar and store in the refrigerator for up to 1 month.

ingredient guide/
common substitutions

Chiles: Fresh   Bird's eye chiles are my favorite source of spiciness. They have a bright heat to them. They are red or green in color and rather small in size (1 to 2 inches), especially given their potency. If I can't find them, serrano chiles are a good substitute—they are slightly mellower in heat, so you might want to use more to get the same firepower.

Chiles: Dried Red   Any bag of small (2 to 3-inch-long and ½-inch-wide) dried red chiles will do the trick. Thai, de árbol, or japones chiles are good options. Look for them at Asian or Latin markets.

Coconut Milk   Make sure you don't buy "lite" coconut milk. The recipes in this book were developed with full-fat coconut milk, and lite will not give you the same thick and rich result. Thai brands such as Aroy-D, Savoy, and Chaokoh are my preferred picks, but any can or box that seems thick and creamy is fine with me. Be sure to give the can a good shake before opening to mix any solids that have separated.

Curry Pastes   A quality Thai red curry paste is an ingredient to always have in your cupboard or fridge. For some recipes, I call for specific kinds of curry paste (like green curry or Massaman curry paste), but red curry paste is generally the standard. I use store-bought curry paste because it saves so much time and the flavor is spot-on.

Dried Shrimp   Most Asian or Latin supermarkets will stock dried shrimp in the seasoning or bulk items section. If you're not sure what size to buy, go with the ones labeled small or medium. Store in a sealed container and they'll keep in the cupboard forever.

Fish Sauce   A salty, sharp seasoning sauce with lots of umami, fish sauce is a must for this cookbook. I like the briny, sweet flavor of Thai fish sauce best, but any Asian brand is fine.

Galangal   Galangal is a more citrusy, pine-smelling cousin of ginger and is used in many Thai dishes. Like ginger, it should be peeled before using, though if you're throwing slices into a soup or broth for flavor you can leave them unpeeled since they won't be eaten (too fibrous and tough). If you can't find galangal fresh or frozen at Asian supermarkets, using fresh regular ginger is the way to go.

Lime Leaves/Lime Zest   The leaves of the makrut lime (sometimes known as kaffir lime, but we don't like using that term since it has derogatory origins) have an amazing aroma that people in Thailand are obsessed with. You can usually find them at Asian or Indian supermarkets in the produce or frozen section (they last a long time frozen). Otherwise fresh lime zest is the next-best option.

Oyster Sauce   Thick, brown, and savory-sweet, oyster sauce adds another layer of flavor to the simplest stir-fries (and yes, it's made with oysters). Lee Kum Kee is a common brand.

Palm Sugar   Palm sugar is made from the sap of the palm tree and is usually sold in jars or in hard discs, which can be chopped as needed or softened in the microwave before using. When I can't find palm sugar, I use light brown sugar as a one-to-one substitute.

Soy Sauce: Light   Soy sauce comes in many varieties, but what you want for many of the recipes in this book is "light soy sauce." Not to be confused with reduced-sodium soy, the "light" refers to the sauce's lighter color and thinner consistency. In fact, light soy is saltier than regular soy. My favorite Thai brand of light soy sauce (also called thin soy sauce) is Healthy Boy, but if you can't find Thai light soy, Chinese light soy (look for the Lee Kum Kee brand) will work instead.

Soy Sauce: Sweet Dark   This syrupy style of soy sauce, which is used in some stir-fried noodle dishes and soups, is dark and sweet because it's blended with molasses. Thai brand Healthy Boy makes a good version, or you can substitute Chinese sweet soy or Indonesian kecap manis. If all else fails, you can make your own version at home with dark brown sugar and regular soy sauce (see page 232).

Soybean Sauce   Thai soybean sauce is a salted soybean paste that comes in large bottles and adds a salty fermented flavor as a seasoning. If you can't find it at an Asian supermarket, the next best thing is to use brown Japanese miso paste, which is saltier and bolder than sweet white miso. Mix 2 parts brown miso with 1 part water to create the consistency of soybean sauce.

Tamarind Concentrate   This tangy paste is made from the sour-tasting fruit of the tamarind tree. Though some Asian supermarkets sell blocks of tamarind pulp, I use a more commonly found "tamarind concentrate" (also labeled tamarind paste), which is a strained and reduced tamarind pulp that is ready to use. Look for it in plastic and glass jars in the Indian or Asian ingredients section.

Thai Basil   Thai basil is sometimes called sweet basil and has a more licorice-y aroma than the Italian kind, though they're close enough that you can use either one in these recipes.

Pepper's Table

Here are a few of my favorite menu suggestions—pick one that fits the occasion or mood and make it your own.

acknowledgments

I can't believe I'm writing the acknowledgments for *my own cookbook*. I have to say THANK YOU to all of the people who helped me make this book.

First of all, I want to thank my daughter Chrissy. Thank you for being proud of your Thai mom and the food from my country. Thank you for featuring me in your *Cravings* books and giving me the confidence to write my own cookbook.

Thank you to my cowriter, Garrett Snyder. He came to the house so many times, and we cooked and wrote everything together. I'm not used to measuring things and putting everything in writing, but he helped me put down all my ideas so that you could make my dishes at home.

Thank you to Kate Malay Hopewell for testing all my recipes, and making sure that everything is easy to follow and perfect for all of you!

Thank you to the team at Penguin Random House: editor, Raquel Pelzel; publisher, Aaron Wehner; designer, Sonia Persad; art director, Stephanie Huntwork; marketing team, Stephanie Davis and Windy Dorresteyn; and public relations team, Jana Branson and Kate Tyler.

Thank you to Chrissy's amazing team who adopted me and helped me with this entire process: Luke Dillon at 3Arts Management, Christine Shim from Cravings, and Erin Malone, our book agent at WME.

Thank you to all the people who helped make this book look so beautiful: photographer, Jenny Huang, assisted by Pierce Liu; food stylist, Tyna Hoang, assisted by Scotty Fletcher; prop stylist, Beatrix Chastka, assisted by Stephanie de Luca.

My glam squad was so sweet and so great: makeup by Kristine Studden and Nova Kaplan Zekofsky; hair by Irinel de Leon; styled by Alana Van Deraa.

And thank you to my wonderful family. I'm so lucky—I couldn't do anything without their love and support.

Thank you to my daughter Tina, for always being with me in the kitchen and for becoming such a great cook yourself. I am so proud of the woman you've become. Thank you to my son-in-law, John, for tasting everything! You are such a wonderful man. And thank you to my beautiful grandchildren, Pasha, Luna, and Miles.

index